Dikson

o Norilsk

• Krasnoyarsk

• Novosibirsk

Omsk

Okhotsk o

Lake Baikal

Irkutsk •

Nikolayevsk •

Khabarovsk •

Spassk-Daini •

o Vladivostok

Peking o

• Pyong-yang

• Seoul

D0935569

"The man
who fights
for his
ideals
is the man
who
is alive."

CERVANTES
author of
DON QUIXOTE

Raymond H. Hoffman

The Red Falcons

A gift to
Fitzgerald
Library

FROM
Arlene Hoffman
IN MEMORY OF HER HUSBAND
Raymond H. Hoffman
CLASS OF 1950

The Red Falcons

The Soviet Air Force
in Action, 1919-1969

by Robert Jackson

CLIFTON BOOKS

New England House, New England Street, Brighton, BN1 4HN

Registered Office:
Clifton House, 83-117 Euston Road, London N.W.1

ISBN 0 901255 16 5

Printed in Great Britain by
Strange the Printer & Sussex Printers Limited, Eastbourne, Sussex

Contents

List of Plates

Preface

On the night of August 20th 1968, waves of Soviet transport aircraft swept down out of the darkness to land on Prague's international airport. The invasion of Czechoslovakia had begun.

Distasteful though the invasion was in the eyes of the Western world, the initial surprise capture of the Czech air-fields by the Soviet airborne forces was one of the best planned and most efficient operations of its kind in history, and revealed the Soviet Air Force as being well equipped to meet the type of emergency it might have to face during the 1970s.

Fifty years ago, the Red Air Force consisted of a motley collection of British, French and German aircraft, many of them gleaned from the scrap-heaps of European battlefields. This book traces the course of its development since those early days, when the Red and the White fought for mastery of the Russian skies in one of history's bloodiest revolutions; we see its emergence, with foreign help, as a coherent fighting force during the 1920s and 1930s, when Russian pilots fought in the skies of the Far East against Chinese and Japanese and in Spain against Franco and his Italian and German volunteer airmen.

Then, following the shattering defeat inflicted on the Soviet airmen by the tiny Finnish Air Force, come the near-annihilation of Soviet air power during the German blitz-krieg on Russia; the long retreats of 1941 and 1942, followed by the stand at Stalingrad and the turning-point of the war in the East, the Battle of Kursk. The bitter fighting of the Eastern air war is seen through the eyes of the men who helped to forge the Soviet Air Force into a massive instrument of destruction. Men like Alexander Pokryshkin, the cool air fighter who spent hours after every dogfight working out better ways to shoot down the enemy and who virtually wrote the Russian air fighting manual; Ivan Kozhedub, the impetuous air fighter who became Russia's top-scoring ace with 62 victories; Alexei Maresyev, who lost both legs in an air crash but who returned to fly and fight again; and many others. Stripped of the thin veneer of communist propaganda, the Soviet Air Force pilots are found to be very much like their British, American and German counterparts; men who flew not for an ideal, but because they loved flying. Their experiences are set against those of the men they fought, up to the last great battles in the sky over Berlin—where all the Russian aces were reunited in the final drive to victory.

After the holocaust of World War Two comes the Cold War, with the part played by the Soviet Air Force in harassing the Berlin Airlift and the commitment of whole Soviet fighter squadrons to Korea, where Russian MiGs fought it out with American Sabres in the first-ever jet-versus-jet battles over the Yalu River. Then the tragedy of Hungary, when the resistance of the Soviet-trained Hungarian Air Force was smashed before it had begun, and in that same year the Suez crisis, when Soviet airmen were caught in the middle of the Arab-Israeli conflict and the Anglo-French invasion. We see the secret 'radar war' fought in the stratosphere between Russian and American reconnaissance aircraft, culminating in the U-2 incident and the Cuban Crisis.

Finally, for the first time, the story of the part played by the Soviet Air Force in the invasion of Czechoslovakia and the massive manoeuvres that led up to it is told in detail; and there is a glimpse into the future, to the possibility that the Soviet Air Force may yet have to fight its greatest battle —in an armed conflict with China.

Chapter 1

The Red and The White

On March 3rd 1918, the long and bitter war between Imperial Germany and Russia came to an end with the signing of the Treaty of Brest-Litovsk. The road had not been an easy one; early negotiations had broken down and final agreement had been reached only after the Central Powers had launched a massive attack along the whole of the Eastern Front in February. For the Bolsheviks, the cost of peace with Germany was harsh; Russian territory amounting to a million square kilometres, with a population of 46 million people, was to be ceded to the temporary victors, who also claimed reparations to the total of 3,000 million roubles in gold.

Reaction to the treaty by the Allies—now faced with the prospect of a spring offensive supported by massive reinforcements of German troops withdrawn from the East, and with the occupation of large areas of Russia by the Central Powers —was immediate. During the third week of March 1918, the British cruiser *Glory* arrived at Murmansk and disembarked the first units of the Allied intervention force. More landings were made during May and June by British, French and American troops, supported by Fairey Campania seaplanes from the aircraft carrier *Nairana*. The first task of the intervention force was to occupy the strategically important ports of Archangel and Bakeritza, and *Nairana*'s seaplanes were used to bomb Red gun positions.

Soon after the Bolsheviks had been driven from these objectives, early in August, a small Royal Air Force contingent arrived with eight DH 4 bombers. With it were 37 pilots and ground crew of the former Imperial Russian Air Service, under the command of Captain Alexander Kazakov; a redoubtable officer who had shot down 17 German aircraft while flying with the famous 19th Squadron—known as the 'Death or Glory Boys' because of the skull-and-crossbones insignia painted on the tails of their aircraft. The 19th

Squadron collapsed after the October Revolution; in fact, most of its aircraft were wrecked when the ground crews tried to fly them after the pilots had gone. Kazakov had been luckier than some of his comrades, many of whom had been captured by the Bolsheviks and shot out of hand.

At Bakeritza, the Allies discovered some Sopwith $1\frac{1}{2}$-Strutters and Nieuport 17C-1s, still in their crates. The aircraft—nine in all—had been delivered to the Imperial Russian Air Service in 1917, but the revolution had prevented their use. They were now hurriedly assembled by RAF mechanics and formed into two flights, manned by Kazakov's airmen but with a small number of RAF personnel attached as advisers. Before they had a chance to go into action, however, the Bolsheviks launched an offensive in October and part of the intervention force—including Kazakov's Slavo-British Squadron—was cut off by enemy infiltration. Undeterred, the airmen loaded their aircraft on to sleighs and battled their way towards safety for two days, struggling through deep snow and fighting off constant attacks by Red guerrillas. They took refuge in a convent, where they stayed for a week while a strong force of Red soldiers made determined attempts to winkle them out. The Bolshevik onslaught was once again beaten off, and Kazakov's men—still dragging their aircraft—made their getaway under cover of darkness, reaching the Allied lines the following morning. The pilots went into action almost immediately, mounting a series of strafing attacks on Red forces that were threatening to overwhelm some British artillery positions.

During this period, the Allied operations in northern Russia were never seriously opposed by Red aircraft, although the Reds were known to have a dozen or so Caudron G IIIA 2 reconnaissance aircraft in the area, as well as one Nieuport 28 fighter. The Caudrons were employed to drop grenades and primitive bombs on the Allied positions on a number of occasions, but they never did any damage. During the winter months, there was a lack of air activity on both sides; on all but a few occasions flying was prohibited by the intense cold.

At the time of the first Allied intervention, the total

operational strength of the 'Workers' and Peasants' Air Fleet' —as the embryo Red Air Force was then known—stood at not more than 150 aircraft. Most of them were British and French types—Farmans, Spads, Nieuports, Caudrons, Morane-Saulniers and Sopwith Strutters, the great majority rapidly approaching obsolescence. There were also some Albatross D IIIs, Fokker E Types, Halberstadt CL IIs and LVGs, left behind by the Germans in the Ukraine. All the serviceable aircraft were divided among 36 squadrons, most of which had only two or three machines. Many of the initial Red Air Fleet units were in fact ex-Czarist squadrons, whose personnel had defected *en bloc* to the Bolsheviks. Often they had no choice; the alternative was death. However, several aviators who were 'aces' in their own right joined the Red Air Fleet of their own free will; one of them was Latvian-born Colonel Jezup Bashko, who had fought with distinction against the Germans as a bomber pilot and won ten decorations. He served with the Red Air Fleet until 1921 and was awarded the highest Bolshevik medal, the St George Soldier's Cross with Palms.

Every squadron suffered from a critical shortage of trained personnel, both aircrew and mechanics; this fact was quickly recognized by the Aviation Board, which had been responsible since December 1917 for the organization of the Red Air Fleet, and by mid 1918 two flying and technical training schools had been set up, one at Petrograd and the other near Moscow. Personnel for the naval aviation units of the Red Fleet—there were four squadrons in the spring of 1918, with a total strength of about 20 seaplanes—were trained at Oranienbaum. Two more naval aviation schools were later set up at Sevastopol and Nizhni Novgorod.

In May 1918, a few weeks after the first Allied units landed at Murmansk, the Czechoslovak Legion, an army corps made up largely of Czech and Slovak prisoners of war, rebelled against the Bolsheviks while travelling eastwards along the Trans-Siberian Railway to Vladivostok. With the approval of the Bolsheviks, who feared that the Czechs—whose leaders numbered many Czarist officers—might get involved in

Russia's internal struggle, the Legion was to embark in Allied ships at Vladivostok, with the Western Front as its eventual destination. By the end of June, six weeks after the revolt, the Legion had seized control of the entire Trans-Siberian Railway from Penza in the Ukraine to Vladivostok, with the exception of Irkutsk, and had set up what was virtually a state within a state at Chelyabinsk.

In September 1918, the Bolsheviks launched a strong counter-attack in the Samara region, where an anti-Bolshevik regime had been set up under Czech protection. For the first time, aircraft were used extensively by the Reds, both for reconnaissance and for strafing enemy concentrations. The Czechs, who had been hanging on grimly in the hope that an Allied force would invade Siberia and attack Germany from the east, now abandoned their positions in the Volga area and began to make their way eastwards to join Admiral Kolchak, the White Russian leader, in Omsk. The Volga area was reoccupied by the Reds, and aircraft of the Red Air Fleet made frequent sorties along the railway to harass the Czechs during the early stages of their withdrawal.

When the Armistice of November 11th 1918 brought the First World War to an end, the Bolsheviks immediately made a determined effort to take over territory abandoned by the withdrawing forces of the Central Powers, but they met with fierce resistance from the Ukrainians and the Don Union, an alliance of the Don Cossacks and southern Whites. The Reds were now committed to a war on three fronts, for the Siberian Whites had by this time built up a powerful army under the shield of the Czech Legion. The White plan of attack envisaged a simultaneous advance on Moscow and Petrograd from the south, east and north-west. From the south, the White armies under General Anton Denikin were to thrust northwards into the Ukraine, partially occupied by the Bolsheviks; the left wing of Denikin's forces was to capture Kharkov and Kiev, while the right, led by General Wrangel, was to advance along the Volga and link up with the armies of General Yudenich, thrusting down from Estonia. Kolchak's Siberian armies were to move westwards across the Volga, heading directly for Moscow.

The onset of winter meant that the White plans had to be postponed until the following spring. In the meantime, the respite allowed both sides to marshal their forces in readiness for the onslaught. By the end of 1918, the strength of the Red Air Fleet had increased to 52 squadrons, some of them equipped with Fokker D VII fighters discovered on former German airfields. These aircraft were as good as anything the Whites possessed, including the Sopwith Camel F 1s which were now beginning to reach the White air units in small numbers. By January 1919 the Slavo-British Squadron at Archangel had re-equipped with Camels and Snipes, and it was flying one of the latter aircraft that Captain Kazakov shot down one of the few Red aircraft encountered in combat in the far north: a Grigorovitch M 9 seaplane.

In March 1919, Admiral Kolchak launched his offensive from Siberia and initially his armies enjoyed considerable success. Then the Red Army counter-attacked in strength and the White armies broke in panic. A general rout followed and the Reds pushed through the Urals into Siberia. The Red Air Fleet was active during these operations, its aircraft being used to mount strafing attacks on the retreating Whites with devastating results. Both Kolchak and the Czech Legion had received small numbers of aircraft during the previous months, but the morale of the White pilots was at rock-bottom and many of them flew over to the Reds. In the end, the disastrous campaign resulted in the Czech Legion abandoning the Whites to their fate and concluding an armistice with the Reds; they handed Kolchak over to the Bolsheviks, who shot him at Irkutsk. The Reds then began a two-year pursuit of the remnants of the White armies towards the east and the Pacific, 3,000 miles across Siberia.

The advance of Denikin's armies from the south also went well at the start. By the second week in April they had driven the Reds from the Donets Basin, and the following month they began a general offensive against the Soviet Southern Front. As well as several White squadrons equipped mainly with Camels and DH 9s, Denikin also had at his disposal two

RAF squadrons, Nos. 47 and 221—the former commanded by Wing-Commander Raymond Collishaw, a redoubtable fighter who had destroyed 68 enemy aircraft during the First World War—and 'A' Flight of No. 17 Squadron. The aircraft—Camels, DH 9s and RE 8s—had been rushed to the White Russian airfield at Ekaterinodar from Salonika, and they were almost worn out; nevertheless, they were soon to be engaged in some bitter air fighting. The Reds had assembled some of their best squadrons on the Southern Front, and during the spring of 1919 the Red pilots became increasingly aggressive—a sure sign that their quality was improving.

The RAF Camels were employed mainly for reconnaissance, strafing, and escorting formations of White DH 9 bombers. No. 47 Squadron was the first to meet the Reds in air combat, during the advance on Tsaritsyn in April; three Camels were carrying out a reconnaissance to the north of the town when they were bounced by a flight of Red Nieuport 28s. One of the Nieuports was shot down by Captain Aten, crashing on the banks of the Volga; all the Camels returned safely to base. A few days later, Red fighters made an unsuccessful attempt to attack the DH 9s of 47 Squadron 'A' Flight, escorted by Camels, which were bombing a Bolshevik headquarters in Tsaritsyn; one Spad was shot down by the British pilots, and a Fokker Triplane was damaged. A more spirited fight was put up that same week by a mixed formation of half a dozen Red Spads and Nieuports which attacked the DH 9s and Camels during a raid on an enemy flotilla sailing up the Volga. A whirling dogfight developed over the river and two of the Camels were badly damaged before the Reds broke off the combat, leaving a Spad and a Nieuport burning on the ground.

In mid April, the White fortunes suffered a severe blow when the French Colonial Division—which had been the first Allied force to land in southern Russia the year before—began to evacuate Sevastopol. Then, in May, General Wrangel's cavalry smashed the Reds at Velikoknyazheskoye, and the stage seemed to be set for further advances by Denikin's armies. Crossing the Volga, Wrangel's Cossacks fell on the

10th Red Army and cut it to pieces, taking 15,000 prisoners. While the White armies continued the advance on Tsaritsyn, the Camels of 47 Squadron patrolled the front, on the lookout for Red bombers that were reported to have arrived in the area. No bombers appeared, but there were several scraps with Bolshevik fighters, and No. 47's score began to mount steadily.

Several of the Red squadrons in the area were based on Urbabk airfield, and during the second week in May this was attacked by two squadrons of White Russian DH 9s escorted by 47 Squadron's Camels. The raid did very little damage, and the Reds came up in strength to meet the attackers. The enemy formation was led by an all-black Fokker triplane, and the pilot was no novice. For the first time since they arrived in Russia, the Camel pilots found themselves fighting for their lives, unable to protect the bombers, which were soon subjected to savage attacks by the Reds. Two DH 9s went down in flames, but the Camels accounted for five of the Red fighters for no loss to themselves.

In June, while Denikin prepared an offensive on the Kharkov front, General Wrangel's troops made a series of rapid forced marches across the steppes and arrived at Tsaritsyn, defended by the remnants of the 10th Red Army. On the 14th, news reached the Whites that General Budenny was on his way to relieve the town with 3,000 cavalry, and the pilots of 47 Squadron were at once ordered to attack the advancing Reds. Budenny's cavalry brigades were threading their way through a pass to the north of Tsaritsyn when the Camels screamed down on them. The slaughter was frightful; within minutes, the pass was choked with dead and dying horses and men, cut down by the storm of machine-gun fire from the air. Only a fraction of Budenny's force reached Tsaritsyn; many of those who survived the air attacks were caught and butchered by Shkura's Wolves, the Cossack division that was hated and feared above all others by the Reds.

The battle for Tsaritsyn began on June 15th, and by July 1st Wrangel had cleared the last Red troops out of the shattered city. There was hardly a building left intact. Throughout July, 47 Squadron was occupied in reconnaissance and the bombing of enemy supply lines. During one of these raids, on Cherni-Yar, a DH 9 flown by Captain W. Elliot was hit by ground fire and brought down; the pilot of a second DH 9 landed close by and picked up Elliot and his observer right under the noses of a troop of Red cavalry. He flew back to base with the two shot-down airmen in the rear cockpit, and his own observer standing on the wing, hanging grimly to a strut and plugging holes in the fuel tank with his thumbs.

August was a hectic month, with the Reds throwing everything they had in a bid to recapture Tsaritsyn. 47 Squadron carried out almost daily strafing attacks; the pilots were frequently challenged by Red aircraft, 10 of which were destroyed during the first two weeks of the month. On one occasion, the Red fighters attacked 47 Squadron's base at Beketovka, killing six men; fortunately, the squadron was out on a mission and no aircraft was lost. One Red aircraft—a Pfalz—was brought down by ground fire.

The Red offensive failed, and the Bolsheviks fell back on Saratov. By the beginning of September, Denikin was less than 400 miles from Moscow; during his summer campaign, he had taken nearly a quarter of a million Red prisoners. In the north-west, Yudenich was advancing on Petrograd. Six weeks later Denikin captured Orel and Novosil, bringing him to within 200 miles of Moscow. The triumph, however, was short-lived; on October 19th, overwhelmed by a new Red onslaught, the Whites were forced to evacuate Kursk and Orel, and the Bolsheviks had occupied Kiev several days earlier. Denikin, his lines overstretched, was forced to begin the long retreat from which the White armies would never recover.

By this time, No. 47 was the only RAF squadron in south Russia. No. 221, which had been based at Petrovsk for much of the time since its arrival—its aircraft being used mainly for reconnaissance over the Astrakhan area—had been disbanded in September, following the collapse of the White armies in that region. No. 47 was earmarked to carry on the fight in support of General Mai-Maevsky's Volunteer Army, engaged in bitter fighting around Kharkov, but both men and machines were swept up in the chaos of retreat and 47 Squadron was also disbanded in October, the crews making their way to Rostov. They were finally evacuated in March 1920, after destroying those of their aircraft that were left.

The evacuation of the Allied intervention forces left the Red Air Fleet in undisputed mastery of the sky on all fronts. Scattered White air formations continued to fight on, but by February 1920—the month when Archangel fell to the Reds —they were outnumbered and outclassed. The élite of the White Russian pilots were dead; men like Captain Kazakov, killed when his Snipe dived into the ground after stalling at low altitude on August 1st 1919. Those who were left were easy prey for the Red pilots, many of whom had now developed a high degree of skill. Among the Red pilots who carved out names for themselves during the bitter campaigns of 1919 were Ivan Pavlov, who commanded the first Soviet Military Aviation Group which flew in support of the 5th Red Army in the fighting around Kazan; G. S. Shaposhnikov, who chalked up a considerable score while flying a captured Snipe and later died while stunting over his airfield in 1920; Ivan V. Satunin, who also flew in support of the 5th Army; and Yuri Bratolyubov, who commanded a Special Duties Unit on the Southern Front. It was widely rumoured that some Red formations were led by German pilots, veterans of the First World War, and although this was never confirmed Allied pilots reported that Red air combat tactics in some sectors during 1919-1920 were reminiscent of those employed by the wartime German Flying Corps.

Red air operations on the Southern Front had been stepped up considerably towards the end of 1919, considerable numbers of aircraft having been transferred to this area after the defeat of Kolchak's forces in the east. During operations against Kolchak, the Red Air Fleet had made considerable progress in the development of various air fighting techniques, notably close support.

Some bombing missions had also been carried out at night.

On the Southern Front, the biggest concentration of Red air units had been around Tsaritsyn, with up to 50 aircraft committed to the defence of the town—an important target for the White bombers because of the location there of a major Bolshevik headquarters, which was frequently visited by Trotsky and other Red leaders. The Whites made several attempts to destroy these squadrons on the ground, but the Reds usually received plenty of advance warning of an approaching raid and the attacks were generally unsuccessful. The Red squadrons were successfully evacuated shortly before Tsaritsyn was captured by General Wrangel's forces. Aircraft of the Red Air Fleet based in this area, in addition to providing limited close support for the Bolshevik armies, also carried out a number of night attacks on White lines of communication, mainly railway stations. These raids had a certain nuisance value, but no significant damage was inflicted.

In the north, the activities of the Red Air Fleet had been limited mainly to reconnaissance, but since cavalry scouting patrols could not be used successfully because of the difficult terrain, the part played by aircraft in this respect was an important one. British naval forces operating in the Baltic in support of Latvia and Estonia encountered a few Red aircraft, but no combats were recorded during five months of operations in this area, even though British seaplanes made a series of devastating attacks on the big Russian naval base of Kronstadt.

On April 4th 1920, with the major part of his forces penned up in the Crimea, General Denikin handed over his command to Wrangel and left Russia for ever. By this time, Wrangel's total air strength numbered only 40 or so aircraft, under the command of General Tkatchoff, and although Britain and the United States had both promised to send replacement aircraft there was no prospect of their arriving in time to assist in stemming the Red onslaught.

Meanwhile, bitter fighting had broken out between the Reds and the Poles. Poland, which had been partitioned between Russia, Germany and Austro-Hungary for 100 years, had finally emerged as an independent state at the end of the First World War, but fierce fighting had broken out almost immediately in the Lvov area, where the Ukrainian minority had attempted to set up its own government. The Poles hurriedly began to expand their army and formed a small air force, consisting of 200 or so German aircraft—most of which were unserviceable. In April 1919, the new Polish army had captured Vilna, Lida, Baranovichi and Lvov, afterwards taking up defensive positions along the Beresina River in anticipation of a possible attack by the Bolsheviks. But the latter were fully committed to the struggle with the Whites during the ensuing months, and the expected offensive never materialized. In the spring of 1920, the Allied leaders made an unsuccessful attempt to bring about a frontier settlement between the Polish and Soviet Governments; the Poles refused to consider any frontier that did not include territory already occupied by their own troops, together with a large slice of the Ukraine.

With the military balance very much in his favour, the Polish commander, Marshal Pilsudski, resolved to launch a strong spring offensive against the relatively weak Soviet Western Front. When the battle started, the Poles had 20 squadrons with about 150 combat aircraft, far more than the Red Air Fleet could muster in the area. Initially, the Polish airmen caused considerable destruction, their bombing and strafing attacks being directed mainly against Soviet shipping on the Dnieper and against rolling stock.

Late in May, the tide began to turn against the Poles when the 1st Cavalry Army under Budenny attacked the Polish southern flank and broke through a week later, recapturing Kiev on June 10th. Budenny had an air group of 25 aircraft, fighters and reconnaissance machines, many of which had been captured from the Whites, and these were used extensively during the Russian breakthrough and subsequent Polish retreat. During this period, the Polish Air Force suffered badly from an almost complete lack of replacement aircraft and spares; by the beginning of July, the effective Polish air strength had been reduced to some 35 combat machines of all types.

The Russians also suffered from a shortage of spares and fuel; nevertheless, their aircraft—of which there were now about 170 along the entire front—maintained pressure on the Poles throughout the Red advance, although much attention was paid to the dropping of propaganda leaflets instead of bombs.

Early in August, with the Soviet advance threatening Warsaw itself and the Polish forces still in general retreat all along the front, the Poles appealed to the Allies for help. The French immediately sent a military mission under General Weygand, and a substantial quantity of British aircraft—mainly Bristol Fighters—arrived just in time to take part in the defence of the city. Losses were high, but the Poles managed to establish a measure of air superiority over the Reds. On August 15th, the Soviet armies were decisively beaten and began a disorderly withdrawal. Russian resistance crumbled everywhere, and by the beginning of October the victorious Poles had advanced through Byelorussia to the outskirts of Minsk. Hostilities came to an end on October 23rd, with the signing of the Treaty of Riga.

In the south, General Wrangel was still in control of the Crimea, and his forces were still capable of dealing sharp blows to the enemy. In June 1920, as the Reds were beginning to throw back the Poles, Wrangel made a lightning thrust into the Ukraine and succeeded in drawing off several Soviet divisions which might otherwise have enabled the Reds to smash the Poles once and for all. In this action, the Whites destroyed the 13th Red Army and, later, the 1st Cavalry Corps. During this fighting, heavy casualties were inflicted on the Red ground forces by General Tkatchoff's DH 9 ground-attack squadrons. In one of these attacks, in July, an astonishing incident occurred when Tkatchoff found himself involved in a mid-air battle with his opposite number in the Red Air Fleet, Peter Mesheraup—the only occasion in the history of air fighting when the commanders of two opposing air arms met in combat. This incident took place near Melitopol, when Tkatchoff—leading a flight of six DH 9s —was attacked by a pair of Red Nieuports, one of them piloted by Mesheraup. After a battle lasting three-quarters of an hour—in the course of which Tkatchoff's aircraft was hit five times—both sides broke off the combat and headed for home. Subsequent White offensives in the Caucasus and on Rostov, however, were checked by the Reds in September; and with the end of the war against Poland the following month, the Soviets concentrated all their forces in an all-out bid to smash Wrangel for good.

The Soviet preparations for a general offensive were assisted by the Red Air Fleet and the seaplanes of the Red Navy, which—in addition to reconnaissance—repeatedly bombed White shipping in the Black Sea and the Sea of Azov. For the first time, formations of up to three squadrons—15 aircraft—assembled to attack certain targets, mainly shipping and harbour installations. On November 16th, the Red Army smashed its way into the Crimea, forcing the remnants of the White Army back towards Sevastopol and Kerch. Throughout their retreat, the Whites were continually harassed by strafing Red aircraft; many of the surviving cavalry units—those that still retained some semblance of discipline—were torn to shreds by air attack.

On November 21st Sevastopol fell, and a few days later the last of the British, French and American ships that had been standing by to evacuate refugees pointed their bows away from Russia, overflowing with terrified people and leaving thousands more to the mercy of the Reds. The Imperial Standard had flown over Russia for the last time, and the Civil War was almost over. Almost, but not quite.

In March 1921, elements of the Red Baltic Fleet mutinied and seized control of the naval base of Kronstadt. On the 7th, two Soviet divisions attacked the port from north and south, across the ice-covered Gulf of Finland. During the advance, which was supported by the Red Air Fleet, at least two Naval Aviation seaplanes—flown by rebel pilots—attacked the Soviet troops, causing some casualties. The first assault was beaten off with heavy losses by Kronstadt's big naval guns, but the island fell the next day. During the preceding week, the Red airmen had flown 137 sorties against the island.

The Red Falcons

Meanwhile, White Russian forces were still holding on at Vladivostok and Khabarovsk, in the Far East Maritime Territory controlled by the Japanese. Khabarovsk was recaptured by the Reds in February 1922, and the Whites were forced to retreat steadily down the Ussuri River towards Spassk, where they made their last stand. This town also fell on October 9th, and two weeks later the first Red units were in Vladivostok. The Japanese evacuated the area shortly afterwards.

The numbers of aircraft used by both sides in the Far East were negligible. There had been an American unit equipped with Maurice Farmans at Spassk up to the summer of 1920, but it had withdrawn together with the rest of the United States forces. Afrer that, the only aircraft possessed by the Whites in the area were two Nieuports, one Farman and a pair of Morane-Saulnier Type N monoplanes—most of which were permanently unserviceable. Red aircraft in the Far East probably did not exceed 20 in number at any time before the end of 1922, and for most of the time these were engaged in reconnaissance and strafing missions against renegade Cossack and Mongolian bands.

When the Civil War finally ended, the strength of the Red Air Fleet had grown to some 325 aircraft, with 54 land-based units (including detachments of three or four aircraft) and at least 13 seaplane units. Already, by the end of 1922, great efforts were being made to streamline the Air Fleet and to standardize its equipment, at least partially. Most important of all, steps were being taken to organize a Soviet aviation industry; before 1917, 240 aircraft had been produced by the Russo-Baltic factories at Petrograd and a further 300 by other factories; but with the Revolution plans for further production and design had collapsed, technicians and designers emigrating or drowning in the tide of war.

With the worst of the internal strife over, an Aviation Research Institute—later to be known as the NII VVS—was created in September 1920 and staffed by those of Russia's aeronautical élite who had chosen to remain in the country. The following January, Lenin personally ordered the setting up of a Commission with the formidable task of working out a full aircraft construction programme for the next 10 years, down to the minutest detail. The Commission's first practical decision, taken in 1921, was to invite constructors to submit designs for an indigenous fighter aircraft.

Two designs were submitted: the Grigorovitch I-1 and the Shishmarev and Korvin MK-21. Neither was successful, and as a temporary replacement for their ageing equipment the Soviet were compelled to manufacture foreign types under licence. These included Nieuports and Spads; wide use was also made of captured types, including Ansaldo Balillas, Sopwith Pups, Martinsyde F 4 Buzzards and Fokker D 13s. Then, in 1922, an experienced aircraft engineer was appointed to organize a new design study bureau at GAZ-1, the Soviet State Aircraft Factory near Moscow. His name was Nikolai Polikarpov, and in 1923 his bureau produced its first combat aircraft design: the I-400 fighter, a single-seat low-wing canti-lever monoplane of mixed wood and metal construction, armed with two 7·62-mm machine-guns and fitted with a 400-hp Liberty engine that gave it a maximum speed of 150 mph. After some modification—which included the fitting of additional armament and a 450-hp M-5 engine, the licence-built version of the American Liberty—the fighter was produced in small numbers for the Red Air Force under the designation I-1M-5, but the type was not a success and only one unit was equipped with it.

For two decades, the GAZ-1 factory was to remain the nucleus of Soviet fighter production; and the little I-400 was the start of a long line of Polikarpov combat aircraft which, up to the middle of the 1930s, was to provide the Soviet Air Force with equipment as advanced as any produced by the Western aviation industries.

Chapter 2

The Growth of Soviet Air Power

In October 1922, under conditions of strict secrecy, 350 German aircraft engineers and fitters arrived in the Soviet Union. Within days of their arrival, they had begun work at a modern aircraft factory at Fili, near Moscow—a factory created by Professor Hugo Junkers, whose advanced D 1, CL 1 and J 1 combat aircraft had made their appearance on the Western Front during the closing stages of the First World War.

The clandestine movement of German personnel and equipment to the Soviet Union was the first fruit of an agreement on military collaboration drawn up in April 1922 between the Soviet Politburo and the Reichswehr, the post-war German army. The Russians realized that the Germans had a great deal to offer not only technically, but also in training and organizing elements of the Soviet armed forces; the Germans saw Russia as a base for the secret expansion of their own military power, crippled by the Treaty of Versailles. After tentative talks between German and Soviet agents, negotiations proper began in the spring of 1920, between Trotsky, the Soviet Commissar for War, and General von Seeckt, the Reichswehr commander.

Early the following year, a steady flow of German officer cadets entered various military training establishments in the Soviet Union. Many went to the flying school at Lipetsk, which in 1921-2 was entirely under German control. During their period of service in Russia, most German personnel wore Red Army uniforms, and some assumed Russian identities. It was during this time that Junkers and Krupp were invited to take part in further discussions, with a view to setting up factories on Russian soil. Ostensibly, the Krupp factory would be engaged in producing tractors and other farm machinery; but this was merely a cover for its true purpose, which was to study the design of tanks and other military vehicles for the Reichswehr and the Red Army.

In January 1922, three months before the agreement to provide industrial facilities for the Germans on Soviet territory was signed, plans were laid for German assistance in training the Red Army. By the end of the year, over 500 German officers were engaged in instructor duties with the Red Army and Air Fleet. Over the months that followed, several joint German-Soviet military exercises were held, involving the widespread use of aircraft; the lessons that emerged from these exercises enabled the Red Air Fleet planners to draw up a manual of air fighting, based largely on the tactics evolved by the Germans during the war. These were reflected in the use by the Russians of large, often unwieldy air formations on the lines of the Geschwader such as Richthofen's 'Circus' during the First World War. Although the Germans later revised their tactics completely as a result of the lessons they learned during the Spanish Civil War, the Russians made only a number of insignificant changes; in the main, the air fighting tactics used by the Red Air Force when it found itself locked in combat with the Luftwaffe in 1941 were 20 years out of date, and the consequences were disastrous.

While the training of personnel and the expansion of the Red Air Fleet went on at a steady rate, a number of squadrons were actively engaged in assisting the Red Army to put down a series of rebellions and 'brushfire wars' that sprang up in various corners of Russia during the early 1920s. Peasant revolts in the Ukraine and the Caucasus—caused by famine and opposition to the Soviet Government's collectivization policies—were put down ruthlessly by regular Red Army units under the command of NKVD officers and the Red Air Fleet was called in on several occasions to bomb villages where resistance was particularly stiff. In Central Asia, roving bands of Basmachi tribesmen continued to be a thorn in the Soviet Government's flesh, but the Basmachi ceased to be a dangerous fighting force after their leader, the former Turkish soldier Enver Pasha, was killed in a skirmish with Red troops in August 1922. During operations against the tribesmen, several Red aircraft were brought down by ground fire. On one or two occasions, the Basmachi returned surviving airmen to their comrades—minus various parts of their bodies. The Basmachi held out in the mountains of Tadzhikstan and Uzbekistan for nearly a decade; the Red Army was completely incapable of winkling them out, and for lengthy periods offensive operations were maintained by units of the Red Air Fleet in the area. Between 50 and 60 aircraft were involved, the majority being DH-9s and 9As—known as the R-2 and R-1 in Russian service.

The year 1923 saw the beginning of a substantial reorganization programme for the Soviet Armed Forces, including the Military Air Forces of the Workers' and Peasants' Red Army, as the former Air Fleet was now known. Although squadrons still came under the direct control of the army commands to which they were attached, overall administration was now the responsibility of a separate headquarters, the Chief Directorate of the Air Forces of the Red Army. An Air Force General Staff was formed in 1925, and the systematic numbering of Red Air Force squadrons began the following year. The size of air units was also standardized to a certain extent, with approximately five squadrons to an Air Brigade and three flights, each of three sections, to a squadron. In 1928, all air units came under the direct operational control of the Chief Directorate of the Air Forces, although their primary task was still to support the Red Army.

In 1929, the new organization of the Soviet Army and Air Force was put to the test under combat conditions when a crisis suddenly flared up in the Far East. The trouble started when the Chinese, under General Chiang Kai-shek, began to move large troop concentrations up to the Manchurian border to threaten the Soviet-controlled Chinese Eastern Railway, which ran through the fringes of Manchurian territory and linked the Trans-Siberian Railway with Vladivostok. In August 1929, the Russians formed a Special Far Eastern Army under Marshal Blukher, with its headquarters at Khabarovsk; its organization was still incomplete when the Chinese—mainly troops of the provincial Manchurian Army—began a series of lightning raids on installations inside Soviet territory.

Blukher had some 65 aircraft at his disposal, some of which

had been hurriedly flown to the Far East from bases west of the Urals. The majority were DH 9s, but there was also a small number of Farman bombers and Fokker reconnaissance and fighter aircraft. Most of the reconnaissance missions were in fact flown by the DH 9s, which also attacked infiltrating groups of Chinese infantry during August. The Farmans made several trips across the border to bomb military targets; a few of these raids were carried out at night.

It was not until October, however, that the Red Army counter-attacked in strength in an effort to reoccupy the territory seized by the Chinese troops of Marshal Chang Tso-lin. On the 12th of that month, large numbers of Soviet troops crossed the Amur River and established a foothold in Manchuria to the south of Khabarovsk, advancing rapidly on the strategically important town of Fukdin. Throughout the advance, Soviet aircraft strafed ahead of the army units and bombed targets in Fukdin itself. The final assault on the town began on October 31st, and Fukdin fell three days later. The Manchurian garrison was all but wiped out, and the Soviet force withdrew across the river after blowing up enemy communications and supply dumps.

Two weeks later, on November 17th, three Soviet divisions and one cavalry brigade of the 18th Corps advanced on Manchouli, the meeting-point of the Soviet, Chinese and Mongolian frontiers, to clear Chinese troops from a stretch of railway. The Russians crossed the railway at two points and encircled the enemy in a huge pincer movement, cutting the Chinese off completely from any outside help and moving up tanks and artillery to finish them off. During this operation, Red Air Force units—mainly those using DH 9s—were called in to bomb the enemy-occupied towns of Manchouli, Suifenho, Dalainor, Hailar and Tunkiang. The raids had a serious effect on Chinese morale, particularly since the Chinese had no aircraft in this sector to oppose the Soviet machines. Some anti-aircraft fire was put up, but it was totally ineffective. There is no record of any Soviet aircraft being lost through enemy action during the entire campaign.

Nevertheless, the Manchurian forces fought back hard as

the Russian net began to tighten, and some units managed to break out. The defence was undoubtedly aided by the fact that there was complete confusion between the Soviet infantry, tanks and artillery; there was virtually no co-operation or effective support. Soviet casualties were very heavy, but sheer weight of numbers—together with valuable air reconnaissance —saved the situation, and by November 27th the Manchurians surrendered. Meanwhile, another Manchurian force had been cut to pieces by the Soviet 19th Corps at Mishan, north of Vladivostok. Two flights of Soviet Air Force aircraft were reported to have been involved in this operation.

Peace finally returned on December 22nd 1929, when the Chinese signed an agreement returning the railway to Soviet control. For both sides, the conflict had been brief and costly; but the Russian success forced Chiang Kai-shek to abandon any ideas of bringing further military pressure to bear on Soviet administration in the Far East. The Russians, anxious to avoid any further confrontations in an area where their resources were badly overstretched, later sold their interests in the Manchurian section of the railroad to the Japanese when the latter invaded Manchuria in 1932.

The Sino-Soviet conflict was a direct reflection of the Russians' inability to extend their influence to China during the mid 1920s; their aspirations in this field had received a severe setback with the series of defeats inflicted on the Chinese Communists by Chiang Kai-shek's forces. China, however, was only one of the areas subject to Soviet political interference during this period, subversive activities also being directed against Mongolia, India, Afghanistan, Persia, Java and Turkey. The Red Air Force played a considerable part in these political manoeuvres by 'showing the flag' and providing direct assistance in the form of military missions. In addition to long-distance flights and prestige tours carried out by Soviet aircraft in western Europe and the Far East during the mid 1920s, formations of Soviet military aircraft also visited Afghanistan, Turkey and Persia, participating in numerous air displays. At the same time, the Red Army and Air Force undertook the training of increasing numbers of personnel from several 'sympathetic' countries; as early as 1923, the Red Air Force sent a special military mission to Afghanistan to help found a small air arm, and in 1927 a civil air service was inaugurated between Tashkent and Kabul. In Persia, an embryo air force was also created with Soviet equipment in the face of stiff competition from the West, particularly Britain; while in Mongolia, the Russians founded a flying school at Urga in 1929 and equipped it with 30 Soviet aircraft. Negotiations with Turkey were less successful, even though Kemal Ataturk had received substantial aid from the new Soviet Government in his campaign to drive the Greeks out of the country in the early 1920s; nevertheless, Soviet aircraft were frequent visitors to Turkey throughout the twenties and a small number of Red Air Force advisers were stationed there more or less permanently.

Meanwhile, the Soviet aviation industry had been rapidly getting off the ground. In the beginning, as we have already seen, the plan had been for a large part of the modern aviation industry to be based on German technical prowess and financial assistance; but results had been generally disappointing. Hugo Junkers had produced a number of transport and bomber aircraft for the Soviet Air Force, but the aircraft of his design that had looked the most promising on the drawing board, the H-21 fighter—a parasol monoplane fitted with a 185-hp BMW in-line engine—had proved a failure. Following this, the Soviet Government had taken over control of the Fili factory, and the man they had appointed as chief designer was Andrei N. Tupolev.

In 1908, at the age of 20, Tupolev had entered the Advanced Technical College in Moscow, and it was there that he first met N. E. Zhukovsky, the 'Father of Russian Aviation'. Specializing in aeronautics, Tupolev formed a syndicate with several friends and built a series of small gliders. In 1918, together with Zhukovsky, he founded the Central Aero-Hydrodynamic Institute, or TsAGI, and three years later he built his first powered aircraft, the ANT-1 single-engined sporting monoplane. This was followed, in 1924, by the all-metal ANT-2 single-engined three-seater. While this type was

still being flight-tested Tupolev completed the prototype
ANT-3, a single-engined biplane which was later produced
in series for the Red Air Force. It was in an aircraft of this
type that Mikhail M. Gromov, a test pilot at the NII-VVS
research centre, made a tour of European capitals in 1925,
and in 1927 another test pilot named Shestakov flew an ANT-3
from Moscow to Tokyo and back.

In 1927, Tupolev embarked upon the construction of several
new prototypes. The first was the ANT-4, a twin-engined
bomber and reconnaissance aircraft known as the TB-1 in
Red Air Force service; next came the ANT-5, an all-metal
sesquiplane fighter conceived by Tupolev, Pavel O. Sukhoi
and Vladimir Petlyakov. By this time, Tupolev had established a firm reputation as a pioneer of all-metal construction,
and the ANT-5—known as the I-4 in Air Force service—
was the first Soviet fighter built in this way; its appearance
marked an important turning-point in the evolution of aircraft
construction in the USSR.

A single-seater with a fixed undercarriage, the I-4 was built
of Kolchugalumin—a type of duralumin produced by the
Kolchuga factories. It was fitted with a nine-cylinder radial
M-22 engine (the licence-built version of the French Gnome-
Rhône Jupiter) developing 480 hp, and armament comprised
two fixed 7·62-mm machine-guns firing through the propeller.
With a maximum speed of 170 mph, the I-4 was superior to
contemporary Soviet fighter designs, and quantity production
continued for several years after 1928. By 1932, Factory No. 22
at Fili had turned out 242 examples, and the total number
built was about 370. Several different versions of the I-4
were produced, including a twin-cannon variant, a monoplane
variant, a seaplane variant and a version fitted with six solid-
fuel rockets for short take-off.

Concurrently with the I-4, Tupolev produced the ANT-9,
a three-engined transport aircraft. Perhaps the most famous
ANT-9 was one named 'Wings of the Soviets', which Gromov
took on a second tour of Europe in 1929. That same year,
an ANT-4 named 'Land of the Soviets' made a flight from
Moscow to New York. Also in 1929, Tupolev produced the

ANT-6 four-engined bomber, known under the military designation of TB-3; 818 examples were built over the next decade.

The other highly successful Soviet aircraft designer of this period, Nikolai N. Polikarpov, was also turning out new prototypes in rapid succession. In 1924, following his unsuccessful I-1M-5 fighter, he produced a single-engined transport biplane known as the PM-1, a formation of which flew to Peking the following year under the command of Mikhail Gromov. In 1925 Polikarpov designed a more advanced version, the P-2, which was capable of carrying seven passengers. It was in 1925 that M. V. Frunze, the head of the Soviet War Commissariat, announced to the Third Congress of the Soviets that Russia's aviation industry had become independent of foreign aid.

In 1927, Polikarpov produced a new single-seat fighter, the I-3, fitted with a 600-hp M-17 engine, a licence-built version of the German BMW VI. Armament was two fixed 7·62-mm machine-guns, and maximum speed was 160 mph. Next came the R-5, an excellent reconnaissance biplane that was subsequently produced in large numbers, together with an assault variant known as the R-Z. In 1929 Polikarpov modified his I-3 and produced the DI-2 two-seat fighter, fitted with a 680-hp M-17 engine and an armament of one fixed 7·62-mm gun in the nose and two movable 7·62s in the rear cockpit. Maximum speed was 160 mph.

In the spring of 1930 Polikarpov, in collaboration with Dmitri Grigorovitch, produced the I-5, a single-seat biplane fighter with exceptional manoeuvrability and an armament of four PV-1 machine-guns with a rate of fire of 800-900 rounds per minute. Polikarpov conceived this aircraft in prison, where he and his colleague found themselves for a short time after being charged with sabotage during the first Stalin Purge. The first prototype flew in April 1930, and about 800 I-5s were subsequently built.

By this time, the design of fighter aircraft in the USSR was progressing along two distinct lines, with the traditional highly manoeuvrable biplane fighter designs now competing with early low-wing monoplane designs, fitted with retractable undercarriages and either radial or in-line engines. Grigoro-vitch adhered to the first formula, and in 1930 he produced the I-6 single-seat biplane, a very light and manoeuvrable machine with a nine-cylinder M-15 radial that gave it a maximum speed of 200 mph. He then produced a two-seat biplane fighter, the DI-3, characterized by its twin fins and rudders; it was fitted with a 600-hp M-17 engine and three 7·62-mm machine-guns. The I-7, which appeared shortly afterwards, was a landplane version of a proposed floatplane fighter for the Soviet Naval Aviation, which in fact was not built. The I-7 was powered by a 680-hp M-17 engine; speed of the I-7 was 210 mph, and armament comprised four 7·62-mm guns.

The years 1930-3 saw the appearance of a further three designs which never left the drawing-board. These were the twin-engined I-9, which was to have been equipped with two 480-hp M-22 engines giving it an estimated maximum speed of 215 mph; the I-10 single-seat gull-wing monoplane with a 625-hp M-25 radial and a maximum speed of 220 mph; and the I-11, a Polikarpov biplane with a 820-hp AM-34A in-line engine, also with an estimated top speed of 220 mph.

In 1933 Polikarpov designed the I-13 biplane, forerunner of the famous I-15 or TsKB-3, which made its first flight in October of that year. The I-15 was a biplane with a fixed undercarriage; the upper wing was gull-shaped, giving an excellent view forwards and upwards. It was fitted with a 750-hp M-25 engine (the licence-built version of the American Wright Cyclone) which gave it a top speed of 220 mph. Armament comprised four 7·62-mm machine-guns and there was provision for light bombs in racks under the wings. On November 21st 1935, test pilot Vladimir Kokkinaki reached a record altitude of 14,575 metres while flying an aircraft of this type. In 1934, the I-15 was followed by the I-15 bis, with an improved M-25V engine that raised its top speed to 230 mph. In a bid to raise the speed still further, Polikarpov then produced the I-153, with a retractable undercarriage, but the maximum speed of the early I-153s—240 mph—was still insufficient when compared with that of the new fighter aircraft which were beginning to enter service with the British, French and German air forces. The M-25V engine was consequently replaced by an M-62R developing 1,000 hp, and then by a 1,100-hp M-63, which gave the I-153 a top speed of 265 mph.

The I-153, dubbed 'Chaika' (Seagull) because of its distinctive wing shape, was a first-rate combat aircraft and was subsequently to prove its worth in air fighting. It was able to outturn almost every aircraft that opposed it in action. The last single-seat biplane to be produced in series in the USSR, the I-153 had an armament of four ShKAS 7·62-mm synchronized machine-guns, and could carry a bomb-load of 150 kg or six RS-82 air-to-ground rockets.

On December 31st 1933, two months after the I-15, a new Polikarpov fighter made its first flight: the I-16 or TsKB-12, a low-wing monoplane with a retractable undercarriage, two wing-mounted 7·62-mm guns and a 480-hp M-22 engine which gave it a maximum speed of 270 mph. The I-16 was the first Soviet fighter to incorporate armour plating round the pilot's cockpit. The first production versions, the I-16 Types 4, 5 and 10 (TsKB-12 bis), were fitted with a 750-hp M-25B, which raised their speed by 20 miles an hour. On these variants, wheels and flaps had to be wound down by hand, which required some mild gymnastics on the part of the pilot.

During the mid 1930s, the basic I-16 design was progressively modified to carry out a variety of different tasks. Among the variants produced was the TsKB-18, an assault variant armed with four PV-1 synchronized machine guns, two wing-mounted machine guns and 100 kg of bombs. The pilot was protected by armour plating in front, below and behind.

In 1938 the I-16 Type 17 was tested, armed with two wing-mounted cannon. This version was produced in large numbers. Then, with the co-operation of the armament engineer B. G. Shpitalnii, Polikarpov produced the TsKB-12P—the first aircraft in the world to be armed with two synchronized cannon firing through the propeller arc. The last fighter version of the I-16 was the Type 24, fitted with a 1,000-hp M-62R engine which gave it a top speed of 325 mph. Two more versions of the I-16 were built: the UTI-4, a two-seat trainer with a fixed undercarriage, and the SPB, a dive-bomber version. Altogether, some 20,000 I-16s of all types were built. The little fighter never had an official name; its nickname Rata, by which it was widely known during its operational career, was only one of many applied to it.

Concurrently with Polikarpov's I-16, Andrei Tupolev developed the ANT-31 or I-14, a low-wing single-seat mono-plane which was the first Soviet aircraft to feature stressed-skin construction. The prototype flew late in 1933, and the aircraft was produced in small numbers. A year later, in 1934, Tupolev converted his SB-1 bomber into a long-range fighter for the Naval Aviation. Designated MI-3, the aircraft was powered by two 850-hp M-58 engines and carried a heavy armament: one fixed 25-mm cannon and two fixed 7·62-mm machine guns in the nose, plus two movable 7·62-mm guns in the dorsal turret.

Also in 1934, the Grigorovitch design bureau produced the IP-1 cannon-armed fighter, armed with two machine guns and two DRP-76 recoilless cannon. Both the IP-1 and the IP-4, a modified version, were produced in fairly large num-bers. September of that year saw the first flight of the prototype Polikarpov TsKB-15 or I-17, a low-wing fighter with a retractable undercarriage and an in-line engine, armed with two wing-mounted cannon and two machine guns. The second prototype, known as the TsKB-19 or I-17 Type 2, was shown at the Salon International de l'Aeronautique in Paris in 1936. It was equipped with a 840-hp M-100 engine and armed with four 7·62-mm ShKAS machine guns in the wings and a 20-mm cannon in the propeller hub. The I-17 was modified once more in 1935, when it was armed with three machine guns and 100 kg of bombs and designated TsKB-33. Maximum speed was 310 mph at sea level. The type was not a success and did not go beyond the prototype stage.

During this period, with considerable emphasis being

placed on the creation of a strong bomber force, many experiments were carried out in an effort to find ways of adapting existing fighter designs for long-range escort duties. One of the possibilities investigated was the use of 'parasite' fighters, where the fighter was carried on board the bomber and launched to provide on-the-spot defence over the target area, afterwards being retrieved in flight. The responsibility for working out the technical details was given to Vladimir S. Vakhmistrov, a member of the Scientific Research Institute of the Red Air Force, who had already designed a number of small gliders which were carried aloft by aircraft and then released for use as aerial gunnery targets.

Parasite fighter experiments began in December 1931, with two I-4 fighters attached to the upper surface of the wings of a TB-1 bomber. The two fighters were flown by test pilots Alexander Anisimov and Valerii Chkalov, with Adam Zalevski piloting the TB-1. The experiment nearly ended in disaster when the TB-1's co-pilot released the attachment of Chkalov's I-4 too soon and without warning, causing the fighter to pitch up violently. Chkalov's skill, however, saved the situation; both fighters separated safely from the parent aircraft, carrying out a simulated mission before flying back to land on their own airfield.

Further development of the idea was ordered by Marshal M. N. Tukhachevski, the C-in-C of the Soviet Armed Forces, and more experiments were carried out in April 1934—this time with two I-5s attached to a four-engined TB-3 bomber, and later with two I-16s attached. The fact that these experiments were successful was due entirely to the exceptional skill of the test pilots; it was quickly realized that fighters would have to be specially designed for missions of this type if they were to be carried out by the average Red Air Force pilot.

Vakhmistrov accordingly took a Grigorovitch TsKB-7 fighter and modified it extensively, giving it the designation I-Z (Istrebitel Zvyeno). The I-Z was extremely sturdy and robust, featuring stressed-skin construction. Hook-on experiments with this type began in 1934, and in April of that year test pilot Vasilii Stepanchonok successfully linked up with a special trapeze slung under a parent TB-3 bomber, afterwards detaching the I-Z and bringing it in to land safely. Nevertheless, the use of the I-Z was only an interim measure; Vakhmistrov's real hopes were pinned on a version of Polikarpov's I-17, fitted with a retractable hook, and on a projected design for a huge mother aircraft capable of carrying up to six fighters. In 1937, however, Vakhmistrov's plans received a severe blow when his chief supporter, Marshal Tukhachevski, was arrested and shot during a purge. Vakhmistrov's funds were drastically cut, and he was forced to abandon the idea of an advanced 'Zvyeno' combination. However, some further experiments were made with SPB (modified I-16) fighters slung under the wings of a TB-3-AM-34 bomber, and in fact this combination was used operationally on one occasion: in August 1941, when two SPBs dive-bombed a bridge in Rumania after being carried within range by a TB-3.

In 1938, with the speed of new bomber aircraft having improved to such an extent that it matched and sometimes even surpassed the speed of the fighter aircraft that were supposed to catch them, the manoeuvrable biplane v. fast monoplane controversy at last came to an end in the Soviet aviation industry. The Soviet Air Staff now issued a requirement for a new monoplane fighter which, although possessing a high maximum speed, still retained good manoeuvrability and an acceptable landing speed.

The first attempt to meet this requirement was made by the engineers Nikitin and Shevchenko, whose IS-1 fighter prototype was a combination of old and new—a biplane on take-off and a monoplane in flight. Once the aircraft was airborne, the two small lower wings were raised automatically to become part of the centre section of the gull-shaped upper wing. The undercarriage was retractable. The IS-1 never went into production; although ingenious in its conception, its complexity gave rise to insurmountable problems of handling and maintenance.

Meanwhile, the fighters and bombers that formed the

first-line equipment of the Soviet Air Force had been severely tested under all kinds of combat conditions in a war that was a dress rehearsal for the greater conflict to come, as Russian aircrews fought and died and stubby-winged Ratas and Chaikas tangled with Nationalist aircraft in the skies of Spain.

Chapter 3

Into Combat

It was bitterly cold in the open cockpit of the little Fiat
CR 32 biplane fighter. The icy wind tore at Captain Garcia
Morato's face as he leaned forward, his eyes probing the
dangerous sky above the horizon.

It was the morning of February 18th 1937. Half an hour
earlier, Morato had taken off from his base at Talavera
together with 20 other CR 32s to escort a flight of Nationalist
Junkers 52 bombers on a raid over the Republican lines. Most
of the fighters belonged to the Italian Legion and were flown
by Italian pilots. Only three, Morato's 'Blue Patrol', were
flown by Spaniards. On their tails, standing out against the
green and sand-yellow dappled camouflage, was Morato's
insignia—a trio of birds, a buzzard, falcon and blackbird,
inside a blue circle with the old bullfighting motto 'Vista,
Suerte y al Toro'.

Suddenly, dirty yellow puffs of smoke began to blossom
among the Nationalist formation as it crossed the front line.
The Italian fighters began to jink about wildly, then they
formed up and turned for home, leaving Morato's Blue Patrol
to escort the bombers alone. The Italians were obeying orders
from the Italian Air Ministry, instructions strictly forbidding
the fighter squadrons of the Italian Legion to fly over enemy
territory under any circumstances.

The Blue Patrol was under the orders of the Italian Legion,
and should have turned back with the other fighters; but
Morato and his two wing-men stubbornly refused to leave
the slow, lumbering Junkers 52s to the mercy of the ever-
growing hordes of Republican aircraft. The bombers were
just beginning their run-in towards the target when Morato
saw them: a cluster of brilliant dots at ten o'clock, a couple
of thousand feet higher up. They were Republican fighters,
there was no doubt about that; stubby little Russian-built
I-15 Chato biplanes. Morato counted them as they closed
in rapidly: 10 . . . 20 . . . 25 . . . 36 of them. Thirty-six

against three! The Blue Patrol would be lucky if it came out of this in one piece.

Still maintaining a slack formation, the Chatos dived towards the bombers and the three Nationalist fighters. Morato waited, timing his next move with a skill born of 50 air combats. Suddenly, he slammed open the throttle and brought the stick hard back into his left thigh, bringing the CR 32 round in a steep climbing turn. His wing-men, anticipating the move, clung grimly to his tail.

The manoeuvre took the Republicans completely by surprise. They broke and scattered in all directions as the three Fiats raced head-on towards them, guns chattering. A Chato zipped across Morato's nose and he got in a solid burst; the Republican fighter flicked away into a tight spiral, coughing smoke. There was no time to follow the enemy aircraft down to make sure it was finished; the three pilots of the Blue Patrol found themselves enmeshed in a web of darting, twisting fighters, all queueing up to attack the bombers. Desperately, the gunners in the Junkers fought to bring their weapons to bear on the aggressive little biplanes that came boring in from all directions. Already one Junkers was trailing smoke from a shot-up engine.

A Chato rocketed past Morato and he got on the Republican's tail, raking the fighter's fuselage. The pilot flung up his arms and collapsed in the cockpit, and the Chato fell away in a vicious spin. Sweating, Morato rolled frantically to the left as bullets crackled past his own aircraft from an I-15 sitting a few yards behind his tail. Then, suddenly, the Republicans put down their noses and dived away, their tubby shapes dwindling rapidly into the distance. Looking round, Morato saw the reason: the sky was full of Nationalist CR 32s. The Italian fighter leader had decided to disobey orders after all; he and his pilots had returned and hurled themselves into the fray in the nick of time. . . .

When the Spanish Civil War began in July 1936, the Republicans held all the cards as far as air superiority was concerned; and they were to retain their commanding position throughout the first year of the conflict. On the outbreak of war they had 214 aircraft of all types, against the 50 or so —mostly unserviceable—that were available to the Nationalists. The Republican air strength was increased still further during August, when the predominantly anti-Fascist French Government supplied 70 Dewoitine D-371, D-500 and D-510 single-seat fighters, together with a smaller number of Loire-Nieuport 46s and Bleriot-Spad S-510s.

Nevertheless, it was the Nationalists who had been the first to receive military aid from abroad. On July 26th 1936, Franco had sent emissaries to Adolf Hitler, who promised German support for the Nationalist cause. A department of the German Defence Ministry was given the task of sending war material to Spain and recruiting 'volunteers'. A training contingent was formed under the command of General von Scheele and on July 31st 85 men and six Heinkel He 51 fighters sailed from Hamburg on the ss *Usaramo*, bound for Cadiz. The ship also carried spares for a number of three-engined Junkers 52 bomber-transports, which had reached Spain by way of Italy. The Junkers' first task was to transport thousands of Franco's Moorish troops across the straits from Morocco to the Spanish mainland; grossly overloaded, each aircraft made up to seven trips a day, and it was thanks to them that Franco was able to consolidate his position on the mainland in an amazingly short time and begin his march on Madrid. The Junkers also bombed and sank the Republican battleship *Jaime I* and dropped supplies to the defenders of the Alcazar de Toledo, enabling General Moscardo to hold out until he was relieved by Franco's forces.

Meanwhile, the Soviet Government appeared to be approaching the Spanish situation with a good deal of caution. On August 23rd 1936, Stalin formally accepted the international Non-Intervention Agreement, and on the 28th of that same month he issued an open decree forbidding the export of Soviet military equipment to the Spanish Government. In fact, Stalin planned not only to supply arms and military advisers, but also to assist in the formation of the International Brigades by sending experienced Comintern leaders to Spain, and ultimately to gain control of the Spanish Communist and Socialist Parties.

On September 10th 1936, 33 Red Air Force technicians arrived at Cartagena and immediately took over various facilities at the nearby airfields of Carmoli and Los Alcazares. Their immediate task was to prepare for the arrival of 18 crated Polikarpov I-15s, which were then in the process of being loaded on board the Russian freighter *Bolshevik* at Odessa. The *Bolshevik* reached Cartagena on October 13th, and the I-15s were rapidly off-loaded and transported to Los Alcazares for assembly. On the 16th, another Soviet freighter rendezvoused on the high seas with a Spanish Republican vessel, the *Lavamendi*, and 12 more crated I-15s were transferred to the latter, which then proceeded to Cartagena. That same day, 150 Red Air Force personnel under the command of Colonel Yakob Shmushkievich—who was known by the pseudonym of 'General Douglas' throughout Russia's commitment in the Spanish conflict—arrived at an airfield south of Alicante. The group included 50 fighter pilots, and it was in their hands that the I-15—immediately dubbed 'Chato' (Snub-nose) by the Spaniards—made its operational debut on the Madrid front, while the first squadron of Republican pilots were converting on to the type under the supervision of Russian instructors at Los Alcazares.

The I-15's first combat over Spain took place on November 4th 1936, when a formation of 10 fighters attacked an Ro 37 reconnaissance aircraft of the Italian Air Legion over the Manzanares River. The Ro 37 got away when a pair of Fiat CR 32s came up and engaged the I-15s, but the Russian pilots were no novices and both the Fiats went down in flames. Other Italian fighter pilots, who came racing up to the scene just as the I-15s were disappearing over the horizon, returned to base and reported that they had identified the enemy aircraft as American Curtiss biplanes. Because of this mistake, the I-15 continued to be referred to as the 'Curtiss' by many Nationalists for the duration of the Civil War, and it was years before the myth was finally dispelled.

During October and November 1936, a dozen Soviet

freighters kept up a shuttle service between Odessa and Cartagena. By the end of October, there were 200 Russian pilots and 1,500 technicians in Spain, the majority having arrived aboard the freighters *Rostock*, *Volga* and *Neva*. These vessels did not return to the Soviet Union completely empty; on the return trip, they carried Spanish Government gold to the value of £63,265,684—the agreed payment made by the Republicans in exchange for Russian aid.

Strangely enough, the first Russian combat aircraft to see action over Spain was not the well-tried I-15, but a type which had entered service with the Red Air Force only a matter of weeks before the first batch arrived at Cartagena: the Tupolev SB-2, a fast twin-engined bomber with a maximum speed of 250 mph at 16,500 feet. Armed with three 7·62-mm ShKAS machine guns and able to carry up to 1,100 pounds of bombs, the SB-2 Katiushka presented the Nationalist pilots with a real headache when it first appeared in Spanish skies during the second week of October 1936; it was not only faster than the Fiat CR 32s that were sent up to intercept it, but it could also outclimb them once it had got rid of its bomb load. It was a real triumph when, on October 28th, a Nationalist pilot named Captain Salas managed to shoot down the first SB-2; and an added boost for the Nationalists' morale came five days later when Captain Mantelli, an Italian Legion pilot, destroyed a second bomber over Talavera.

The Republican SB-2 units, which were commanded by a Russian Air Force officer named General Denisov, were used for both bombing and reconnaissance. The Russian bomber bore a strong resemblance to the American Martin 139, and —as with the I-15—this led to the completely erroneous belief that it was the American aircraft which the Republicans were using. In fact, this belief—which the Republicans deliberately did their best to foster by issuing photographs of the Martin bomber from which the American markings had been carefully erased and replaced by Republican ones—very nearly caused a major international crisis when formations of SB-2s began to bomb Nationalist-held cities, causing civilian casualties.

For weeks the SB-2s ranged at will over Nationalist territory, virtually unopposed by any fighters. To deal with them the Nationalist fighter pilots had to evolve a completely new set of tactics. These involved flying standing patrols at 16,500 feet over the front line; as soon as an SB-2 was sighted, the fighter pilots would build up speed in a dive—their only hope of catching the Russian aircraft.

It was Garcia Morato who developed these tactics to a fine art. During December 1936 and January 1937, a pair of SB-2s made repeated bombing attacks on Cordoba, and every attempt to intercept them failed. Then Morato discovered a significant fact: the SB-2s always arrived over the city at the same time and the same altitude.

One morning late in January, Morato took off to patrol over the city at 16,500 feet, and saw the two bombers appear below him right on schedule. With the sun at his back, he dived on the leading bomber and raked it with his Fiat's twin 12·7-mm machine guns. Pieces broke away from the Russian aircraft and thick black smoke poured back from one engine. Then the SB-2 rolled over and dived vertically earthwards, exploding just before it hit the ground.

Tracers flicked over Morato's own cockpit and he broke away sharply to see the second SB-2 blazing away at him with its nose guns from a range of 200 yards or so. Morato dived, then pulled up the nose of his Fiat steeply. The oil-streaked fuselage of the Russian bomber passed a few feet above him and he hung there on the edge of a stall, finger crooked around the trigger and watching his two machine guns sew jagged holes along the full length of the SB-2's pale blue belly. The bomber lurched and fell away in a spin, breaking up as it plummeted and finally hitting the ground in a cloud of blazing wreckage. The myth of the SB-2's invulnerability had been shattered once and for all.

The third Russian aircraft type to enter service in Spain was the I-16, 12 of which—a complete Red Air Force squadron —arrived at the northern Spanish port of Bilbao on October 25th 1936. From there they were transferred to an airfield near Santander, where they were hastily assembled and hurled into battle on November 5th. Their first task was to provide air cover for a Republican offensive against Nationalist forces advancing in Valdemoro, Sesena and Esquivias. The I-16—nicknamed Mosca (Fly) by the Republicans and Rata (Rat) by the Nationalists—proved itself to be markedly superior to the German Heinkel He 51. It was also faster than its most numerous Nationalist opponent, the Fiat CR 32, although the Italian fighter was slightly more manoeuvrable and provided a better gun platform. Apart from that, the Nationalists' tactics were better; the Republicans tended to stick to large, tight, unwieldy formations that were easy to spot and difficult to handle. During the early stages of their commitment, both I-15s and I-16s were used extensively for ground attack work, but the responsibility for most missions of this kind was gradually undertaken by the fourth Russian type to enter combat in Spain—the Polikarpov R-Z Natasha, the attack version of the R-5 reconnaissance biplane.

By the beginning of January 1937, 17 Soviet pilots had been designated Heroes of the Soviet Union as a result of their service in Spain; ostensibly, the decoration was given for 'the successful completion of difficult Government missions'. One of them was Captain S. F. Tarkhov, who commanded the 107th (I-15) Squadron; two flight commanders in the same unit, Captain N. F. Balanov and Lieutenant I. A. Lakeyev, received similar awards later in the year. Also a recipient of the award was test pilot A. K. Serov, who became the top-scoring Russian ace in Spain with 16 'kills' to his credit. He was later killed in a flying accident in May 1939. The second top-scorer was P. V. Rychagov, who destroyed 15 Nationalist aircraft, and third—with 14—was Captain I. T. Yeremenko, who was a flight commander in the 119th (I-15) Squadron. In 1937, Yeremenko took over command of a Soviet fighter group in Spain from Major-General I. I. Pumpur, also a Hero of the Soviet Union, who—like Rychagov, Shmushkievich and several others—was later arrested and shot during Stalin's infamous purges. Also high on the list of Soviet aces in Spain was Stepan Suprun, although his score is uncertain; some sources put it at 12, others at more than 15.

Meanwhile, as the Russians continued to step up their aid to the Republicans, increasing numbers of German personnel had been arriving in Spain on the Nationalist side. Their presence was kept a closely guarded secret. Luftwaffe personnel posted for a tour with the Condor Legion—as the German contingent was known—reported to a secret office in Berlin where they were issued with civilian clothes, Spanish currency and papers. They then left for Döberitz, where they joined a 'Kraft durch Freude' tour ostensibly bound for Genoa via Hamburg.

The main body of the Condor Legion sailed for Spain during the last days of November 1936. It consisted of three fighter squadrons equipped with He 51s, four bomber-transport squadrons operating Junkers 52/3ms, a reconnaissance squadron equipped with Heinkel 70s, a seaplane squadron operating He 59s and He 60s, six anti-aircraft batteries, four signals companies and one repair section. After settling in, the Legion began a series of bombing raids on Mediterranean ports held by the Republicans, but the Ju 52s encountered severe icing difficulties over the Sierra Nevada and were later transferred to Melilla in Spanish Morocco, from where they made low-level attacks across the straits.

One of the most active elements of the Condor Legion was Jagdgruppe J/88, comprising the three He 51-equipped fighter squadrons. Nevertheless, the Heinkel fighter's limitations soon became apparent; it proved utterly incapable of intercepting the Republican SB-2 bombers even under the most favourable conditions and was usually forced to avoid combat with I-15s and I-16s, although it could hold its own against many of the older types in service on the Republican side. On August 18th 1936, for example, while flying He 51s, Garcia Morato and another Nationalist captain named Julio Salvador shot down two Nieuport 52 fighters, a Breguet XIX and a Potez 54 during their first sorties in the German fighter. But in spite of its early success, the He 51—which already equipped two Nationalist fighter squadrons by the time the three Condor Legion squadrons became operational in November—came off a poor second best as soon as it began to encounter the first Russian I-15s in October 1936. By the spring of 1937 about 200 I-15s had reached Spain, and the He 51 could no longer carry out its intended task as a fighter without suffering severe losses. From March onwards, fitted with bomb racks, the Heinkels were confined to close-support duties.

On February 6th 1937, in an attempt to isolate the Republican forces holding out in Madrid, the Nationalists attacked in strength on the Jarama front. Their first objective was the village of Arganda, straddling a vital junction on the Valencia road five miles to the east of the Jarama River. A Red counter-attack, supported by Russian tanks, was beaten off with heavy losses four days later, and on the 12th Nationalist cavalry units and troops of the Moroccan Legion crossed the river and secured a strategic hill on the east bank.

In the air, however, the Nationalists were unable to gain the necessary superiority to cover a further advance. The Reds had concentrated some 200 I-15s, I-16s, R-Zs and SB-2s in the Madrid area, and the five fighter squadrons assigned to the Arganda sector inflicted heavy losses on the Nationalist Junkers 52 units operating in the area. The fact that the Italian fighter escort abandoned the bombers as soon as the front line was reached contributed greatly to the Reds' success. It was a different story on the 16th, when the Italians belatedly followed Garcia Morato's Blue Patrol into the attack; in spite of their superior numbers the Reds took a severe mauling, losing at least ten I-15s and I-16s for the destruction of three Nationalist aircraft.

Nevertheless, the Republicans maintained their overall air superiority until the end of the month, when Franco called off the Nationalist offensive after it had become obvious that the attempt to encircle Madrid had failed. One last attempt was made, however—this time by the Italian Volunteer Expeditionary Force, supported by tanks and artillery. The plan was a good one in principle, envisaging a lightning thrust across the country towards Guadalajara, 35 miles north-east of Madrid on the main Barcelona road. Having secured this objective, the Italians were to join up with an advance by Nationalist forces in the Jarama sector, the two spearheads meeting at Alcala de Henares and cutting off Madrid's only line of supply to the east.

The attack was launched on March 8th, with five Italian divisions—some 30,000 men, under the command of General Roatta—advancing rapidly down the Barcelona highway from the village of Algora and meeting hardly any opposition. Within 48 hours the Italians had advanced 20 miles, the Reds falling back ahead of them in suspiciously good order. In fact, the Reds had known all about the attack several days before it developed, and the reason for their orderly withdrawal became apparent on March 10th, when over 100 R-Zs, I-15s and I-16s swept down on the congested highway in successive waves and systematically began to cut the Italians to pieces. The road quickly became clogged with burning transport and the Italians fought to get out of the bottleneck, only to get bogged down in clinging mud caused by a heavy rainfall the day before. Thanks to the proximity of their airfields at Alcala de Henares and Barajas, the Red fighter-bombers were able to mount incessant attacks throughout that day. The two Italian fighter wings and three bomber squadrons which had been supposed to cover the advance, however, were operating from Soria, to the north, and there was high ground between their base and the combat area. Consequently, when bad weather clamped down on the 9th, only small numbers of Italian aircraft managed to find their way safely through the fogbound hills and oppose the deluge of Red aircraft. The Italian position became completely untenable on the 12th, when the best units of the International Brigades— which had been held in reserve until the air attacks had done their job—counter-attacked in strength, supported by armour, and rolled the Italians back 10 miles. The Italians had lost over 4,000 dead and wounded, and large quantities of their equipment had either been destroyed during the strafing attacks or had been abandoned in the mud.

Much of the credit for the Red success in shattering the advance on Madrid was due to one man in particular: Commander Ivan Berzin, head of the Intelligence Directorate of the Soviet General Staff, who was responsible for organizing the defence of the Spanish capital. Berzin was a firm advocate of the use of air power in support of the army, and the Battle of Guadalajara had certainly vindicated his faith. During the operations in Spain he worked under the code-name of 'Goriev'. He was recalled to Moscow late in 1937 to face charges of being a Trotskyite; the tribunal found him guilty and he was shot shortly before the German invasion in 1941—as were several other notable airmen, including Shmushkievich.

In March 1937, shortly after the Guadalajara battle, the Republican Air Arm was substantially reorganized, with many of the I-15 and I-16 squadrons which had hitherto been staffed exclusively by Soviet personnel now being turned over to the Spaniards. The first all-Spanish I-16 unit was Grupo 31, which began to exchange its Breguet XIXs for Ratas just in time to take part in the final stage of the Guadalajara counter-attack. The other I-16 squadron which figured prominently in the strafing attacks on the Italians was a Red Air Force unit based on Barajas, which was also the base of the Voluntary International Squadron commanded by André Malraux and equipped with I-15s.

March also saw the reorganization of the Condor Legion and the appearance in Spain of new types of German aircraft. The first of these was the Heinkel He 111B-2, which replaced the Junkers 52s serving with the two squadrons of Kampf-gruppe 88. The Heinkels were sent into action immediately in support of the campaign against Bilbao; their first operational mission was flown on March 9th, when they bombed the Republican airfields of Alcala and Barajas. At the end of March, the two Heinkel squadrons of K/88 made a series of attacks on the Bilbao 'Iron Belt'. They proved outstandingly successful right from the start. The Heinkels went on to see service on every battlefront and were flown by both German and Spanish crews. Altogether, 75 were supplied to the Nationalists; 58 stayed behind when the war ended and equipped two Air Regiments.

In April 1937, Jagdgruppe J/88's No. 1 Squadron, re-equipped with new Messerschmitt Bf 109B fighters, hurriedly rushed out from Germany. No. 2 Squadron followed suit soon after. These two squadrons, whose emblems were a marabou and a top hat respectively, were commanded by Lieutenants Lützow and Schlichting. The third squadron, still operating He 51s, was commanded by a man whose name was to become legendary: Adolf Galland. The Condor Legion itself was commanded by Major-General Hugo Sperrle, with Colonel Wolfram von Richthofen as his Chief of Staff. It was von Richthofen's responsibility to evolve the ground-attack techniques that were later to become standard procedure throughout the Luftwaffe; on many occasions he personally supervised close-support operations from a hill overlooking the battle area.

Galland's pilots, nicknamed *cadenas* or *trabajadores* by the Nationalist infantry, flew six or seven missions a day against the Republicans and caused considerable havoc among the enemy troops. Losses began to mount, however, when the Republican anti-aircraft defences became more efficient. In spite of this, III/J 88 soldiered on with its He 51s until July 1938, when it too received Messerschmitt 109Bs. Galland had by this time flown 280 missions and he was now recalled to Germany, the squadron being taken over by Werner Mölders —the man who was to become the Condor Legion's top-scoring pilot. A fourth squadron was formed to take over the remaining He 51s, which fought on until the end of the war. The total number of Heinkel fighters shipped to the Condor Legion and the Nationalist Air Arm during the conflict was 135; 46 were still airworthy when the shooting stopped.

On the opposing side, a steady flow of Russian equipment still continued to reach the Republican air units. By the end of May 1937, 150 SB-2 bombers were in service, the great majority still flown by Red Air Force crews. Although their raids continued to present something of a problem for the Nationalists, the Russian crews were notable mainly for the inaccuracy of their bombing and for their general indiscipline. On several occasions, General Denisov employed his SB-2 units with complete disregard for the wishes of his nominal superiors, the Republican General Staff; on one occasion, for example, he was asked to send his aircraft in to attack military targets near Salamanca, but he deliberately altered these orders and briefed his crews to attack Valladolid instead. This town was not a military objective, and the immediate result of the SB-2s' attack on it was a heavy reprisal raid by Nationalist aircraft on Barcelona. On another occasion, a pair of SB-2s bombed the German battleship *Deutschland* while she lay at anchor off Ibiza; one bomb exploded in the seamen's mess, killing 22 of the warship's crew and wounding 83 more. It was an utterly pointless and provocative attack —and the Germans were not slow to retaliate. Five days later, on May 31st 1937, a German cruiser and four destroyers appeared off Almeria and lobbed over 200 high-explosive shells into the defenceless town.

On July 6th 1937, seven Republican divisions totalling 60,000 men drove a deep wedge in the Nationalist left flank at Brunete, 15 miles west of Madrid. The offensive was supported by 180 aircraft grouped on the airfields of Barajas, Alcala, Guadalajara, Villafranca, Tembleque, Manzanares el Real and Santiana. By July 9th, the Nationalists had managed to assemble 150 aircraft of all types on the Madrid front to oppose the Republicans, and the latter slowly began to lose the overwhelming air superiority which they had enjoyed during the first phase of the battle. While the Nationalist Junkers 52s, Heinkel 111s and Savoia 79s hammered the enemy airfields, Galland's Heinkel 51 *cadenas* maintained constant strafing attacks on the Red troop concentrations. In the sky above, Fiat CR 32s of the Italian Fighter Wing and the Bf 109s of I/J 88 tangled with big formations of Ratas and Chatos. The Reds sustained heavy casualties, both on the ground and in the air; their R-Z Natasha attack biplanes in particular suffered heavily, eight being shot down on July 13th alone. Three days later the Nationalists counter-attacked, and savage dogfights developed between formations of 30 and 40 aircraft over the battle area. By the 25th, after some of the bloodiest fighting of the whole Civil War, the Republicans were in full retreat, having suffered 25,000 casualties. Sixty Red aircraft had been destroyed—roughly one-third of the total Republican air strength in this sector. The Nationalists had lost 30 aircraft.

The scene now shifted to the northern front, where, on August 22nd, the Reds began a major offensive in the Belchite area, with Saragossa as the ultimate objective. Eighty thousand troops were committed, supported by 150 aircraft operating from Figueras, Reus, Sitges, Sarinena and Balaguer. The Red offensive finally ground to a halt during the first week of September, the Red troops continually harassed by air attack. Red fighters continued to appear in strength during the battle, but they were unable to gain mastery of the air: 30 were shot down between September 1st and 6th. Nevertheless, the Reds did succeed in mounting several attacks on Nationalist air-fields; the most devastating was a dawn raid on Saragossa air base on October 15th, when 12 Polikarpov R-Zs, escorted by 30 Ratas and Chatos, destroyed 15 aircraft on the ground in the space of five minutes. A week later, however, the Nationalists captured Gijon and the Republicans were decisively defeated, resulting in the collapse of their entire northern front.

By the beginning of December 1937, the Nationalists had gained definite air superiority; this was demonstrated during the Battle of Teruel, which began on December 15th when the Reds launched an offensive against the town with 100,000 men. The town was completely encircled by the 19th, but its garrison of 5,000 Nationalist troops managed to hold out until January 7th before being forced to surrender. Meanwhile, reinforcements had been pouring in on the Nationalist side, and the Nationalists counter-attacked vigorously on December 29th, after several days of fierce blizzards which had grounded all aircraft and brought operations to a complete standstill. During the first day of the counter-offensive, a new type of aircraft made its appearance over the front: the Junkers 87A dive-bomber, three of which had arrived in Spain only a matter of days earlier. Now, for the first time, infantrymen learned to dread the banshee wail of the plummeting Stuka.

Another blizzard on January 1st once again brought operations to a halt, but by the second week in January the Nationalists had begun to move forward slowly. The Teruel offensive developed into the Battle of Alhambra, which began on February 5th 1938 and ended, after some bitter fighting under appalling conditions, in the complete defeat of the Reds. Throughout these operations, the Nationalists had almost complete control of the air; while the Heinkels and Junkers bombed intensively, packs of Nationalist fighters roved well inside enemy territory with orders to seek out the Red air formations and engage them in combat. Thanks to these tactics, the Reds were forced on to the defensive right from the start.

In spite of the severe losses sustained, however, the majority of the Red air units continued to operate at full strength throughout the first half of 1938; although the supply of aircraft by sea was becoming increasingly less practicable because of the growing Nationalist naval blockade, considerable quantities of Russian aircraft—mainly I-16s—were off-loaded at the French ports of Le Havre and Bordeaux, and from there shipped to Spain by rail across the frontier. Most of these aircraft continued to be flown by Red Air Force pilots, who served a six-month tour of duty in Spain.

In June 1938, however, it was becoming increasingly obvious to the Soviet Central Committee that the Republican cause in Spain was already lost, and the decision was taken to recall most of the Soviet personnel serving in the country. Although a number of Russian advisers were allowed to remain, virtually all combat personnel had been withdrawn by the middle of October, after handing their aircraft over to Republican air units; all the surviving SB-2 bombers, for example, became part of the Republican 24th Bomber Wing. With the loss of the Russian crews, the effectiveness of the Republican air operations diminished still further; by the end of 1938 there was an almost complete lack of co-ordination, with surviving air units widely scattered and operating for the most part on the initiative of their own officers. The Soviet Union continued to supply aircraft to the Republicans, albeit in greatly reduced quantities, and the supply dried up altogether when France closed her frontier. The attrition suffered by the Republican squadrons during the last year of fighting was fearful; out of the total of 475 Ratas delivered to Spain from November 1936 onwards, only 18 were salvaged intact by the victorious Nationalists when the war ended. No fewer than 415 were claimed as having been destroyed in the air or on the ground. The same was true of the SB-2 Katiushkas; out of the 210 aircraft delivered in all, only 20 or so survived the war. The exact number of I-15s delivered to Spain was never revealed, but it must have exceeded that of any other type. In spite of the fact that 140 I-15s were destroyed during 1937 alone, the type continued to appear in strength right up to the last days of the war.

Months before the shooting was over, Russians, Germans and Italians were already incorporating, in both aircraft production and air force organization, the lessons being learned the hard way in Spanish skies. On the German side, the deficiencies of the Heinkel 51 marked the virtual death of the fighter biplane in operational Luftwaffe service. The Italians, on the other hand, had been so impressed with the performance of their CR 32 that they decided to go ahead with the production of its successor, the CR 42—another biplane. The Germans did in fact evaluate another biplane fighter—the Arado Ar 68—in Spain; two of them flew in the role of night fighter with Grupo 9 from La Cenia airfield in 1938, but their performance only served to confirm the Luftwaffe's opinion that the day of the biplane fighter was over.

As far as the early model Messerschmitt 109 was concerned, the Germans believed with a good deal of justification that it was superior to every other type of aircraft flying over Spain. However, its armament of three MG 17 machine guns was found to be inadequate, and was replaced by four MG 17s. It was also found that the fighter's range was not sufficient to provide effective escort for bombers engaged in deep penetration missions over enemy territory; a discovery that led to the development of external fuel tanks. In combat, the Bf 109 pilots also found that the tight, wingtip-to-wingtip battle formations used by most air forces at that time were not only unsuitable but also dangerous, with pilots concentrating more on keeping station than maintaining a good lookout.

The 'vic' of three aircraft was dropped in favour of the loose pair, two of these making up a 'finger four'. These basic formations, which were introduced to the Luftwaffe by Mölders on his return to Germany in 1939, are still used almost universally by the world's air forces today.

The need for fast reconnaissance aircraft, able to outrun enemy fighters, was a lesson impressed upon both sides. The Russians solved the problem more or less successfully with the SB-2, but the Nationalists learned the hard way. During the first few months of the war they used a squadron of Breguet XIXs in the reconnaissance role, and by March 1937 it was proving suicidal to operate them without a strong fighter escort. The situation improved when the Condor Legion's A/88 reconnaissance group, which had re-equipped with the Dornier 17F-1, transferred its 12 Heinkel 70s to the Nationalist Southern Army in April to form Grupo 7-G-14. The Heinkels played a vital part during the Battle of Brunete, and the following November they were split into two groups which took part in the Teruel offensive during the winter of 1937-8.

Paradoxically, however, the very fact that the German combat types—particularly the bombers—that were tested operationally in Spain were generally superior to their opponents was to prove a disservice to the Luftwaffe in the long run, for it led to the formation of the Luftwaffe's Blitzkrieg tactics, which were based on two misconceptions that arose out of the Spanish conflict. The first was that strong formations of fast bombers could operate in daylight over enemy territory without fighter escort; the second was the infallibility of the Stuka. Admittedly, the tactics worked only too well during the later campaigns in Poland, France and the Low countries; but it was to be a very different story when the Luftwaffe came up against determined fighter opposition during the Battle of Britain.

The Russians fell into much the same pitfalls; like the Germans, they failed to realize the potential importance of accurate long-range bombing, independent of army support operations. One lesson they did learn, however, which was to stand them in good stead during the later German-Soviet war, was the value of night intruder operations by fast bomber aircraft flying over enemy territory either singly or in twos and threes. They found that psychologically the harassing effect of such operations was as great as, if not greater than, the actual damage done. The intruder technique was pioneered with the SB-2, which usually operated in vics of three, crossing the front line at low level and then climbing to 16,500 feet. They then passed over the target in tight formation, dropping their bombs simultaneously and diving away at high speed to escape the worst of the anti-aircraft fire.

The appearance of the Messerschmitt 109 in Spanish skies underlined the urgent need for a really modern Soviet fighter with speed and altitude performance at least capable of matching that of the German type. The result was the appearance, in 1939-40, of the prototypes of the three aircraft that were to form the backbone of the Soviet fighter force until 1945: the Yak-1, MiG-1 and LaGG-3.

The Yak-1 'Krasavyets' (Beauty) made its first public appearance during an air display on November 7th 1940. It was Alexander S. Yakovlev's first fighter design, and it earned him the Order of Lenin, the gift of a Zis car and a prize of 100,000 roubles. The fighter was powered by a 1,100-hp M-105PA engine and carried an armament of one 20-mm ShVAK cannon, two 7·62-mm ShKAS machine guns and sometimes had six RS-82 rockets. The Yak-1 was of mixed construction, fabric and plywood covered; it was simple to build and service, and a delight to fly. Maximum speed was 360 mph.

The second type, the MiG-1, was the fruit of collaboration between the two aero-engineers Artem I. Mikoyan and Mikhail I. Gurievitch. Heavier than the Yak-1, it was powered by a 1,350-hp engine that gave it a maximum speed of 380 mph at 23,000 feet. The third fighter, the LaGG-3, took its name from the initials of the three engineers who conceived it: Lavochkin, Gorbunov and Gudkov. It was a remarkable little aircraft, built entirely of wood and bearing a strong resemblance to the French Dewoitine D 520. It was armed with one 20-mm ShVAK cannon, two ShKAS 7·62-mm machine guns and one 12·7-mm BS (Beresin) machine gun. Its 1,100-hp M-105PA engine gave it a top speed of 345 mph. Series construction of all three types was begun in 1940-1, the first machines entering squadron service in mid 1941, shortly before the German invasion.

Apart from the fighter question, the other main lesson to emerge from Russia's commitment in the Spanish Civil War was the need to develop an aircraft designed specifically for ground attack and close support duties. The decision to go ahead with the development of such aircraft and their subsequent quantity production was of far-reaching importance, for it was to provide the Soviet Union with the world's most formidable short-range attack force, as well as dictating the tactical thinking of the Red Air Force's strategists for years to come.

Chapter 4

The Bitter Frontiers

In the summer of 1938, half a world away from where men were dying by the thousand in the yellow dust of Spain, Russian forces once again became involved in a limited war, on the eastern frontiers of the Soviet Union. Since the previous autumn, Japan and China had been engaged in a full-scale undeclared war on two fronts, in the valley of the Yangtse River and in northern China, and there had been several border incidents between Soviet and Japanese troops along the Amur River, dividing Siberia from Japanese-occupied Manchuria.

Soviet-Japanese tension had been on the increase since August 1937, when the Soviet Union concluded a non-aggression pact with Chiang Kai-shek. Soon afterwards, the Central Committee agreed to supply quantities of aircraft and equipment for use by the Chinese Central Government. The first contingent of Soviet Air Force personnel arrived in China during the last week of September, and by the beginning of 1938 the number of Russian 'advisers' serving in the country had risen to over 350.

The total included 80 Soviet Air Force fighter pilots. Although their task was ostensibly to give flying instruction to Chinese crews converting to Soviet aircraft types, their real purpose was to fly four squadrons of I-152 (I-15bis) fighters in combat against the Japanese. Two squadrons of SB-2 bombers also arrived at the same time, and they too were manned exclusively by Soviet crews. Operational flying began almost immediately from bases in the vicinity of Nanking, the Chinese capital, which by that time was coming under heavy Japanese air attack. In January 1938, two of the I-15 squadrons were pulled out of the front line and replaced by two fresh units operating I-16 Type 10s, which proved able to meet the Japanese A5M2 fighters on more equal terms. The Soviet 'volunteers' were commanded by Lieutenant-Colonel Stepan P. Suprun.

Meanwhile, Chinese units had begun to receive the first of the 400 I-152s and I-16s promised by the Soviet Government, and Russian-trained Chinese pilots were flowing through the flying and technical schools at Nanchang, Langchow and Hami at a fast rate—so fast, in fact, that many of them were far from ready to take on the highly skilled Japanese aircrews in combat. Nevertheless, they were immediately flung into battle in the defence of Nanking, replacing the four Soviet Air Force fighter squadrons which were withdrawn for a rest. That was in mid November. Four weeks later, their pilots completely outclassed by the Japanese, the Chinese squadrons defending Nanking had been decimated and had to be withdrawn to Nanchang, leaving the capital naked to the onslaught from the air.

The Russian squadrons, meanwhile, had regrouped near Langchow, where a new batch of crews had arrived to start their four-month tour of duty in China. There was little air activity on either side during the spring of 1938, but in April and May Japanese reconnaissance aircraft began to appear in increasing numbers over Langchow and other places in north-west China where the combat aircraft being supplied by Russia were assembled. The first heavy air raids on these centres were carried out late in May and continued for five weeks, heavy losses being inflicted on the attackers by the defending fighters.

Two months later, in July 1938, a major clash between Soviet and Japanese forces occurred near Lake Khasan, 80 miles south-west of Vladivostok on the Soviet-Manchurian border. Two miles to the west of Khasan, between the lake and the Tumen River—in what had virtually become no man's land—there was a high ridge known as Chang-ku-feng by the Chinese and Zaozernoe by the Russians. The ridge was of little strategic importance; nevertheless, on July 9th, the Russians began to move troops up to it and set up a well-defended observation post on its summit. A few days later the Japanese ambassador in Moscow demanded the withdrawal of the Soviet forces, but the Russians—quoting the terms of a Russo-Chinese treaty drawn up in 1888—

replied that the ridge legally belonged to them. While the wrangling was going on, the C-in-C of the Soviet Far Eastern Forces—Marshal Blukher—quietly moved the 40th Division and several V-VS (Soviet Air Force) squadrons into the Khasan area in readiness for a possible Japanese attack. It came on July 29th, when the Japanese 19th Division attacked the ridge in strength and drove the Russians off it, pushing them back nearly three miles inside their own territory.

The Russians counter-attacked on August 6th with shock units of the 39th Corps, under the command of Grigori M. Shtern—fresh from a tour of duty in Spain, where he had worked under the code-name of 'Kleber'. Before the assault began, four squadrons of TB-3 heavy bombers, escorted by I-152s, pounded the Japanese positions for several hours. While the Soviet infantry and tanks fought their way towards the ridge, several squadrons of I-16s and I-152s strafed ahead of them, and waves of SB-2s took over from the TB-3s and continued to pound the summit of the ridge. Shattered by the continual air attacks, the Japanese were unable to hold on and by nightfall the ridge was once again in Russian hands. The Japanese counter-attacked the following day, but their formations were broken up by concentrated air attacks and the bid to recapture the ridge failed. In the end, a cease-fire was agreed on August 11th. The Russians had owed their success almost entirely to overwhelming air support; the number of aircraft of all types committed was about 180. Nevertheless, the 39th Corps had suffered nearly 50 per cent casualties.

The defeat of their forces at Chang-ku-feng was a serious loss of face for the Japanese, and during the early months of 1939 their military leaders laid careful plans for revenge. This time, the place they chose for their surprise attack was a poorly defended stretch of frontier between Manchuria and Outer Mongolia; a barren expanse of steppe stretching 50 miles to the east of the Khalkhin River, a tributary of the Amur.

On May 11th 1939, the Japanese Kwantung Army swept over the border into Mongolian territory. Fierce fighting broke out between the Japanese and the Soviet 57th Independent Rifle Corps, which was immediately ordered forward to try to stem the onslaught. Further reinforcements arrived soon afterwards in the shape of the 11th Soviet Armoured Brigade, the 6th Mongolian Cavalry Division and a Soviet rifle regiment, and by the end of May they had succeeded in establishing a foothold on the east bank of the Khalkhin River. Skirmishing continued until the first week of July, when the Japanese struck from the north with close on 40,000 men, driving back the Russian and Mongolian forces. Then, on July 5th, the Japanese thrust was checked and forced back across the river by a rapid deployment of Soviet armour.

Throughout this phase of the battle there had been sporadic air fighting, with aircraft used for bombing and strafing by both sides. The fighting of August, however, was to be marked by the biggest air battles the world had seen since the 1914-18 War. During July, the Japanese assembled a total of 475 aircraft of all types in Manchuria, including considerable numbers of Mitsubishi A5M and Nakajima Ki 27 fighters. There were also some bomber squadrons equipped with Mitsubishi Ki 21s, fast twin-engined bombers which had entered service with the Japanese Army Air Force the previous year and which were later to be known by the Allied code-name of Sally.

The Russians, meanwhile, had been pouring troops and equipment into Mongolia, and the First Army Group—commanded by Georgi K. Zhukov, who was to achieve fame during the Second World War—was rapidly deployed along the disputed frontier. At his disposal, by the end of July, Zhukov had 580 aircraft operated by both Soviet and Mongolian squadrons. The total included 125 SB-2s, 25 TB-3s, 150 I-16s, 200 I-15s and I-152s, and 80 reconnaissance and transport aircraft of various types. The I-15s had already clashed with Japanese fighters over the Khalkhin River on several occasions, and had proved inferior to the Nakajima Ki 27; during subsequent operations, they were relegated mainly to the ground-attack role, leaving the I-152s and I-16s to tangle with the enemy.

The Japanese had planned to launch another offensive on August 24th, but it was the Russians who got in the first blow. At dawn on August 20th, 130 SB-2s and TB-3s struck hard at Japanese positions across the river and at Japanese lines of communication to the rear. While the air attack was still in progress, Soviet and Mongolian forces moved forward in a giant pincer movement from north and south. By August 23rd, the Japanese were completely encircled. For five days they tried desperately to break out of the trap, while bitter dogfights developed overhead between the opposing fighter forces. By this time, four of the Red Air Force squadrons had exchanged their I-15s for the more modern I-153, with a retractable undercarriage, and the appearance of these aircraft over the Khalkhin-Gol took the Japanese fighter pilots completely by surprise—particularly as the Russian pilots evolved tactics which were deliberately designed to mislead the Japanese. They would approach the combat area with their undercarriages lowered, giving the impression that they were slower I-15s or I-152s and inviting the Japanese to attack. Once the latter had committed themselves, the I-153 pilots would cram on full power and tear into the middle of the enemy formation, causing complete confusion. The Japanese Ki 27s suffered heavy losses at the hands of the I-153s before their pilots woke up to what was happening.

Occasionally, the sky above the river was covered by a twisting mêlée of 200 aircraft as big formations clashed head on. The Japanese usually emerged the worse from these encounters; although the Ki 27 could hold its own against the I-153 and was superior to the I-152, it was outclassed in speed and firepower by its most frequent opponent—the I-16, which the Japanese pilots nicknamed 'Abu' (Gadfly). Figures of the air losses sustained by both sides are, unfortunately, somewhat vague and conflicting. The Russians were reported to have lost 145 aircraft of all types between May 11th and September 15th, when a cease-fire was finally arranged; the Japanese are said to have lost over 600, 200 of them during the last ten days of fighting, but these figures seem over-optimistic. What is certain is that very heavy aircraft losses were suffered by both sides, and particularly by the Japanese.

During the bitter air fighting of August, several Soviet pilots became the first to win the coveted Hero of the Soviet Union award for a second time. Among them were Yakob Shmushkievich, who had been awarded his first HSU for commanding the Soviet air contingent in Spain; Major V. M. Zabaluyev and Major S. I. Gritsevets, commander and deputy commander of the 70th Air Regiment; and Major G. P. Kravchenko, commanding the 22nd Air Regiment. Another pilot, V. F. Skobarikhin, also a member of the 22nd Air Regiment, was made a Hero of the Soviet Union for deliberately ramming a Japanese aircraft.

Although there had not been a great deal of difference in terms of skill between Russian and Japanese pilots, the Russian tactics had been better. So had the armament of their aircraft —four 7·62-mm machine guns carried by the I-16 Type 10 compared with the twin 7·7-mm weapons mounted in both the Ki 27 and A5M. The I-153 also had four 7·62s, as well as provision for six RS 82 air-to-ground rockets under the wings. On several occasions, RS 82s were launched at Japanese aircraft by rocket-carrying I-16s to break up the enemy formations.

In spite of their defeat at Khalkhin-Gol, the Japanese immediately began to plan another offensive for the autumn of 1939, but these plans were abandoned on orders from the military authorities in Tokyo—possibly as a result of intervention on the part of Japan's ally, Germany, anxious at this stage to show an outwardly friendly attitude to the Soviet Union. On August 23rd von Ribbentrop, the German Foreign Minister, had reached agreement with Stalin and Molotov over the spheres of influence of the two countries in eastern Europe. The price of this agreement was Poland; following the imminent German invasion, Poland was to be occupied by Soviet forces as far as the rivers San and Bug, and the Soviet Union was also free to make territorial gains in Latvia, Estonia and Lithuania.

With the nagging fear of opposition from the Soviet Union finally removed, Hitler was now able to go ahead and put the finishing touches to the invasion plan. The assault on Poland began at 4.45 on the morning of September 1st, when—15 minutes before the advance armoured units of the Wehrmacht rolled into the country—a squadron of Junkers 87 Stukas swept over the Vistula and bombed the railway line near the bridge at Dirschau, paving the way for the capture of this vital river crossing by an army task force. By September 8th —the turning-point of the Polish campaign, when several Polish divisions were surrounded near Radom and shattered by concentrated Stuka attacks and the 4th Panzer Division reached the defensive perimeter around Warsaw—the situation of the Polish Air Force was desperate, with more and more aircraft being put out of action by lack of spare parts and shortage of fuel. Only the Polish Bomber Brigade was still able to operate in any strength, owing to the fact that its main supply base at Deblin was still functioning. Nevertheless, attrition was considerable and the last major mission was flown by Polish bombers on September 12th. Scattered attacks were made after that date by aircraft operating in twos and threes, but they were of little significance.

Then, on September 17th, the Russians attacked from the east. Shortly after first light, nine I-16s swept down on the Polish airfield near Buczacz, strafing installations and the handful of aircraft that were left. The timing was perfect; the Russians had waited until all Polish resistance had been effectively smashed before making their move. For the Polish Air Force, it was the coup de grâce—the final, bitter stab in the back. The following day, the remaining aircraft were evacuated to Rumania. On the ground, there was some spirited opposition to the invaders by pockets of Polish troops along the frontier, and the Red Army suffered some 2,500 casualties. During the later stages of the Russian advance, Luftwaffe and V-VS formations began to run into one another more frequently, and although both sides had strict instructions to steer clear of the other there were a number of incidents caused by faulty aircraft recognition—usually on the part of the Russians. During one of them, a squadron of I-16s mistook a formation of Heinkel 111s for Polish Los bombers and attacked them, damaging one of the Heinkels slightly before the mistake was discovered.

On September 28th, following a few minor territorial adjustments, the Russians settled in along the new Soviet-German frontier defined by the rivers Bug, San and Narev, and a number of first-line V-VS units immediately occupied Polish air bases close to the border. Over the next 18 months the Russians were to assemble large quantities of their combat aircraft on these airfields—a serious mistake, as it turned out, for it meant that they were within easy striking distance of Luftwaffe bases in eastern Europe, and when the Luftwaffe struck at the Soviet Union at dawn on June 22nd 1941 it was consequently able to paralyse a large part of the Red Air Force's first-line strength on the ground.

But that was still in the future. Meanwhile, in November 1939, the Red Air Force found itself committed to a war against Finland—a bitter struggle in which the Finns fought back with incredible and totally unexpected ferocity, inflicting on the Red Air Force the worst losses it had yet sustained.

Chapter 5

Battle in the Winter

On November 30th 1939, the Soviet 7th, 8th, 9th and 14th Armies launched a full-scale invasion along the whole length of the Soviet Union's frontier with Finland. The attack came after months of negotiations over territorial rights, in which the Russians claimed a large slice of Finnish territory, had broken down. As a pretext for launching their offensive, the Russians alleged that Finnish artillery had opened fire on a Soviet village.

The initial Soviet attacks were supported by four bomber brigades, some of them operating from bases in Estonia, and two fighter brigades—a total of some 900 aircraft. The bomber and reconnaissance units were equipped with SB-2s, TB-3s, Ilyushin DB-3s, Polikarpov R-5s and R-Zs; the main equipment of the fighter units was the I-15 and I-152, with only a small number of I-153s and I-16s. Because of their conviction that there would be no serious opposition from the Finns, the Russians had not thought it necessary to commit their more modern fighter types to the battle.

The assumption that the Finns would offer no dangerous resistance had been an easy one to make, for to oppose the formidable Russian air armada the Finnish Air Force had only three air regiments with a total of 150 aircraft—mostly obsolescent types which included Fokker C Xs and C VEs, Blackburn Ripon floatplanes, Junkers K 43s and Bristol Bulldogs. The only Finnish aircraft that could really be classed as modern were 16 Bristol Blenheim bombers and 36 Dutch Fokker D 21 fighters.

On the first day of the war Russian SB-2s and DB-3s attacked several targets in Finland, including the capital, Helsinki. Finnish fighters were hurriedly scrambled to intercept them, but all the bombers got away safely. The following day, however, a pair of SB-2s was intercepted by Lieutenant Eino Luukkanen of the 24th Squadron, flying a Fokker D 21, and he shot down one of them. During the next two weeks, air operations were brought to a virtual standstill by heavy and continual falls of snow. Nevertheless, by December 12th the Soviet 7th Army—driving through the Karelian Isthmus —had succeeded in reaching the Mannerheim Line, the main Finnish defensive bastion, and Commander K. A. Meretskov was preparing to break through with his armour.

On December 16th the Russians threw in everything they had, concentrating their main assault in the Summa sector. The attacking Red Army units were preceded by wave after wave of SB-2s, DB-3s, I-15s and R-5s—200 aircraft in all— which pounded the Finnish positions mercilessly for several hours. The Russian tanks went in first, in groups of 25 or 30. Scores of them ground to a halt against the Finnish anti-tank barrier and were picked off one by one. Then the infantry attacked, the troops of the 123rd and 138th Soviet Divisions moving forward in a solid mass behind a ragged artillery barrage, falling in their thousands as the defensive fire mowed down rank upon rank. In spite of the fearful losses, 50 Russian tanks managed to break through to the town of Summa on the 19th, but they were all but wiped out when an attacking Finnish force cut them off from their supporting infantry.

In spite of the terrible odds stacked against them, the pilots of the Finnish Air Force were very active during this phase of the fighting. Their orders were simple: establish complete air superiority over the Summa area. By the 18th, the Fokker D 21s were maintaining standing patrols at squadron strength over the battle area, and encounters with large Soviet forma- tions became more frequent. The Finns usually managed to throw the Russians into complete confusion by charging straight into the middle of them, breaking up the enemy formation and then concentrating on picking off individual Russian aircraft. These tactics worked well, and several Finnish pilots began to build up an impressive score of enemy aircraft destroyed. One of them was Lieutenant Jorma 'Zamba' Sarvanto, who shot down his first Russian—an SB-2 —over Summa on December 19th. His squadron, the 24th, had been on patrol for nearly an hour over the front without seeing any Russian aircraft—apart from one R-5 on an artillery-spotting mission, which was promptly shot down by four Fokkers—when suddenly a squadron of nine SB-2s appeared from behind a bank of cloud. Sarvanto, leading the second flight of D 21s, immediately slammed his throttle wide open and climbed to meet the enemy. Stick hard over, a kick on the rudder-bar and he was swinging in behind the Russian formation as it slid past him. An SB-2 drifted into his sights and he fired, seeing his bullets flash and sparkle on the enemy's dark green wings. Tracer lanced past the Fokker's cockpit and Sarvanto hauled back the stick frantically, the little fighter bouncing skywards as though on a ball of elastic. Sweating, the pilot stall-turned and dived vertically on the bomber which had fired on him. For a split second the SB-2 seemed to hang motionless, spreadeagled in his sights. A quick burst, and then he was hurtling past, terrifyingly close. A glance to the rear: the bomber was nosing earthwards, blazing furiously.

The remainder of the SB-2s crammed on power and turned for home. One of them, trailing a thin stream of smoke from its starboard engine, began to lag behind the rest. Sarvanto closed in and fired at point-blank range, killing the rear-gunner. The Russian pilot jettisoned his bomb-load and twisted away from the Fokker's bullets. Grimly Sarvanto clung to his tail and fired again. The SB-2 skidded and lost altitude. The pilot levelled out and desperately tried to ditch his aircraft on the frozen surface of Lake Vuoksa. At the last moment, the SB-2's wingtip ploughed into the ice and the bomber cartwheeled in a cloud of fragments. Sarvanto climbed away, elated; he had scored his first two 'kills' in the space of five minutes.

Farther north, the Soviet 14th Army had meanwhile succeeded in capturing the town of Petsamo and had made some gains on the highway leading south-westwards. At the centre of the front, however, the intended Soviet thrust across the narrowest part of Finland to the Gulf of Bothnia had ended in disaster. The town of Suomussalmi was captured by the 44th and 163rd Divisions on December 9th, but they were driven out again the following day by crack Finnish ski troops and forced into full retreat. The Finns concentrated their attacks on the 44th Division as it straggled eastwards in temperatures as low as —40° F, cutting off the Russians' line of retreat and sweeping down out of the forest to strike at isolated pockets of exhausted Red soldiers. By the end of the first week in January, the 44th Division had virtually ceased to exist. Because of the nature of the terrain and the almost ghost-like elusiveness of the Finnish units, the Soviet Air Force had been powerless to intervene.

It was a different story to the north of Lake Ladoga, where almost non-stop operations by Red Air Force units had saved a large part of the 8th Army from what might have been complete annihilation. By the middle of December the 8th Army had advanced 35 miles inside Finland, before grinding to a halt in deep snow and under constant Finnish attacks. Then the Finnish 11th Division counter-attacked ferociously, splitting up the Soviet 56th Corps into three sections which were promptly surrounded. The trapped Russians put up a fierce resistance and managed to hold on to their positions, thanks to daily supplies dropped by TB-3 bombers.

As 1939 drew to a close the tempo of air fighting over Finland increased significantly. The Russians now realized that the tiny Finnish Air Force was proving a formidable opponent, and many of their bombing raids during late December were directed against the Finnish airfields. They found it impossible to destroy the Finnish aircraft on the ground, however, for by this time the Finns had vacated their major bases and scattered their squadrons among a series of small and exceedingly well-camouflaged emergency airstrips. The 24th Fighter Squadron was no exception; on Christmas Eve its pilots flew their Fokkers to Vuoksenlaakso, a frozen lake not far from the front line.

Christmas morning dawned red and bitterly cold, with a cutting north wind whispering in the pine trees around the lake. Scattered snowflakes drifted down as the mechanics swarmed around the Fokkers, while the duty pilots sat huddled around the stove in the crew-tent, drinking scalding coffee. From time to time, the muted rumble of heavy artillery reached them.

The sky grew steadily lighter. A sudden yell from outside startled the pilots into action: vapour trails had been sighted, apparently heading for Vuoksenlaakso. Coffee forgotten, the Finns dashed for their aircraft, cursing as the full impact of the icy air hit them. A Mercury engine started up with a crackling roar, followed by another and another. The pilots slammed their cockpit canopies shut and pushed the throttles wide open, sending the Fokkers tearing across the makeshift airfield in a cloud of snow just as the first bombs erupted in fountains of earth on the shore of the lake. The Fokkers climbed hell for leather; they were just in time to catch a second formation of SB-2s heading for their airfield, and the Russians jettisoned their bombs and headed flat out for home as soon as they spotted the Finnish fighters.

By the New Year, the 24th Squadron's score had risen to 100 Russian aircraft destroyed. On January 3rd 1940 the Squadron moved north-west to Utti, which was close to the Russian bombers' main route to targets in central Finland—and it was while flying from this base that Jorma Sarvanto scored the most spectacular success of any Finnish pilot during the Winter War. It happened on January 6th. Sarvanto was flying a lone patrol over the devastated town of Mikkeli when he spotted a formation of Ilyushin DE-3 bombers—seven in all. He climbed at full throttle and attacked out of the sun, closing in rapidly on the rearmost flight of three enemy bombers. Four hundred yards to go. Safety catch off. Three hundred. A gentle pressure on the rudder bar to bring him in line with the bomber on the extreme left of the formation. Sarvanto fought to hold the Fokker steady as she hit the Russians' slipstreams. The enemy gunners had spotted him at last, and glittering strings of tracers zipped past his cockpit. Sarvanto clenched his teeth and held his course as bullets ripped through the wings of his little fighter. Fifty yards. Thirty. Now!

A long, hammering burst from the Fokker's guns and suddenly the Russian bomber's starboard wing became a mass of flame. The DB-3 slewed out of formation and spun down towards the white snowscape in a mushroom of smoke.

Sarvanto shifted his attention to the next DB-3 in line, watching his bullets chew up the bomber's starboard engine cowling. A bright flicker, and then a river of flame shot back from the engine. The bomber followed its companion in a last plunge earthwards.

Frantically, Sarvanto flung his fighter away from the deadly cone of fire that reached out towards him. As he did so, the pale blue belly of a DB-3 filled his sights for a fraction of a second. It was enough. A quick jab on the gun-button and his bullets stitched a jagged seam up the bomber's fuselage. The DB-3 faltered, a wing dropped and it fell, turning over and over.

Three down! Sarvanto drew off a little and calmly selected his next victim. He closed in again and fired, and a fourth DB-3 went into a spin with its rudder shot away. A few seconds later it was joined by a fifth, the crew dead in the bullet-shattered cockpit. The sixth bomber banked into the sun in a desperate effort to escape. Sarvanto noticed the manoeuvre and turned to intercept. The pilot of this DB-3 was no novice: he tried every trick in the book to get away from the fighter worrying at his tail. It was no use. Controls shot away, the bomber went down in a tight spiral and crashed in a fountain of snow and earth. Sarvanto immediately chased the seventh Russian, who was diving flat out towards the Russian lines. He crept within range and pressed the button. Nothing happened: he was out of ammunition. Swearing, he reluctantly turned away and set course for Utti, practically out of fuel, his Fokker riddled like a colander.

A short while later, as Sarvanto was relating his account of the scrap to a horde of jubilant mechanics, two more Fokkers touched down on the frozen lake. The grinning pilots —Lieutenant Sovelius and Sergeant Ikonen—hoisted themselves from their cockpits and joined the small crowd. It turned out that they had seen the whole dogfight, but had been too far away to get there in time. However, that seventh Russian had not been so lucky after all; they had caught him as he was crossing the line and shot him to pieces.

January wore on. Day after day, in the bitter cold, the

Finnish pilots took off from the frozen lake in their worn-out aircraft and flung themselves tirelessly on the Russian formations. On January 11th a Swedish volunteer squadron joined the Finns in action. Known as Flygflottilj 19, it was equipped with 12 Gloster Gladiator and four Hawker Hart biplanes, operating from a frozen lake at Kemi under the command of Major Hugo Beckhammar.

The Swedish squadron's first mission—a ground-attack sortie against Russian positions at Markajarvi—proved disastrous. Three Harts were shot down by ground fire and fighters, although one Russian I-15 was destroyed by Ensign Jacoby, flying a Gladiator. A couple of days later, the squadron was split up and its aircraft dispersed among four small emergency landing-strips code-named Svea, Nora, Oskar and Ulrik. On January 17th, four Gladiators led by Major Beckhammar ran into an equal number of I-15s over Salla; the Swedes shot down two of the Russians without loss to themselves.

Early in February, an SB-2 bomber was shot down by Ensign Solvane over Oulu. Two weeks later, on the 21st, four Gladiators intercepted a Russian attack on Rovaniemi, and Ensign Steniger destroyed one SB-2 and possibly destroyed another. The Swedish unit remained in action until March 10th, when Ensign Carlsson closed the score by shooting down a big four-engined TB-3 bomber near Rovaniemi. During 59 days of operations, the squadron had destroyed 12 enemy aircraft for the loss of three Gladiators and three Harts.

By the beginning of February 1940, the Russians had assembled a total of 1,500 aircraft of all types on the Finnish front in preparation for the major offensive which, they hoped, would bring them victory. The I-15s were now supplemented by I-153s and I-16s, which began to appear in strength from the end of January onwards, and by a small number of I-17s.

The Soviet offensive began on February 2nd, with a series of probing attacks all along the front and an intensive softening-up air bombardment of the Mannerheim Line fortifications and of the lines of communication to its rear by the Red Air

Force. The main assault came at dawn on February 12th, with the Russian infantry advancing in the wake of a highly accurate creeping barrage. They had learned their lesson; they did not attack in closely packed waves this time, but in small and highly mobile groups. The task of the Finnish defenders, already reeling under the hammer-blows of the Russian artillery, was made doubly difficult by blinding snow that swept across the countryside. As before, the Russians concentrated their heaviest attacks in the Summa sector, and on the 14th they succeeded in driving a wedge over two miles wide and three miles deep through the Finnish defences, forcing the Finns to fall back on their second line of fortifications.

The following day, the weather cleared sufficiently to allow both sides to commit their aircraft to the battle. The Finnish 24th Squadron was up in force from Utti over the Russian lines when it was bounced by an avalanche of enemy fighters. The sky quickly became a whirling confusion of white-painted I-153s and dark green I-16 Ratas. Jorma Sarvanto, commanding one of the 24th Squadron's flights, found himself isolated in the middle of a mêlée of Russian fighters. Slamming open the throttle, he clawed for altitude and looked down; below him, the twisting aircraft looked like flies against the snowy background.

A red-nosed I-16 sped past, a couple of hundred feet beneath, and Sarvanto went after him in a shallow dive. Just before he fired, he glanced rearwards as a matter of habit. It was just as well he did: two I-153s were sitting on his tail, about to give him the coup de grâce. Sweating, he hauled back the stick and shot upwards, losing both his pursuers and his erstwhile target.

Far below, a Fokker was diving towards Lake Saimaa, trailing a thin streamer of smoke, an I-153 hot on its tail. Sarvanto flicked his aircraft over and plunged after them. Suddenly, his Fokker shuddered as bullets ripped into the starboard wing. An I-153 was close behind him, blazing away madly. The Fokker dropped away in a spin. Desperately, Sarvanto wrestled with the controls as the earth gyrated around him. It was no good—the Fokker continued to tumble

out of the sky like a falling leaf. He had to get out, quickly.
He reached for the handle to jettison the cockpit canopy, and
at that precise moment the Fokker came out of the spin by
itself. Sarvanto had had enough; there was no telling what
damage the I-153's bullets had done. Flat out, he raced for
home, a few hundred feet above the snow. Back at Utti, he
anxiously counted the rest of the squadron as they came in
to land. There were two aircraft missing; they had been
flown by two young Danish volunteer pilots, Erhard Frijs
and Fritz Rasmussen, who had joined the 24th Squadron
only 10 days earlier.

Four days after this episode, on February 19th, Sarvanto
was leading his flight on patrol near Lappeenranta when he
spotted a cluster of black dots away to the east. The dots
grew rapidly bigger until they resolved themselves into the
shapes of 27 DB-3s with an escort of 10 I-16s. Four against
37—not very good arithmetic! Luckily, while Sarvanto was
making up his mind whether to attack or not, more friendly
fighters arrived on the scene: four more Fokkers and 10 Gloster
Gladiators, the latter part of a batch of 30 which had been
rushed out to Finland from Britain during January.

The Gladiators hurled themselves at the I-16s and were
soon engaged in a whirling dogfight while the Fokkers climbed
to intercept the bombers. The enemy formation spotted the
approaching fighters and pulled up into a layer of cloud a few
thousand feet above. Ice began to form on the Fokkers' wings
as the pilots plunged into the cloud in pursuit. Suddenly a
huge, ghostly shape loomed up in front of Sarvanto; he had
flown smack into the middle of the Russian formation. His
tracers lit up the murk as he fired. Lurid sparks bounced
from the DB-3's wings and it turned slowly over on its
back and dropped out of sight. At the same instant a
Fokker plunged past, minus a wing and blazing furiously.
Sarvanto peered around, unable to see a thing in the murk,
expecting to collide with something at any second. He
dived free of the cloud and turned south, spotting a formation of eight DBs slipping away towards the Gulf of Finland
as he did so. He could have caught up with them easily,

but he was low on fuel and ammunition so he let them go.

Russian fighters roamed the sky of Finland freely now, outnumbering the defenders by 10 to one. By this time, the Russians knew the location of every airfield in Finland, and the Finnish air bases suffered heavily towards the end of February. Several of the Russian I-16 units became adept in hit-and-run intruder tactics, ranging deep inside Finnish territory in flights of three or four aircraft. On several occasions Finnish aircraft were caught by marauding I-16s just as they were landing or taking off, a number being lost in this way.

On February 21st, the worst blizzard in living memory screamed across Karelia, bringing both land and air operations to a halt for three days. The Russians made use of the respite to withdraw the exhausted shock troops of the 7th and 13th Armies, replacing them with fresh soldiers who launched a new offensive on the 28th. The Finns enjoyed no such respite; there were no reserves to relieve the battle-weary defenders of the Mannerheim Line. Nevertheless, for four days two undermanned Finnish divisions fought off 12 Soviet divisions and five tank brigades until they were finally driven back to the city of Viipuri, where—encircled and without hope—they made their last stand.

The main Soviet thrust against the city came across the ice-bound bay of Virolahti, and suddenly the Finnish pilots got the opportunity they had been waiting for. The first Russian attempt to land a large force from the ice had been thrown into confusion by accurate artillery fire, and now every available Finnish aircraft—including the 24th Squadron, now operating from its original base at Kakisalmi—was ordered into action against the disorganized masses of enemy troops.

Roaring low across the coast under a thick blanket of fog, the pilots dived on the tangled columns of men and horses, guns hammering. The slaughter was frightful. Streams of bullets ricocheted across the ice, mowing down the enemy in great swathes. The Russians broke and ran, trampling their wounded comrades into the bloodstained snow. They tried again, this time on the northern shore of Viipuri Bay. Soon the ice was littered with corpses, strewn among the carcases of burnt-out tanks. Twenty Fokkers dived on the survivors, lighting up the fog with the glare of their darting tracers. It was getting difficult to see: dusk was falling, a dusk pierced by the ruddy glow from burning Russian transport. Suddenly, a squadron of tubby I-153s tumbled out of the gloom and the Fokkers, out of ammunition, fled for home.

For days the massacre went on. For days the Russians tried to smash through the last line of Finnish defence and were slaughtered in their thousands. They lay in heaps on the ice, their blood freezing in the cold. Above the carnage the fighters roared endlessly, diving and strafing, diving and strafing. Hundreds more Russians were drowned in freezing water when the Finns opened the locks of the Saimaa Canal, flooding the area around Viipuri.

But it was the last act of the drama. The 10 decimated Finnish divisions at the front, starved of reinforcements and ammunition, could no longer hold out against the 22 Soviet divisions, five tank brigades and 21 artillery regiments which had been hurled against them. On March 12th the armistice was signed, and Soviet troops moved in to occupy the disputed territories.

Crushed by the armistice, the Finnish airmen looked to the east and longed for revenge. They had fought vastly superior numbers of Russians, and they had exacted a fearful toll of the enemy. At the beginning, they had been pledged aircraft and material by several nations, including Britain. Only the first trickle of that equipment had begun to arrive a week or two before the end, when it was too late.

Towards the end of March, a fortnight or so after the armistice, the Soviet Defence Commissar—Marshal Voroshilov —presented a full report on the Finnish campaign to the Central Committee. It was hardly a shining chapter of Soviet military achievement. Apart from a few isolated cases, Red Army and Air Force commanders had shown a complete lack of initiative and tactical sense—a direct result, perhaps, of the great purges of 1937-8, which had robbed the Soviet armed forces of many of their best leaders. Whatever other conclusions might be drawn from the disastrous campaign, there was no escaping the fact that it had taken 1,200,000 Russian troops to force the Finns into an armistice—a number equivalent to one-third of Finland's total population.

Although over 150 major targets in Finland had been repeatedly bombed by the Red Air Force, the latter had completely failed to achieve its primary objective: the neutralization of a large part of the Finnish war effort. Because of the marked inefficiency of their navigation, formation flying and bombing accuracy, the Russians had persisted in attacking in broad daylight and under clear weather conditions right up to the last phase of the campaign, when some of their raids had taken place at night. Two hundred and eighty Russian aircraft had been shot down by the Finnish fighters, and a further 314 had been destroyed by anti-aircraft fire. About 300 more aircraft of all types were written off during the four months of the campaign through accidents, mechanical defects resulting from the fearful operating conditions, and battle damage—bringing the total losses to something of the order of 900. Against this staggering total, the Finns had lost only 62 aircraft in combat, although 69 more were so badly damaged that they could no longer operate.

The lack of success of the Soviet bombers over Finland had considerable influence on future Russian policy with regard to strategic bombing. The failure of the bombers to score any real success in the Finnish war, however, was undoubtedly the result of extremely poor training among the Russian crews rather than of any fault in the concept of this type of operation. Because of the ever-present fear of a surprise attack by the Germans—the Nazi-Soviet Pact notwithstanding—most of the best V-VS units were held in reserve along the Soviet-German frontier, and only began to make their appearance during the latter stages of the conflict with Finland. Towards the end of the campaign, the Russian bombers—which at the beginning had operated in formations of up to 50 or 60—began to operate in units of 25 or 30, under strong fighter escort. Bombers and fighters had been used extensively in support of ground operations, but their effectiveness had been drastically reduced by haphazard co-ordination and lack of co-operation between army and air force commanders.

The Finnish war had, however, been notable for one thing: the world's first large-scale use of airborne troops. On several occasions, commandos and saboteurs had been dropped behind the Finnish lines, and two airborne brigades had been used in action against the Mannerheim Line and during the attacks on Petsamo. Although the Russians were later to develop the use of airborne troops to the point where they became an important and hard-hitting tactical weapon, these early operations were generally unsuccessful, the paratroops suffering from the same inaccuracy on the part of the Russian aircrews that saved many important Finnish targets. The airborne assaults lacked both planning and cohesion, the paratroops becoming widely scattered during the drops and consequently unable to attain their objectives. Several new airdrop techniques were carried out experimentally during the campaign, including the dropping of airborne troops without parachutes. The men jumped from low-flying TB-3s, relying on deep snowdrifts to break their fall. Surprisingly, the casualty figures incurred during these dramatic experiments were quite low.

During the spring and summer of 1940, while Soviet aircraft manufacturers strove to step up their combat aircraft production and the Red Air Force's front-line squadrons began to receive the first of a series of more modern types, the Russians kept a close watch on the German offensive in Western Europe. The longer the Germans remained fully committed in the West the better, for it gave the Soviet aviation industry and Air Force a breathing space for expansion and modernization. New factories were set up in the autumn of 1940, some of them east of the Urals—a fact that was to save the aviation industry from obliteration during the German invasion, for the Luftwaffe had no bomber capable of covering the immense distance into the heart of Siberia. By mid 1941, these factories were engaged in the series production of Yak-1, MiG-1 and LaGG-3 fighters, in addition to the SB-2, DB-3, Pe-2 and Il-2 bomber aircraft. The Petlyakov Pe-2, a twin-engined light bomber, was subsequently produced in large quantities and became one of the most versatile aircraft in service with the Soviet Air Force. The heavily armoured Ilyushin Il-2 Shturmovik attack bomber had just began to enter service with the V-VS when the German invasion came; in several units it replaced the Su-2, a low-wing single-engined bomber designed by Pavel O. Sukhoi. The Su-2—about 100 of which were built—served as an interim aircraft until quantity production of the Il-2 got under way. No fewer than 35,000 Il-2s were manufactured during the four years of war in the east, and it may be claimed with some justification that this aircraft made a bigger contribution to the eventual Russian victory than any other.

But when the German Luftwaffe struck the first blows of Operation Barbarossa—the invasion of the USSR—at dawn on June 22nd 1941, it was a question not of Russian victory but of Russian survival as squadron after squadron of Ratas, Chaikas and SB-2s was turned into blazing wreckage by the Stukas and Messerschmitts, and the old adversaries of Spain met in mortal combat for the second time.

Chapter 6

Fire from the Skies

June 22nd 1941. 03.20 hours.

It was going to be a beautiful Sunday morning. In the east, the stars were already fading out in a cloudless sky before the spreading dawn. Soon, the rising sun would evaporate the thin layer of condensation of the wings of the 23rd Air Division's fighters, parked in immaculate rows on their airfield near Rovno, south of the Pripet Marshes.

A pair of sentries moved slowly among the aircraft, their voices loud in the morning silence. There would be no flying that day; many of the pilots and ground crews were on week-end leave. They had been training intensively during the past few days, converting to the new MiG-1s which had just begun to replace the Division's I-16s. The MiGs were still factory-fresh and uncamouflaged, their all-metal finish contrasting sharply with the dark green of the Ratas.

Suddenly, the deep-throated roar of engines cut through the silence. Out of the shadows to the west three aircraft swept, skimming low over the airfield boundary, heading straight for the long ranks of Russian fighters. Seconds later they were overhead, and from their bellies showers of four-pound fragmentation bombs whistled down, exploding among the parked aircraft with devastating results. Red-hot splinters tore through wings and fuselages, ripping open fuel tanks which erupted with a dull thud. Streams of burning petrol reached out to engulf fighter after fighter and a pall of oily smoke began to drift across the airfield.

The three Heinkel 111H2s of Kampfgeschwader 53 turned lazily at the end of their bombing run and swept over the field a second time, machine-gunning the burning wreckage. Then, their job done, they droned away westwards again as the dazed Russian personnel tumbled from their beds. In less than two minutes, the 23rd Air Division had ceased to exist as a fighting force. Not a shot had been fired in its defence.

The Divisional Commander, Colonel Vanyushkin, stood among the wreckage and wept.

At nine other major Soviet airfields between Bialystok and Lvov, the story was exactly the same. Between 03.15 and 03.20, German bombers swept down on the Russian bases, taking the V-VS personnel completely by surprise and cutting a swathe of destruction through the ranks of Soviet fighters and bombers with their clusters of small four-pounders. Yet only 30 bombers—Heinkel 111s, Junkers 88s and Dornier 17s —were involved in this initial attack; drawn from KGs 2, 3 and 53, they were flown by picked crews—men on whom depended the success or failure of Operation Barbarossa, the German invasion of Russia.

The task of the Luftwaffe in the opening phase of Barbarossa was far from easy. The whole invasion plan hinged on a surprise attack by the Wehrmacht's shock units at first light, but at the same time the Luftwaffe was required to prevent the Soviet Air Force from intervening by striking first. The problem was simple enough: if the Luftwaffe formations went in at the same time as the ground forces launched their offensive, making use of the spreading daylight—which Field-Marshal Kesselring, the C-in-C Luftflotte 2, insisted was absolutely necessary—the Russians would have anything up to an hour to get their aircraft into the air before the Luftwaffe's bombers arrived overhead to deliver the knockout blow. If the Luftwaffe attacked at night, before the offensive got under way, the drone of large numbers of aircraft crossing the frontier would give the whole game away and the offensive would run into trouble as soon as it began to roll forward.

It was a problem that had to be solved. Scattered over the dozens of airfields beyond the German-Soviet frontier the Red Air Force possessed some 4,000 aircraft of all types against the 1,945 that were theoretically available to the Luftwaffe on the Eastern Front. In fact, the disparity in the Russians' favour was much greater, for on June 21st only 1,280 German aircraft were serviceable. If Barbarossa was to succeed, the Luftwaffe needed to establish overwhelming air superiority right from the start.

One important point was in the Germans' favour: they possessed highly accurate target intelligence. For several months now—ever since February 1941, in fact—German long-range reconnaissance aircraft had been systematically photographing military airfields and installations all over the western part of the Soviet Union, ranging as far as Kiev. High-altitude Junkers 88s and 86Ps, operating from Budapest and Cracow, had covered the Ukraine, while Heinkel 111s and Dornier 215s—all with specially modified engines to increase their ceiling—had roved over Byelorussia and the Crimea from bases in East Prussia and Rumania. All these flights had taken place at altitudes of between 30,000 and 39,000 feet, and had gone undetected by the Russians. There had been only one incident, when a Junkers 86P made a forced landing with engine failure near Minsk on June 20th, but the crew were able to destroy their aircraft together with its special cameras and equipment, and before the Russians had time to react the invasion had begun.

The reconnaissance flights revealed the full extent of the Russian build-up. A host of new airfields had sprung up near the Soviet-German frontier, and they were crammed with every type of combat aircraft. The photographs also revealed a number of decoy airfields, which were ignored during the initial Luftwaffe strikes—although some were later attacked in error by fighter-bombers when the invasion was under way. In addition, the reconnaissance showed the exact disposition of the Soviet armoured divisions in the vicinity of the frontier —information that proved invaluable to the German Panzer leaders, whose units were to spearhead the assault.

There seemed, however, to be no complete solution to the Luftwaffe's dilemma. Field-Marshal von Bock, the supreme commander of the Wehrmacht's Army Group Centre—which would have to fight its way through some of the strongest Russian defences on the entire front—remained adamant that Barbarossa must be launched at exactly 03.15 hours if full surprise was to be achieved. It was clear that some sort of compromise would have to be reached—and it was General Bruno Loerzer, commander of Fliegerkorps II, who put forward what appeared to be a workable plan after consultation with his opposite number in command of Fliegerkorps VIII, General Wolfram von Richthofen. Loerzer's idea was to select 30 of the best crews from the two Fliegerkorps. They would cross the frontier in their Heinkels, Junkers and Dorniers at maximum altitude to avoid detection, the noise of their engines lost in the night. Then, in groups of three, they would sweep down on 10 carefully selected Soviet airfields on the central front—airfields on which the Russians had massed large concentrations of combat aircraft. There was no question that a mere 30 aircraft could hope to neutralize a major part of the Soviet Air Force on the ground; their task was simply to spread confusion on the Russian bases, and Loerzer was banking on the confusion lasting until the main Luftwaffe assault had time to develop.

The plan worked admirably. The 30 bombers penetrated Soviet airspace without incident and hit their targets at the same instant as a thundering artillery barrage heralded the start of Operation Barbarossa. As the 30 headed for home, the first wave of the Luftwaffe attack force—which consisted of 500 horizontal bombers, 270 dive-bombers and 480 fighters —droned eastwards over the burning frontier, heading for the sunrise and their own assigned targets. In the rear MG positions, the gunners kept a watchful eye open for the Russian fighters that might be expected to attack at any moment— but none appeared. On the airfields that had escaped the first strike, the V-VS commanders, uncertain what to do, simply waited for orders that never came. They were still waiting when the first Stukas howled down out of the morning sky, pulverizing runways, buildings and aircraft with their 550-pound bombs.

On only one air base—at Bug, near Brest-Litovsk—did the Russian squadron commanders appear to have acted on their own initiative. Thirty I-16s and MiG-1s were taxied out hurriedly and the first flight had just lifted clear of the runway when the Messerschmitt 110s of Special Group 210 screamed across the field. The two fighters already airborne exploded and crashed in flames, torn apart by a storm of cannon and

MG fire. When the Messerschmitts departed five minutes later the airfield was littered with burning wrecks. Farther south, near Lvov, the Messerschmitt 109Fs of JG 3—part of Fliegerkorps V, operating in support of Army Group South—had a field day. On one airfield alone the German pilots found nearly 100 Soviet aircraft of all types—bombers, fighters and reconnaissance machines—still lined up in long ranks as though at an air display. For 20 minutes the Messerschmitts roved back and forth, reducing the base to a burning shambles. Two 109s were lightly damaged by anti-aircraft fire, but they returned safely to base.

By 04.30 the majority of the German bombers and fighters were back on their bases, where sweating ground crews strove to refuel and rearm them in readiness for the second strike and the crews were debriefed by their unit intelligence officers. There were no reports of any air combats; the Red Air Force had been taken completely by surprise.

It was a different story later that morning, however, during subsequent Luftwaffe operations. At 09.15, the Messerschmitt 110s of Zerstörer-Geschwader 26 ran headlong into a mass of Russian fighters over Kobrin. They were the I-16s of the 124th Air Regiment. A whirling dog-fight developed, two 110s and three I-16s going down in flames. A fourth Rata, piloted by Lieutenant Dmitri V. Kokorev, collided headlong with another German fighter; the two aircraft spun down, locked together, and exploded on the ground. No one succeeded in bailing out.

On at least five occasions during this first day of the air war in the east, Soviet fighter pilots deliberately rammed their opponents. Three of them were members of the 123rd Air Regiment; the Regiment's political officer apparently set the example and two other pilots followed suit. The first three men to be made Heroes of the Soviet Union during the war were all pilots; their names were M. P. Zhukov, S. I. Zdorovets and P. T. Kharitonov, and they survived the hectic air fighting of the first days to receive their awards on July 8th 1941.

Although the 109s and 110s had the distinct edge in speed over the I-16s and I-153s, the German pilots found themselves out-manoeuvred by the Russians time and again. The Russian pilots fought on the turn and the Germans found it almost impossible to keep the elusive Ratas and Chaikas in their sights. When a Russian pilot found himself in a tight spot, he would simply haul his aircraft round in a tight turn and race head on for the nearest Messerschmitt at full throttle. These tactics usually worked, unnerving the German pilots and forcing them to break away sharply. The Germans found their superior speed more of a disadvantage than an asset, often overshooting to find, seconds later, their erstwhile target sitting a few yards behind their tail.

At 11.00, the first Russian bombers—SB-2s and DB-3s—made an appearance over the Luftwaffe airfields. The Stukas of Geschwader 77 had just landed on their base to the north of Warsaw after bombing enemy positions near Brest-Litovsk when six SB-2s arrived overhead, in perfect formation. They had hardly released their bombs—which did little damage—when the Messerschmitt 109Fs of JG 51 arrived on the scene. It was a massacre; one after the other, the bombers went down in flames. Twenty-five more Russian bombers attacked the airfield during the remainder of that day, and no fewer than 20 were destroyed by the German fighters and flak. It was the same all along the front: the SBs and DBs came in without fighter escort, in close formation and in broad daylight, and were shot down in their dozens.

By noon on June 22nd, 800 Russian aircraft had been destroyed on the ground. At dusk, the figure of aircraft destroyed had risen to 1,489, including 322 shot down by flak and fighters. In Army Group West's sector alone, the Luftwaffe had accounted for 528 aircraft on the ground and 210 in the air. The Luftwaffe's losses during the day's fighting: 35 aircraft.

During the following week, as the German armoured columns swept on to capture Grodno and form a giant pincer movement with Minsk as the objective, the Red Air Force concentrated its available units in attacks on the advancing enemy ground forces. This time the bombers attacked in smaller groups, strongly escorted by fighters wherever possible. On the second day of battle, a young Russian pilot who was later destined to become the second top-scoring Soviet ace chalked up his first victory while on an escort mission: his name was Alexander Ivanovitch Pokryshkin, and he was a member of a crack Fighter Regiment based near the River Prut, not far from the frontier with Rumania. Pokryshkin's regiment had been the first to re-equip with the new MiG-3 fighter, a modified version of the MiG-1.

After a series of uneventful patrols on the first day of the invasion, Pokryshkin's chance came when he was escorting a squadron of SB-2s in an attack on the German 11th Army. On their way to the target, the Russians were attacked by five Messerschmitt 109Es of JG 77. Together with his wing-man, Pokryshkin immediately turned to fight, and although his own aircraft was damaged in the ensuing combat he succeeded in shooting down a 109.

On the morning of June 29th, the citadel of Brest-Litovsk —which had held out for nearly a week in the face of strong attacks by Colonel-General Guderian's Panzer Group 2—fell at last, shattered by the Junkers 88s of KG 3. With this obstacle behind them the German armoured units raced on, supported by Stukas and Messerschmitts. The Germans now justifiably believed that Soviet air resistance had been virtually eliminated, and the four Luftflotten covering the advance now turned their attention to ground attack operations.

Then, on June 30th, came a surprise. That morning, as the German armour pushed on with the intention of completing its ring of steel around Minsk, hundreds of Soviet bombers appeared over the front. Once again they were almost entirely without fighter escort and they suffered fearfully at the hands of the Messerschmitts. JG 51, operating in the Minsk sector in support of Panzer Group 2, shot down 114 of them on the 30th alone. To the north, more waves of bombers attempted to destroy the bridges over the Dvina River to slow up the advance of Panzer Group 4, which was heading north-eastwards for Leningrad. The Panzer Group's spearheads were covered by the Bf 109Fs of the famous JG 54 'Green Heart' Wing, and in a day of fierce air battles they shot down 65 Russian aircraft.

The butchery went on day after day. Luftwaffe fighter pilots who had arrived on the Eastern Front without combat experience found themselves turned into aces almost overnight as Russian after Russian went down before their guns. Yet the apparent suicide of the Soviet Air Force was serving a purpose: at the cost of thousands of aircraft and lives, the Russians were buying time. While the Soviet airmen sacrificed themselves, armies of workmen were hastily taking apart whole aircraft and engine factories at Moscow, Kharkov, Taganrog, Leningrad, Voronezh and Zaparoye; the plant was being shipped hundreds of miles eastwards, to be reassembled at Novosibirsk, Kazan, Komsomolsk, Irkutsk and Semanov—far beyond the Urals and out of range of the Luftwaffe bombers. Because of this massive evacuation—which involved more than half the Soviet aviation industry—the monthly production totals of military aircraft temporarily fell by 50 per cent. By the spring of 1942, however, the figure had once again risen to the pre-invasion total of 1,000 aircraft a month, and from then on it began to increase steadily.

In July 1941, however, the Luftwaffe was undisputed mistress of the Russian sky and the Russians were in retreat along the entire front, from the Baltic to the Black Sea, harassed by the Stukas that blasted a path for the advancing Wehrmacht. On July 2nd, the Germans smashed their way across the Beresina River and forced the remnants of the Soviet 4th and 13th Armies back to the Dnieper, where they were reinforced by four Reserve Armies under the command of Marshal Budenny. In the north-western sector, the Germans captured Vitebsk on July 9th and soon afterwards launched an offensive designed to take Smolensk. The battle for this city, one of the costliest of the whole war on the Eastern Front, was to last for more than six weeks.

On the south-western front, progress had been slower. On the third day of the invasion, von Kleist's 1st Armoured Group had suffered heavy losses near Kovel during a massive tank battle with the Soviet 5th Army, but the Luftwaffe's overwhelming air superiority saved the situation and the Russian armoured formations were broken up by concentrated

Stuka attacks. By July 11th the Soviet 5th, 6th, 12th and 26th Armies had withdrawn to new defensive positions along the pre-1939 western frontier of the Soviet Union, and their retreat enabled the German armies to push forward into the valley of the Dniester. Still farther south, German forces crossed the River Prut into Bessarabia, forcing the Soviet 9th Army also to retreat to new defensive positions beyond the Dniester.

Meanwhile, the German High Command had decided to divert the Wehrmacht's main thrust from Moscow—hitherto regarded as the primary objective—and concentrate on the early capture of Kiev (Army Group South) and Leningrad (Army Group North). While the German 4th Armoured Group advanced through Estonia, the Finnish Army attacked strongly to the north of Lake Ladoga and across the Karelian Isthmus, gradually pushing back the Russians until the two sides once again faced each other across the original frontier that had separated Finland and the Soviet Union before the start of the Winter War. Air fighting on this front was sporadic, with the majority of the Soviet air divisions fully committed on the vital western and south-western fronts.

Farther north, on the Kola Peninsula—with its vital port of Murmansk—air defence was primarily the task of the Soviet Naval Air Arm, which possessed only small numbers of I-153s and I-16s together with a handful of SB-2s. An additional bomber force was provided by the 14th Army, which was responsible for the defence of the Kola Inlet to Kandalaksha and had a mixed wing of SB-2s and Pe-2s attached to it. In this sector, the air war had begun almost a week before the onset of Barbarossa: at two o'clock in the afternoon of June 17th, in fact, when a lone Junkers 88 reconnaissance aircraft swept over Polyarnoe harbour and the town of Vaenga. Two flights of I-153s and I-16s took off to intercept the intruder, but he was faster than they were and got away. Later that day, more Junkers 88s appeared over Ozerko Bay; this time they were met by a barrage of intense but highly inaccurate anti-aircraft fire, through which they passed unharmed. After that, reconnaissance flights over Soviet territory became a daily occurrence. On June 19th, a flight of Messerschmitt 109s attempted to attack an I-153 over Vaenga, but the Russian pilot got away in a bank of cloud. All the German aircraft involved were part of General Stumpff's Luftflotte V and came under the command of the Fliegerführer Kirkenes.

At 04.00 on June 22nd, the Luftwaffe launched a heavy attack on Soviet Air Force and Naval Air Arm bases in the Polyarnoe area. In this case their bid to neutralize the Russian air defences failed, for the Soviet Air Force and Navy commanders in this sector, unlike their colleagues elsewhere along the front, had used their initiative and carefully dispersed their aircraft—in spite of a directive that the German reconnaissance flights of the previous week were purely provocative in nature, and that no action was to be taken. On the first day of operations, the Luftwaffe made several attempts to attack Murmansk with small formations of Junkers 88s and Stukas, but each raid was successfully broken up by the defending fighters. Although a number of German aircraft were damaged during the first two days, it was not until June 24th that the Soviet pilots in the sector scored their first victory, the honour falling to a naval airman named B. F. Safonov. His victim was a Heinkel 111, one of a formation intercepted by Soviet fighters on the approaches to Vaenga. Safonov—whose aircraft was armed with experimental air-to-air rockets—scored a lucky hit on the Heinkel he had selected as his target. He then chased it out to sea and finally shot it down over Zalentsa Bay.

On June 26th, for the first time, Russian SB-2s attacked the German airfield at Lakselven, near North Cape, and the ports of Kirkenes and Petsamo. Four SBs failed to return. Meanwhile, anti-submarine patrols were being maintained by Naval Air Arm MBR-2 flying boats, known as 'Barns' by their crews, and several scraps were recorded between these and Junkers 88s. The MBRs usually managed to escape, and on occasions they even managed to inflict some damage on the German machines. The following day, the Luftwaffe launched a series of heavy attacks on Soviet gun batteries on the Sredni Peninsula; fierce air battles developed, 10 German aircraft being shot down for the loss of six Russian fighters.

On June 28th, the Germans launched their expected offensive across the Norwegian frontier, with Murmansk as their objective. The Soviet 14th Army, largely untrained and poorly equipped, was broken up and fell back on Polyarnoe. Vicious fighting took place along the coast of the Kola Inlet, the Russians clinging desperately to every rock and cliff. In the air, Safonov's fighters hurled themselves against the Luftwaffe again and again, although the fighter situation was so desperate that no more than half a dozen I-16s or I-153s could operate at any one time. The situation was saved by fresh reinforcements—including hundreds of Russian sailors—who were hurriedly rushed into action to bolster the crumbling 14th Army, and by a series of Soviet commando raids behind the German lines. After three weeks the German offensive became bogged down half way to Murmansk and the Russians dug themselves in, forming a strongly fortified front that was to change little during four years of war.

Meanwhile, on the night of July 21st/22nd, Moscow had received its first baptism of fire from the Luftwaffe. On advanced bases at Vitebsk, Orsha, Minsk and Chatalovska, the Germans had assembled 127 Junkers 88s and Heinkel 111s, drawn from KGs 3, 26, 28, 53, 54, 55 and Kampfgruppe 100, the Luftwaffe's 'Pathfinder Force'. In view of the importance of Moscow as a military target, with its massive rail network through which traffic for a large sector of the front flowed—quite apart from the political factor—the number of bombers committed to this initial raid was surprisingly small. The Luftwaffe crews had no way of knowing it at the time, but their expedition to the Russian capital was in fact a gesture on the part of Göring: a reply to Hitler's criticism that the Luftwaffe did not have the courage to fly over more than 300 miles of enemy territory to deliver a serious blow to Russian morale by striking at Moscow.

During this first raid, the Heinkels and Junkers—flying through the worst anti-aircraft barrage they had encountered since the Luftwaffe's night raids on London—dropped over

100 tons of high explosive and 45,000 incendiaries. There was a second raid the following night, with 115 bombers, and on the third night the strength of the attacking force had dropped to 100. Throughout the rest of 1941, the number of bombers committed decreased steadily until most raids were carried out by groups of 10 or 15 aircraft. The Soviet air defence commander in Moscow—Major-General D. A. Zhuralev—continued to strengthen the anti-aircraft forces at his disposal until Moscow was encircled by the biggest arsenal of anti-aircraft weapons in history, with some 300 fighter aircraft also eventually assigned to the defence of the capital. Although handicapped by a shortage of night fighters, the Soviet Air Force never lost its air superiority over the city.

As the first heavy autumn rains turned the summer dust into clinging mud along the Eastern Front, the Luftwaffe began to meet increasing numbers of new Soviet aircraft. Combat experience gained by the V-VS during the first three months of the war was already enabling Soviet designers to incorporate a number of modifications in the three main types that formed the backbone of the Soviet fighter units. The MiG-1 was redesignated MiG-3 after the 2,100th machine had been produced, the main improvements being a fully enclosed cockpit and the addition of an auxiliary fuel tank. Because of the increased combat radius that resulted, MiG-3s were used extensively for fast reconnaissance. The Yak-1 was also modified, its light 7·62-mm machine guns being replaced by one and sometimes two 12·7-mm Beresina weapons. Its M-105PA engine was also replaced by a 1,260-hp M-105PF.

The third fighter, the LaGG-3, had proved a disappointment in combat with German fighters. Although its flight characteristics were excellent in level flight, acceleration was poor and the aircraft was sloppy during the tight manoeuvres necessary under combat conditions, with a marked tendency to spin out of tight turns. The all-up weight was reduced by the elimination of the LaGG's two machine guns, and flaps were fitted to improve the landing characteristics. A method for overcoming the spinning problem was finally evolved by Lieutenant-Colonel Gruzdev, a NII V-VS test pilot, who discovered that the aircraft's unpleasant habit could be cured completely by lowering 10 or 15 degrees of flap, which permitted a pilot to turn as tightly as he liked. In spite of its faults, the LaGG-3 enjoyed a better reputation with Soviet pilots than the MiG-3: conceived as a high-altitude inter-cepter, the latter suffered a marked loss of performance when circumstances forced it to be adapted for other tasks.

In mid July, several V-VS ground attack units on the central front began to re-equip with what was to become the most widely used aircraft in the Soviet Air Force's wartime inventory: the Ilyushin Il-2 Shturmovik. The requirements that resulted in the development of the Il-2 were summed up by the words of its designer, Sergei Ilyushin, who later wrote:

'My task was to build an aircraft which could be used effectively in support of our ground forces. The main function of such an aircraft would therefore be the destruction of enemy ground forces, that is to say infantry, tanks, trucks, artillery, fortifications and so on. For this purpose, the aircraft would have to be capable of carrying a varied weapon-load of machine guns, cannon, bombs and rockets.

'In order to seek out and attack targets as small as tanks and trucks, camouflaged into the bargain, the aircraft would have to operate at very low altitude, between 50 and 500 feet. But this would mean that the aircraft would be subjected to concentrated enemy ground fire, and consequently it would need to be very heavily armoured. Evidently it would be impossible to protect the aircraft against every kind of enemy weapon, and this left me with a serious problem: what type of armour to choose. In the end, I settled for armour-plating of a thickness which, while providing sufficient protection against small-calibre weapons, would not result in a sacrifice of performance.

So the Shturmovik was born, series production beginning in 1940 at Factory No. 18 (Voronezh), No. 22 (Fili) and No. 38 (Moscow). Altogether, 249 Il-2s were built during 1941, but production was drastically curtailed by the removal of the factories to the safe areas of the eastern Soviet Union.

Incredibly, however, full-scale production began once more just two months after the start of the mass evacuation, in spite of the fact that some factories were still only half completed, which meant that the personnel had to work in the open air under the fearful conditions of the Russian winter. Stalin intervened personally, sending a telegram to the director of every factory which read: 'The Il-2 is as necessary to our armies as air or bread!' He was right; the Wehrmacht soon grew to hate and fear the Shturmovik as other armies had feared the wailing Stuka. Known affectionately as 'Ilyusha' by its pilots, the Il-2 was given another name by the Germans: Der Schwarze Tod—the Black Death.

With aircraft such as the Il-2 beginning to reach the front-line squadrons, the Luftwaffe was finding the Soviet Air Force an increasingly formidable opponent. The men were improving too, as well as their machines. During the first weeks of the war, the Russian pilots had laboured under a lack of combat experience and the restrictions of outmoded air fighting tactics. In the beginning, there had been a general and totally erroneous belief among many pilots that the speed of modern air combat was such that it permitted no calculated tactics: there could be no question of teamwork or of working out a plan of action in advance. This dangerous assumption was later rejected outright by several top-scoring Soviet pilots, mainly Alexander Pokryshkin, who developed a series of air fighting tactics that were to become standard throughout the Soviet Air Force.

During this early period, the Russian pilots were able to compensate for their deficiencies only by their courage and general flying skill. There were many instances of Soviet fighter pilots deliberately ramming the enemy, but contrary to popular belief this was seldom an act of desperation but a coolly thought-out manoeuvre demanding the utmost skill and nerves of steel. Several Russian pilots became adept in the ramming technique, notably Lieutenant Khlobystov of the Murmansk Wing, who successfully rammed and destroyed two enemy aircraft during a single sortie. One of the pioneers of the technique was Lieutenant Talalikhin, who rammed a Junkers 88 during a night raid on Moscow.

Towards the end of 1941, however, improvisation began to give way to more organized tactics, which developed steadily as the war progressed. In their early encounters with the enemy the Russian pilots had made considerable use of squadron formations, but this drastically reduced their freedom to manoeuvre. Before long, the 'loose pair' became the basic element of every combat formation. It was an elementary lesson, learned by the Germans in Spain and ignored by the Russians until now. Nevertheless, late starters though they were, the Russians used the pair more offensively than the Germans; in the latter's manual, the destruction of enemy aircraft was the function of the leader, whose tail was to be covered at all times by the number two aircraft. To the Russian way of thinking, this resulted in a double inconvenience: the offensive power of a squadron was reduced by 50 per cent and the wing-men, mostly young pilots, developed a passive rather than an aggressive instinct. Eventually it was agreed that there was a necessity for both pilots of the pair to play an equal part in air combat, each acting as cover for the other.

Once established, the pair remained the basic Soviet air fighting unit. It was first used extensively in October 1941, during the battle for Moscow, when Russian fighters appeared over the front in strength for the first time to oppose the German air offensive against the city. In two months, the Luftwaffe lost 1,400 aircraft to fighters and flak on the Moscow front. On December 6th, Marshal Zhukov went over to the offensive and within a fortnight had pushed the Germans back, and soon afterwards the six air regiments which had particularly distinguished themselves in the defence of the Russian capital were designated Guards Regiments—the first to receive this honour.

Soon after the Luftwaffe's first series of raids on Moscow, the Soviet Air Force had been ordered to retaliate by bombing Berlin. It was easier said than done; the only Russian bomber with sufficient range for the job was the Ilyushin Il-4 (DB-3F), and the only Il-4s that still occupied bases within striking distance of the German capital a month after the invasion were naval aircraft, operating with the Baltic Fleet from airfields on the Estonian islands of Dagö and Oesel. Two squadrons of these (a total of 13) were hurriedly formed into a makeshift strategic bombing force under the leadership of an Air Force colonel named E. N. Preobrazhenski, commander of the 1st Bomber Aviation Regiment of the Baltic Fleet, and on August 7th five Il-4s took off on the 1,500-mile round trip. Two of the bombers were shot down during the outward flight, two more failed to find the target, and one bombed the suburbs of Berlin, causing insignificant damage. Four more raids were carried out between August 7th and September 4th, but few of the attacking aircraft managed to find the target and 75 per cent losses were sustained. Finally, in mid September, the evacuation of the Russian bases in the face of the German thrust through Estonia brought an end to these operations.

The shortage of Soviet combat aircraft in the autumn of 1941 was still critical. The aircraft industry, in the full throes of reassembly and transformation, was hard pressed even to make good the losses due to attrition in combat, and deliveries of combat aircraft promised by both Britain and the United States were anxiously awaited. The first to arrive were 24 Hurricane IIAs of Nos. 81 and 134 Squadrons, RAF, which landed at Vaenga airfield near Murmansk from the aircraft carrier *Argus* on September 7th. They shared the base with a Russian SB-2 squadron and came under the command of the Soviet AOC, Major-General Kuznetsov. The two RAF squadrons were soon in action, escorting the SB-2s on bombing raids behind the enemy lines. On September 17th, during an escort mission over Balncha, the Hurricane pilots shot down four Bf 109Es for no loss to themselves.

Between combat operations, the RAF pilots acted as instructors for the pilots of the 72nd Regiment of the Soviet Naval Air Arm, to whom the Hurricanes were eventually to be handed over. The first two Russian airmen to convert to the new type were captains Safonov and Kuharienko. Safonov, who was a perfectionist, proceeded cautiously in an effort to get everything absolutely right. Kuharienko, however, was different—and typical of many Russian pilots. On his first flight, he somehow managed to pull the Hurricane off the ground after swerving wildly across the airfield, and immediately went into a hair-raising series of aerobatics. When he had finished he brought the aircraft in to land, came to a stop after a couple of enormous bounces, and staggered from the cockpit almost doubled up with laughter. As one astonished RAF onlooker remarked later, anyone but a Russian would have been frightened out of his wits.

By October 22nd all the Hurricanes had been handed over to the Russians and the RAF pilots prepared to leave Murmansk. During five weeks of operations they had shot down 16 German aircraft, probably destroyed four more and damaged seven. One Hurricane had been lost, in an accident. In those five weeks, no Soviet bomber had been lost while being escorted by the RAF Hurricanes.

The twenty-four Mk IIAs were the vanguard of some 2,000 Hurricanes of all types which were delivered to the Soviet Air Force up to the end of 1942. Soon after delivery of the first batch of Hurricanes, 170 Curtiss P-40 Tomahawks arrived in Russia through the northern ports, and some of these also went into service in the Murmansk sector. The Russian pilots had no great love for the P-40; it was prone to sudden engine failure, and they dubbed it the 'Marvel of Engineless Flight'. Nevertheless, the number of P-40s eventually handed over to the Russians was 2,097, and the type saw combat on all fronts. Other types delivered to the Soviet Union by Britain and the United States during the war included the Supermarine Spitfire (143 Mk VBs and 1,186 LF 9s); Bell Airacobra (4,746 delivered and used as ground-attack fighters); Bell Kingcobra (2,400 delivered); Douglas A-20 Havoc (2,908); North American B-25 Mitchell (862); and the Republic Thunderbolt (195). Numbers of transport and training aircraft were also acquired, including 700 C-47s. Altogether, 18,865 aircraft of all types were delivered; a further 638 were lost in transit.

Numerous accounts written about the fighting on the

Eastern Front since the war have stated that the deliveries of foreign aircraft enabled the Russians to turn the tide of the air war in 1942, but this assumption is completely false; it would be no more true to say that the RAF owed its victory over the Luftwaffe to the fact that some of its squadrons were equipped with American types. The fact is that many of the aircraft supplied to Russia during the war were substantially inferior to the combat types being produced on a massive scale by the Soviet aircraft industry; this was certainly true of the Hurricane and the P-40. Also, the fact that the Russians received over half the total number of Bell P-39 Airacobras and P-63 Kingcobras that were built was due mainly to their lack of success in USAAF service; neither type measured up to the Americans' operational requirements. The Russians promptly adapted both aircraft for close-support duties, adding armour and guns, and the Soviet pilots praised them highly—particularly the P-63, which was found to be capable of absorbing tremendous punishment from ground fire.

There is no doubt that the aircraft delivered by the Allies played a big part in bringing about the ultimate Soviet victory in the air. However, there is no escaping the fact that between June 1941 and the end of 1944, the Soviet aircraft industry had produced a staggering total of 97,000 aircraft, so that the Allied contribution could in no way be considered decisive.

In the dark days of 1941, the most important effect of the initial deliveries of Allied combat aircraft was on morale, for apart from their successful defence of Moscow towards the end of the year, things were still going badly for the Russians on all fronts. In besieged Leningrad, people were dying from starvation and the bitter cold in their homes and in the streets. The German encirclement had been completed on August 30th, and after that the city's only hope of supply was by air. Every available transport aircraft was assembled for the job, but the force was pitifully small and the aircraft involved—mostly big four-engined Tupolev G-2s, the transport version of the TB-3, and small Polikarpov Po-2s—suffered heavily from enemy fighters and flak. The airlift was directed by Alexei Kosygin, now the Soviet Premier, and Andrei Zhdanov, who succeeded

Morane-Saulnier Type N of the 19th Squadron, Imperial Russian Air Service, 1917. Pilot on the right is Lieutenant Ivan Smirnoff *(above)* and the Nieuport 11C-1 of the Imperial Russian Air Service, 1917 *(below) (Photos: Original source unknown: via Frank Yeoman)*

Servicing a Yak-3 at a forward airstrip in East Prussia, winter 1944-5 *(above)* and the victors: Yak-3s of the Normandie-Niemen Regiment on their return to Le Bourget, France. Note shadow of camera aircraft: a captured Fiesler Storch *(below)* *(Photos: E.C.P. Armées)*

in working miracles with the limited means at their disposal. During the siege, the transport crews flew in nearly 9,000 tons of food and other essential commodities, 1,200 tons arriving during the fortnight from November 14th to 28th 1941. The total tonnage airlifted into Leningrad represented only a tiny fraction of the city's requirements, but the transport pilots undoubtedly saved many lives—often at the sacrifice of their own.

Throughout the early months of the siege the Luftwaffe enjoyed complete air superiority over the Leningrad sector, as it did elsewhere, although on occasion the German air on-slaught was bitterly contested by the relatively few I-153 and I-16 equipped air regiments on the northern front, as well as by Leningrad's extremely strong anti-aircraft defences. Some of the biggest air battles took place in September, when the Stukas of Major Oskar Dinort's StG 2 'Immelmann' Wing attacked the Red Fleet in the harbour of Kronstadt every day for a week, escorted by the Bf 109s of JG 54. The Stukas sustained heavy osses, lbut sank the battleship *Marat* and the cruiser *Kirov*, as well as inflicting heavy damage on the battle-ship *October Revolution*. The *Marat* fell victim to the bombs of Lieutenant Hans-Ulrich Rudel, who was to become the Luftwaffe's leading 'tank-buster' on the Russian front. The Luftwaffe's losses began to mount still further with the arrival of new combat types on the northern front during the winter of 1941-2, the Soviet 12th Air Regiment being the first to equip with new MiG-3 fighters in this sector.

At the other end of the vast battlefront, while the agony of Leningrad went on during November, the Soviet southern front had been falling back rapidly through the Donets Basin towards Rostov. It was obvious to the Stavka—the Soviet High Command—that this vital port, the gateway to the oilfields of the Caucasus, was the primary objective of General von Kleist's 1st Panzer Army, and steps were immediately taken to meet the German assault. Then, during the third week in November, a sudden complication arose: a dense blanket of fog rolled down across the steppes, with heavy falls of snow, and the Russians lost contact with the Panzers. They had no way of knowing where von Kleist would strike.

On November 20th, Alexander Pokryshkin volunteered to fly a lone reconnaissance mission in a bid to locate the German armour. Although the weather conditions made flying suicidal, permission was granted and he took off accordingly, flying westwards at low altitude through a blinding snowstorm in his MiG-3. The snow and the fog made it impossible to see anything, and after flying around over enemy-occupied territory for what seemed an eternity Pokryskhin decided to abandon the search and head for home. At that moment, purely by chance, he spotted a series of marks on the snow-covered ground through a gap in the murk and identified them as tank-tracks. Following the lines, he swept over a cluster of trucks—and then, carefully camouflaged on the fringes of a wood, he saw von Kleist's tanks; hundreds of them. Light flak started to come up and Pokryshkin roared away into the fog, his one concern now to get back safely with the news. When he landed at his base, there were no more than a few pints of fuel left in his tanks.

Von Kleist's Panzers captured Rostov on November 23rd, but their occupation of the city was not destined to last long. Thanks to the information brought back by Pokryshkin, the Soviet High Command knew the exact direction from which the German attack would develop. Consequently, they were able to redeploy five armies, cutting off the German spearhead in a pincer movement from north and south. On November 28th Rostov was retaken by the Soviet 9th and 56th Armies; for the vital part he had played, Pokryshkin was awarded the Order of Lenin—the first of three similar awards bestowed on him during his career as a fighter pilot. During that career, he became a Hero of the Soviet Union three times. The gold star medal of a Hero of the Soviet Union is Russia's highest award for gallantry, and only one other Soviet fighter pilot was destined to win this honour three times over. His name was Ivan Kozhedub, and he later surpassed Pokryshkin to become Russia's top-scoring ace. We shall hear more of him; but he did not enter combat until

March 1943, which makes his achievement all the more outstanding.

After their evacuation of Rostov, the Germans fell back westward to the River Mius, where—in the face of savage Russian attacks—they succeeded in establishing a defensive line. During the weeks that followed, Pokryshkin's squadron was engaged in many fierce combats over the Mius, escorting Shturmoviks—which, not yet equipped with any rearwards-firing defensive armament, were suffering heavily—and attacking Luftwaffe Stuka formations which continued to appear in strength. During these operations, Pokryshkin took the opportunity to initiate many new pilots into the finer techniques of air combat, taking them along as his own wing-men until they knew the ropes. The ace himself ceaselessly strove to perfect his own combat methods, paying great attention to the Luftwaffe's tactics. The young pilots who came under his wing were often puzzled by his advice: 'Always think and act as though tomorrow were here today'; but after a taste of combat they soon discovered just how sound this maxim was. At the end of the day, Pokryshkin would assemble the pilots of his flight in his tent—which was littered with diagrams of air combat manoeuvres he had worked out—and they would talk tactics for hours. The soundness of Pokryshkin's instruction is demonstrated by one fact alone: 30 of the pilots who saw their first action with him subsequently became Heroes of the Soviet Union, and six won the coveted gold star twice over. Between them, the 30 destroyed 500 German aircraft before the end of hostilities.

One of his early pupils, who saw combat with him during the winter of 1941-2 over the Mius, was Alexander Klubov. Pokryshkin quickly singled him out as a natural leader and a born fighter pilot; although aggressive, Klubov remained completely unruffled even during the most hectic air combats. On one occasion, Klubov set off on a lone reconnaissance mission and became overdue. Pokryshkin, who had stayed behind on the squadron's airfield, tried to call him up over the R/T and eventually made contact, asking Klubov what was going on. 'I'm in the middle of a scrap', was the laconic reply.

As dusk was falling, Klubov's MiG appeared over the airfield, behaving very erratically. It was pitching violently, as though on a switchback. Klubov made his approach, gunning the engine from time to time, and brought the MiG down on its belly with a terrific crash. He climbed from the cockpit, unhurt, as the other pilots—including Pokryshkin—came running up. The aircraft was a complete write-off; it was riddled like a colander with cannon-shell and MG bullet holes. Klubov explained that he had been bounced by six Messerschmitts and that he had shot two of them down before a third had shot away his elevator controls. Nevertheless, he had managed to make his escape and had kept the aircraft flying by careful use of the throttle, cramming on power to bring the nose up when the MiG showed signs of going into a dive. A lesser pilot would have bailed out.

When the Luftwaffe went to war against the Soviet Union, its pilots did so with the impression—carefully fostered by propaganda—that the vast majority of Russian pilots were robot-like morons, and their early crushing successes seemed to bear this out. But the Russians learned rapidly during the dark months of 1941, and in the big offensives of the following year increasing numbers of pilots of the calibre of Alexander Klubov—who finished the war as fifth-ranking Soviet ace with 50 victories—began to tear gaps in the Luftwaffe's ranks.

Chapter 7

1942—The Year of No Retreat

In the middle of January 1942, the Russians—encouraged by their successful defence of Moscow, and with their front-line forces reinforced by fresh combat divisions from Siberia —launched a major offensive on the Kalinin front with the aim of encircling the German Army Group Centre. In bitter cold and deep snow, the 3rd and 4th Soviet Shock Armies— driving through the Valday Hills to the north of Rzhev— hammered a wedge between the German Army Group North and Army Group Centre. On the western front, the Russians advanced along the Smolensk Highway and recaptured Mozhaisk. To the south, the Soviet 33rd Army launched a strong thrust towards Vyazma, and on January 20th the 4th Airborne Corps was dropped to the south-west of this town by an armada of transport aircraft.

On the north-western front, the situation of the German 9th Army—denied reinforcements from the west by the Soviet thrust through Mozhaisk—was becoming desperate. By early February, 100,000 men—a total of six divisions—were completely surrounded at Demyansk, south-east of Lake Ilmen. On February 20th the Germans mustered every available Junkers 52 transport aircraft—some 75 machines—and began airlifting supplies into the Demyansk pocket. Initially, the transports made the trips in ones and twos, but to reach Demyansk they had to fly 100 miles over enemy territory and the Russians quickly set up a formidable flak corridor along their route. Apart from the flak, there were the fighters; when the weather permitted, the Russians maintained standing patrols over Demyansk, and the lumbering Ju 52s were easy game for the MiGs and LaGGs. As losses began to mount the transports were forced to make the flight in close formation, with a strong fighter escort, and—mainly because the Russian fighter pilots had received orders to avoid combat with the Messerschmitts and concentrate on the transports— the situation improved slightly. Even so, operating conditions were fearful; after three weeks only a quarter of the transport force remained serviceable. The airlift continued, however, and for three months—until a narrow supply route was opened by the Germans in May—the transports flew in over 24,000 tons of supplies.

All types of aircraft were pressed into service, including the bombers of Fliegerkorps VIII. During the operation, the Luftwaffe lost 265 machines, the majority being written off accidentally on airfields covered in snow and ice. Supplies were also airlifted to a second German pocket at Kholm; conditions here were even more difficult, for the airstrip was within range of Russian artillery. After a few weeks the Junkers 52s had suffered such crippling losses that they were unable to continue operating, and supplies had to be dropped by parachute from bomber aircraft or landed by glider. On many occasions, fierce battles developed between the Germans and Russians for supplies that fell in no man's land. In spite of everything, the supplies kept the 3,500 troops in the pocket going until they were relieved early in May. The success of these airlifts, under the most adverse conditions, helped to convince Hermann Göring that his Luftwaffe alone could keep huge garrisons of German troops supplied, even in the face of stiff resistance. It was a dangerous assumption, as later events in that fatal year of 1942 were to show.

Although it drove long wedges into German-held territory, the Soviet Winter Offensive of 1942 failed in its primary aim. Notwithstanding desperate Soviet assaults, strongly fortified centres of German resistance—mainly at Staraya Russa, Demidov, Velizh and Velikiye Luki, as well as Demyansk and Kholm—held out grimly until the spring thaw. Throughout the offensive, these positions were under constant attack by the Soviet Air Force's Shturmovik units. The Il-2s were still proving extremely vulnerable, and losses were high in spite of new tactics evolved by their pilots. These included what was known as the 'circle of death', which involved crossing the enemy lines at a poorly defended spot and then circling to attack the German positions from the rear, making full use of the element of surprise.

It was during a Shturmovik attack on a German airfield near Staraya Russa, in April 1942, that a Russian fighter pilot became the central figure in one of the greatest epics of individual courage and endurance in history. His name was Alexei P. Maresyev, and he was flying a Yak-1 fighter on an escort mission with a flight of six Il-2s. The raid took the Germans completely by surprise, the Russian aircraft arriving over the airfield just as two Junkers 52s were taking off. Maresyev shot them both down, but the next instant tracers flickered past his own aircraft as ten Messerschmitt 109s came tumbling down from above. In the twisting dogfight which developed, the Russian pilot found himself out of ammunition. He tried desperately to get away, but cannon-shells smashed into his engine and the Yak went out of control. Maresyev's last memory was of a line of pine trees racing up to meet him, a split second before the shattering impact knocked him unconscious.

When he came to, he found that he was lying in deep snow in the middle of a pine forest. He had been flung out of the wrecked aircraft, and both his legs were shattered. He was in agony, but he knew that he had to keep moving at all costs; the alternative was death from exposure. He had no idea how far he was from the Russian lines; the air combat had carried him away from Staraya Russa and he might be anything between 50 and 100 miles inside enemy territory. All he knew was that the front lay somewhere to the east. Summoning all his strength, he began to crawl in that direction.

Alexei Maresyev crawled through the snow for 19 days, half blind with agony, frequently losing consciousness. His only food consisted of a hedgehog, a few handfuls of berries and some ants, and on one occasion he used his service revolver against a bear that came lumbering towards him out of the forest. Luckily the first shot counted, and the animal fell dead. On the nineteenth day the pilot was picked up by a band of Russian partisans, who made contact with his squadron by radio. His squadron commander, Andrei Degtyarenko, flew a little Po-2 aircraft to an improvised landing strip in the forest and picked up the badly injured

Maresyev, who was immediately flown to hospital in Moscow. There the doctors found that gangrene had set in, and they were forced to amputate both his legs below the knee.

For most people, that would have meant the end of a promising career—and in fact Maresyev almost gave up hope and the will to live. Then another hospital patient lent him a book of stories about the First World War, and in it he read how a pilot named Karpovitch had flown with a wooden leg. Maresyev determined to follow the earlier pilot's example— and he got his wish, in the face of strong opposition from many quarters. He not only flew again, but he was back with his squadron in time to participate in the big air battles during the Kursk offensive of 1943.

Another Soviet pilot who had a remarkable experience during the Winter Offensive was Semyon A. Kuznetsov, who was flying an Il-2 on a reconnaissance mission deep behind the German lines on the Moscow front on January 21st when he got mixed up in a savage dogfight with Junkers 87s and Bf 109s. His aircraft was set on fire and he had to make a forced landing. As he climbed from the cockpit, he noticed a 109 circling overhead and dived behind some bushes, afraid that the enemy pilot would strafe him. Then, to his amazement, the 109 lowered its wheels and flaps and touched down on the hard-packed snow, taxying to a stop 50 yards from the crashed Il-2. The German pilot got out and walked over to the wreck, revolver in hand. As he disappeared round the opposite side of the Il-2 from where Kuznetsov was hiding, the Russian pilot sprinted for the 109 and hurled himself into the cockpit. The German had left the fighter's engine idling. The cockpit was utterly strange to Kuznetsov, but he found the throttle lever and eased it forward. The 109 gathered speed and lurched into the air as its rightful owner came running across the snow, waving his revolver. Using all his skill, Kuznetsov guided the strange aircraft back to his own base and landed safely—although he narrowly missed being shot down by Russian fighters and flak.

Although the Soviet Air Force's contribution to the Winter Offensive had been a far smaller one than it would be called upon to make in future offensives, it had been significant. For the first time, Soviet air units had showed themselves capable of holding their own against the Luftwaffe. This was particularly true on the Moscow front and around Rostov; in the latter case, two Soviet air armies—a total of some 1,000 aircraft —had managed to retain a measure of air superiority since the Germans were driven out of the city in the previous November. Much of the Russian success was undoubtedly due to the more robust nature of their aircraft and equipment, which were better suited to the operating conditions imposed by the most fearful Russian winter in living memory. Throughout that winter, the great majority of Luftwaffe units were forced to operate with fewer than 50 per cent of their aircraft serviceable.

Although both sides had virtually fought themselves to a standstill during the Winter Offensive, there was to be no respite. The Soviet High Command was already planning another major counter-offensive, while the Germans were getting ready for a massive thrust to the Don and the Volga and into the Caucasus, which—in addition to the vast wealth of the region's oilfields—would give them access to the Middle East by the northern route. For their projected offensive, the Germans had assembled 74 divisions and some 1,500 aircraft between Voronezh and the Crimea.

The German offensive opened on May 8th 1942, the first blows falling on the Soviet Crimean front under General Kozlov. The Germans rapidly smashed their way through the Soviet 44th Army and thrust on towards the Sea of Azov. Faulty intelligence had led the Russians to believe that the offensive would not begin in this sector, and consequently they were not adequately prepared to meet it. The Luftwaffe —principally Fliegerkorps IV—quickly established air superiority, enabling Erich Manstein's 11th Army to surround the Soviet 51st Army and capture Kerch. With the Soviet evacuation of the Kerch Peninsula, the Germans captured over 300 Russian aircraft intact on abandoned airfields.

The remainder of the Soviet air regiments in the Crimea were hastily evacuated to airfields in the Caucasus, leaving a token force of 50 fighters and bombers to provide air cover over the Crimea's last bastion: Sevastopol. Although this scratch air defence force put up a stiff fight during the early days of June, it was quickly overwhelmed and Sevastopol was left naked to the Luftwaffe's air onslaught. The garrison—outnumbered two to one—held out amid savage fighting for 25 days before its evacuation was ordered on June 30th.

Meanwhile, to the north, Soviet troops of the south-western front under Marshal Timoshenko had launched a limited offensive with Kharkov as the objective, and had temporarily driven a wedge through the German 6th Army to north and south of the town. The Russian assault was poorly supported by the Soviet Air Force, and the V-VS was consequently unable to be of significant assistance to the attacking ground forces. Nor were the Russian airmen able to intervene when the Russian 6th and 38th Armies were driven back to the Donets River by a strong German counter-attack in mid May, supported by von Kliest's 1st Panzer Army. This thrust effectively sealed the fate of the major part of five Soviet armies, which became isolated by von Kleist's Panzers when Marshal Timoshenko withdrew to form a defensive line on the Donets. Although some units did manage to fight their way out of the trap, the greater part of the encircled armies had to surrender. It was the biggest haul of prisoners the Germans had taken since the war in the east began.

The stage was now set for the massive German offensive that would take them through the eastern Ukraine to the Volga. In readiness for this, Field Marshal von Bock's Army Group South was reinforced until, at the end of June, it comprised 90 divisions, 10 of them armoured. In a desperate attempt to prepare for the coming attack, the Russians re-organized their force in the south-west into four fronts: the Bryansk front, the south-western front, the southern front and the north Caucasus front. For air support, there were the 8th and 16th Air Armies.

It was the 16th Air Army that helped to swing the balance in the Russians' favour—albeit by a critically narrow margin—when the German Army Group B broke through the

Bryansk front towards the end of June and pushed on towards the important strategic town of Voronezh, on the River Don. For the first time, the Soviet Air Force won air superiority. Acting in support of counter-attacks by Soviet armour, rocket-firing Shturmoviks caused havoc among the German armour and transport; the German thrust halted short of its objective and the situation in this sector stabilized temporarily.

The damage, however, had been done. Through the breach created by Army Group B, the German 6th Army struck south-ward and forced Timoshenko's armies into a retreat across the steppe into the great curve of the River Don. Beyond that curve, nestling on the banks of the Volga, lay the city of Stalingrad.

Fourteen hundred miles from Stalingrad, on the Murmansk front, the air war had intensified during the early months of 1942 as the Luftwaffe made determined efforts to destroy the Allied convoys that were bringing supplies to Russia via the northern route with increasing frequency, and fierce air battles took place between Russian fighters and the Germans over the Kola inlet. The 2nd Fighter Aviation Regiment, which had re-equipped with Curtiss P-40s in March 1942, continued to be led by Lieutenant-Colonel Boris F. Safonov; by the following May the ace's score had risen to 22 enemy aircraft destroyed and he had twice been made a Hero of the Soviet Union—the first man to achieve the double award during the war.

The unserviceability rate among the wing's P-40s was high, and when—on May 30th 1942—the fighters were ordered to scramble to provide air cover for the incoming convoy PQ 16, only four aircraft could be made airworthy. The convoy, which was 60 miles offshore, was being savagely attacked by 40 German bombers escorted by Messerschmitt 109s of the Luftwaffe's JG 5 Polar Wing, and the four Russian fighters, led by Safonov, raced up to intercept. The other three P-40s were flown by lieutenants Kukharenko, Pokrovsky and Orlov; the first was compelled to return to base soon after take-off with engine trouble, reducing the fighter force to three machines. In spite of the formidable odds, the Russians did not hesitate to attack; Pokrovsky and Orlov shot down a Junkers apiece and Safonov bagged two. He had just damaged a third when he radioed that his engine had been hit and that he would have to ditch. The crew of a Russian destroyer, escorting the convoy, saw him glide down and hit the sea about two miles away. The warship raced to the spot but Safonov had gone, dragged down into the icy depths of the Barents Sea in the metal coffin of his aircraft. He was the first of the aces to lose his life. His final score was 25 enemy aircraft destroyed.

On the Stalingrad front, the Soviet retreat eastwards continued throughout July. By the middle of that month, the Germans had broken through to the Don; the Soviet southern front narrowly escaped encirclement by a rapid withdrawal behind the Lower Don, and shortly afterwards the armies of this front were transferred to the north Caucasus front under the command of General A. I. Yeremenko. Air support for this front was provided by General Khryukin's 8th Air Army, with the 16th Air Army under General Rudyenko forming part of the Stalingrad front.

While this reorganization went on, the Soviet High Command reinforced the two fronts with several reserve armies, hurriedly brought up from the east, and this helped to check the German advance towards the end of July. Then the Germans too were reinforced by troops from the Army Group A and the Voronezh sector, and this fresh blood enabled them to drive a wedge through the Russian lines and reach the bend in the Don directly opposite Stalingrad.

On the last day of July a new threat materialized in the shape of a thrust from the Caucasus by the German 4th Panzer Army, driving towards Stalingrad from the south-west. A week later, the 6th Army crossed the Don and established a foothold on the river's east bank. The battle for Stalingrad was on. The Russians counter-attacked desperately, fighting for every yard of ground as General Paulus's 6th Army fought its way from the Don bridgehead to the Volga. Behind the Russians' backs Stalingrad lay under a pall of smoke as the city became the focus of a massive air onslaught by the whole of Luftflotte 4.

The first big raid, which coincided with the breakthrough of the German vanguard to the Volga north of Stalingrad, came on August 23rd. In successive waves, 200 German bombers approached the city, escorted by 50 Messerschmitt 109s.

On the approach to Stalingrad, there was a sudden flash of wings in the sunlight and an avalanche of Russian fighters swept down on the attackers. They were the Yak-3s of the 102nd Air Division, and now they dived on the bombers at high speed, scattering the covering Messerschmitts in all directions. A fierce air battle soon spread across the sky, but in spite of their savage attacks the Russian pilots were unable to prevent the great majority of the German bombers from reaching their objective. Nevertheless, during the battles of August 23rd—over Stalingrad and the surrounding front— the Soviet fighters and flak claimed the destruction of 90 enemy aircraft for the loss of 30 Soviet machines. The 102nd Air Division's pilots had proved particularly successful, and were to remain so throughout the battle for Stalingrad. The air defence of the city itself was their primary task, and by the time the last German resistance in Stalingrad ceased on February 2nd 1943, 336 enemy aircraft had fallen to the division's guns, 216 of them bombers.

Many Soviet fighter pilots became aces by destroying five or more enemy aircraft during the aerial slogging-match over Stalingrad. One of the leading pilots was Mikhail Baranov, who eventually went on to score 28 victories. On one occasion, leading a flight of four Airacobras over the city, he ran headlong into a formation of 25 Messerschmitts and took them on, shooting down three before he ran out of ammunition. Then, skilfully manoeuvring his fighter on to the tail of a fourth Messerschmitt, he deliberately closed in and chopped off the fin of the enemy aircraft with his propeller, afterwards coming down to make a safe forced landing. Another pilot, Lieutenant Kostrytzin, attacked a formation of 30 Junkers 88s and shot down three of them single-handed.

Other pilots who achieved fame over Stalingrad were Sergeant Nagorny, who—alone—shot down two out of a formation of four Messerschmitts and drove off the other two,

Riazanov, Makarov, Piatov, Shestakov, Tchembarov and Aleliukhin. The last went on to become the Soviet Union's fifteenth-ranking ace, with a score of 40 kills.

By the middle of September the Germans were in Stalingrad itself, their advance through the city bitterly contested by General Chuikov's 62nd Army. The Russians fought savagely, and every shattered building or stone wall that was seized by the attackers was paid for with dozens of human lives. The battle for Stalingrad became a guerrilla campaign, with individuals or small groups of soldiers stalking each other through the ruins and victory going to the fastest and the stealthiest. Effective air support in the forward areas became impossible on both sides, with the front lines—where they existed—separated by a strip of land only a grenade-throw wide.

Chuikov's forces—the decimated remnants of his original six divisions—quickly found themselves confined to a narrow sector along the west bank of the Volga, some 18 miles long and not more than a mile and a half wide. The ferrying of reinforcements across the river was a hazardous business, as the crossing had to be made under heavy artillery fire and air attack. On September 14th, however, the 13th Guards Division under Lieutenant-General A. I. Rodimtsev made the perilous trip and immediately went into action in the savage fighting for a hill known as Mamayev Kurgan. This hill—Hill 102 on the military maps—was a vital objective. It dominated the river crossing, and whoever controlled it controlled Stalingrad. Twenty-four hours later, Rodimtsev's Guards had virtually ceased to exist—but they had held Mamayev Kurgan.

During this phase of the battle, the Luftwaffe still held overwhelming air superiority over the city, making it impossible for the Soviet Air Force to drop supplies to the city's defenders during daylight hours. For the most part, night supply-dropping operations were carried out by little Po-2 biplanes, and it was the pilots of these flimsy machines who were the real heroes of the air war over Stalingrad. The Po-2s were also used extensively for front-line reconnaissance, and during the preliminary fighting before the battle for the city started General Chuikov himself, the defender of Stalingrad, very nearly came to grief in one of these aircraft. Flying in the back seat, he was making a first-hand survey of Russian troop dispositions along the front when the Po-2 was attacked by a Junkers 88. The pilot tried frantically to escape by jinking across the steppe at low level, but the Po-2 hit the ground and disintegrated. Both Chuikov and the pilot were thrown out violently, but apart from a few bruises neither was hurt.

Another of the Po-2's duties on the Stalingrad front was to assist the bombers. A flight of these little aircraft was attached to most bomber regiments, and they would act as pathfinders, crossing the lines under cover of darkness to drop markers on targets in enemy territory, lighting the way for the bombers that followed. The Po-2s—fitted with machine-guns in the rear cockpit—were also used to strafe enemy flak batteries and searchlights, as well as to carry out nuisance raids in ones and twos with small fragmentation bombs. The German propaganda machine made light of the Po-2s, refer-ring to them contemptuously as 'Russian plywood', but accounts of the fighting on the Eastern Front written by German soldiers since the war have revealed that these nuisance raids had a considerable psychological effect, keeping combat-weary troops in a state of nervous tension during the hours of darkness. The Germans were unable to detect the presence of the Po-2s until the first bombs came whistling down, for the Russian pilots would cross the lines at maximum height and then switch off their engines, gliding down towards their targets.

One air regiment equipped with Po-2s, the 588th, was staffed entirely by women pilots and navigators; they dis-tinguished themselves during the fighting in the Crimea, and in the winter of 1942-3, operating over the Stalingrad and north Caucasus fronts, each aircraft flew up to six missions a night. During this period, the female crews dropped over 50,000 pounds of bombs during 194 raids, totalling 216 hours' flying time. The commander of the Women's Night Bomber

Regiment—as the unit was known—was a veteran woman pilot named Captain Eudocie Bershanskaya.

The 588th Night Bomber Air Regiment in fact formed part of the 122nd Air Division, which was staffed mainly by women aircrews. The Divison made its operational debut during the Battle of Stalingrad, and one of its units—the 586th Fighter Air Regiment, equipped with Yak-7Bs—began to distinguish itself almost immediately. One of the 586th's pilots, Olga Yamshchikova, became the first woman fighter pilot to destroy an enemy aircraft at night when she shot down a Junkers 88 over Stalingrad on September 24th 1942. During the remainder of the war the 586th stayed a first-line squadron, following the Soviet armies in their subsequent advance across Europe. When hostilities ended in 1945 the regiment was in Austria; by that time, its female pilots had flown 4,419 operational missions, engaged the enemy 125 times and shot down a total of 38 German aircraft. Strangely, none of the women fighter pilots was awarded the coveted Hero of the Soviet Union. The other air regiment in the 122nd Air Division was the 587th, which was a Bomber Air Regiment.

Towards the end of September, with the battle still raging with bestial ferocity in the ruins of Stalingrad, the Soviet High Command laid plans for a massive counter-offensive. It would take the form of a giant pincer movement; one arm would strike north-westward from the south of the city, and the other would thrust southward from the middle Don area, the two linking up on the curve of the Don and nipping off the Stalingrad salient. In this salient were the German 4th Panzer Army and Paulus's 6th Army, and the Russian objective was clear enough: trap and destroy them both.

During the preparations for this offensive, large numbers of bomber aircraft as well as transports were used to ferry fresh troops to the Stalingrad front from reserve areas east of Moscow. In addition, the strength of the 8th and 16th Air Armies was increased until the Russians enjoyed slight numerical superiority over Luftflotte 4. The increased air component included a large number of lend-lease types, including Douglas Bostons—known as the DB-7 in Russian service—and the

North American B-25 Mitchell. Both these types served with the 22nd Air Division, under Lieutenant-Colonel Tokayev, during the Battle of Stalingrad. As always, great emphasis was laid on close-support operations, and the strength of the assault divisions of both air armies was increased to 1,000 aircraft.

Later, after the counter-offensive had opened and the Soviet armies were well on their way to victory, the Il-2s on the Stalingrad front began to be progressively replaced by the vastly improved Il-2m3. This was a two-seater, with a 12·7-mm UBT machine gun mounted in the rear cockpit and two fixed 23-mm cannon firing forwards. Maximum speed was 250 mph at 5,000 feet, and the aircraft could carry either a 1,300-pound bomb-load or an 880-pound load with eight RS-82 rockets. The Luftwaffe fighter pilots got a nasty surprise when they first encountered the Il-2m3 in combat near Stalingrad. A squadron of Messerschmitt 109s, taking a formation of unescorted Il-2m3s for earlier single-seat Il-2s, anticipated a series of quick and easy kills when they peeled off and committed themselves to a classic attack from the rear. Instead they were met by the concentrated fire of 20 machine guns and 10 109s were shot down. The Luftwaffe pilots quickly cottoned on and evolved new tactics to deal with the Il-2m3, but it was never quite the same again; the days when the Shturmoviks fell like flies were over.

Several Russian fighter regiments on the Stalingrad front also began to re-equip with new Russian types as the autumn rains of 1942 gave way to the snow of winter. The first of these was the Lavochkin La-5, which was developed from the LaGG-3. Towards the end of 1941, Semyon A. Lavochkin had fitted a standard LaGG-3 airframe with a 1,600-hp Shvetsov M-82A radial engine, and during flight-testing—which began early in 1942—the type was found to be 30 mph faster than the Messerschmitt Bf 109F. The improved fighter —designated La-5—was extremely promising and was ordered into quantity production, the first examples reaching the front-line fighter regiments in October 1942.

The other fighter aircraft which made its operational debut

on the Stalingrad front was the Yakovlev Yak-9, a progressive development of the Yak-1. From this basic type, Yakovlev had developed the Yak-7B and the Yak-7DI, both of which appeared in action during the summer of 1942. The Yak-7B had the same performance, engine and armament as the Yak-1, but it differed externally from the latter in having a redesigned cockpit, which afforded a better view to the rear, and a re-tractable tailwheel. The Yak-7DI was the long-range fighter version of the Yak-7B, and it was in fact a slightly modified version of this type that served as the prototype Yak-9. The main difference between the Yak-9 and the Yak-7B was that the former had additional fuel tanks to extend its range, and the wing structure was modified to accommodate them. The type was initially built in two versions: the Yak-9D armed with a ShVAK 20-mm cannon and a synchronized 12·7-mm BS machine gun, and the Yak-9T, with a 37-mm NS cannon in place of the 20-mm weapon.

By the middle of November 1942, one-quarter of the Soviet Air Force's total combat aircraft strength had been concentrated on the Stalingrad front in preparation for the coming counter-offensive, which was scheduled to start on November 19th. The Russians had laid their plans carefully; the two arms of the giant pincer were to smash their way through the German defences at their weakest points, to the south of Stalingrad and near Serafimovitch, where Soviet forces already held a bridgehead on the south bank of the Don. In both these sectors, the Russians were opposed by Rumanian troops; in addition to being inferior to the Russians in numbers of men and weapons, they were for the most part poorly equipped.

At 7.30 on the morning of November 19th, the Soviet south-western front burst into life with a thundering artillery barrage and a few minutes later the first waves of Russian infantry went into the attack through the fog and darkness, hurling themselves on the Rumanian defences. The infantry were followed by three Soviet armoured corps, and against this massive onslaught the Rumanian resistance quickly crumbled. Twenty-four hours later the Soviet spearheads had advanced 20 miles into enemy territory; the retreat of the 3rd Rumanian

Army had become a rout, and it was only the intervention of the German 22nd Panzer Division that averted the annihilation of the Rumanian forces by slowing up the Russian advance.

Meanwhile, the counter-offensive by the Stalingrad front —which had begun at dawn on November 20th—had also broken through the enemy defences south of the city and was advancing steadily towards the town of Kalach, where the link-up with the armoured vanguard of the south-western front was to take place. Kalach, with its strategic bridge over the Don, fell to General Rodin's 26th Armoured Corps on the night of the 22nd, and the following afternoon the link-up was successfully completed.

Throughout the first three days of operations, the Russian armies had had a powerful ally: the weather. In the first week of November, the weather on the Stalingrad front had suddenly turned bitterly cold and the temperature had dropped to minus 15° C. Then, on November 17th—two days before the Soviet counter-offensive began—a warm air stream had crept over the steppes, bringing with it thick fog and snow combined with severe icing. This meant that the Luftwaffe formations, which might have smashed the counter-offensive in its early stages, were unable to operate. A few units did manage to get off the ground, including Hans-Ulrich Rudel's No. 1 Squadron of Stuka-Geschwader 2, and in spite of the murk they managed to deliver a number of attacks on the advancing Russians; the latter, however, had profited from bitter experience and had made their forward elements stiff with light flak, and the Stukas suffered heavy losses. A signal was sent to the commanders of the Luftwaffe bomber units on the Caucasus front, requesting urgent reinforcements, but the weather was just as bad there and the bombers were unable to get off the ground. Worse still, the German air bases in the Don Basin were being directly threatened by the Soviet drive southwards from Kalach, and if these were seized it would be impossible to airlift supplies to the 6th Army, now encircled in Stalingrad. The airfields were temporarily saved by the rapid deployment of reinforcements, and on November 24th Luftflotte 4's transport units were ordered to fly 300 tons of provisions into the Stalingrad pocket daily, including 30 tons of ammunition.

On the two airfields of Tazinskaya and Morosovskaya, the Germans assembled a total of 320 aircraft to carry out the formidable task of supplying the 6th Army—a task that Göring had assured the Führer was well within the Luftwaffe's capabilities. The Luftwaffe commanders responsible for organizing the airlift, however, knew differently. Two-thirds of their transport force was unserviceable at any given time, and on the first three days of the operation they succeeded in carrying only one-fifth of the required supplies to Stalingrad. Apart from mechanical troubles, there was the weather; the supplies had to be flown in through blinding snowstorms, and the mere task of locating the destination airfield of Pitomnik required a high degree of skill. But the transport crews were grateful for one thing: at least the weather kept the Russian fighters at bay—for the time being.

On the last day of November, the Heinkel 111s of KGs 27, 55 and 100 were also pressed into service as transports alongside the Junkers 52s and 86s of the transport gruppen. The Heinkels—190 in all—were called upon to carry out their transport duties instead of their primary task of bombing the Soviet forces that threatened the all-important airfields. This task now became the responsibility of a handful of Stukas and Henschel 129 anti-tank aircraft.

With the help of the Heinkels, the amount of supplies delivered to Stalingrad on November 30th reached a record total of 100 tons; but this was still only a third of the 6th Army's requirements. Then the weather clamped down again and there was a sharp drop in the tonnage of supplies carried during the first week in December. The area was hit by the worst cold spell so far and the serviceability of the transport aircraft dropped to one-quarter of the total machines available. Those that did keep flying made the trip in twos and threes, escorted by the Messerschmitt 109s of JG 3 when the latter could be spared, but more often unprotected. The trip to the pocket in daylight was becoming extremely hazardous as more Russian fighters began to put in an appearance, and the number of Heinkels and Junkers that failed to return climbed steadily.

On December 19th, in response to a desperate appeal from Colonel-General Paulus, the airlift was stepped up and the transport gruppen flew 450 sorties in three days, taking advantage of a spell of relatively clear weather to fly 700 tons of supplies into the pocket. But the weather clamped down again on the 23rd, and once more the tonnage of supplies that reached Pitomnik dropped steeply. By this time the 6th Army's situation was virtually hopeless. Not only had an attempt to relieve the besieged garrison in Stalingrad by the newly created Army Group Don under Field Marshal Manstein ended in failure, but on December 16th an offensive by the Soviet Voronezh and south-western fronts had broken through the Italian 8th Army, and now the 1st and 3rd Soviet Guards Armies and the 6th Soviet Army were advancing rapidly towards the Donets River. This new offensive was supported by the 2nd and 17th Air Armies, whose Shturmoviks played havoc with the retreating Italian columns. In the face of this threat, Manstein had been forced to abandon all hope of breaking through to Stalingrad; instead, he withdrew his forces to form a new defensive line along the Donets and around Rostov.

For the 90,000 men trapped in the Stalingrad pocket, time was fast running out. Paulus, who had held on to the shattered city on the orders of the Führer, with the latter's assurance that the 6th Army would not be abandoned, now had no choice: the 6th Army was no longer capable of breaking out of the trap without help from the outside.

On Christmas Eve 1942, the vital air supply base at Tazinskaya came under heavy Russian artillery fire. Acting on their own initiative, the transport gruppen commanders ordered their aircraft to take off. Conditions were appalling, with snow and fog reducing visibility to 50 yards. It was incredible that any of the aircraft got away at all, but 125 managed it—although 60 more wrote themselves off during the chaotic take-off or were destroyed by the Russian guns. At one blow, one-third of Luftflotte 4's transport force had been lost. For three days General Fiebig, the commander of Fliegerkorps VIII, had been trying to obtain Göring's permission to evacuate the airfield before it was too late. The permission had still not been granted when the first Russian shells landed on Tazinskaya.

The other supply base, Morosovskaya, was also seriously threatened. The bomber units that had occupied this airfield had already been evacuated to Novocherkassk, but as long as the thick fog persisted they could not be used to disrupt the advancing Russians. Then, on Christmas Day, the fog lifted, and for the first time in days there were clear skies. Before long, the air was filled with the roar of engines as the Stukas and Heinkels swept down on the vanguard of the Russian armour as it crawled over the open steppe. Within minutes, the countryside was littered with the burning remains of tanks, and the remainder fell back. Morosovskaya was saved, if only for the time being. Russian fighters put in a belated appearance over the battlefield, but the clear spell had taken the Soviet Air Force by surprise; the Russian meteorologists were apparently not so efficient as their German counterparts.

With the Heinkel 111s now operating from Novocherkassk and the Junkers 52 units from Ssalsk, another 50 miles was added to the flight to Stalingrad, and in addition tortuous detours had to be made to avoid the flak batteries which the Russians had set up on the approaches to the city. During the first week of January 18 four-engined Focke-Wulf Fw 200 Condors—hurriedly flown in from a Coastal Command wing on the Atlantic coast of France—also joined the airlift, operating from Stalino. On their first operation, seven of them carried thirty-six tons of supplies into Pitomnik, but the next day one was caught by Russian fighters and shot down with a load of wounded on board, a second was hit by flak and badly damaged, two more were grounded with mechanical troubles, and the engines of a fifth were unable to develop sufficient power to lift the big aircraft off the snow-covered Pitomnik airfield.

Two days later, a pair of huge four-engined Junkers 290 transports also began operations on the Stalingrad run. The first, laden with wounded, crashed on take-off from Pitomnik on January 10th, killing 85 of the 86 people on board; the second was caught by a flight of La-5s on the homeward flight from Stalingrad and badly shot up. The pilot nursed the crippled transport back to base, but it took part in no further operations. Forty Heinkel 177 bombers were also flown to the Stalingrad sector from their base at Zaporozhye, where they had been undergoing winter trials, but their small load-carrying capacity made them useless as transports and they were employed on several bombing raids against Russian positions around the city. The He 177's mortality rate was appalling; within a week, the force had been reduced by 50 per cent because of troubles with the aircraft's DB 610 engines; 10 machines burst into flames without warning in mid air and crashed.

On January 10th 1943, the Russians launched a strong offensive against the 6th Army's defensive perimeter around Stalingrad, forcing the Germans to retreat. During this attack the Russians captured Pitomnik, and the airfield's resident units—a squadron of Messerschmitt 109s of JG 3 and a couple of flights of Stukas—escaped by the skin of their teeth, only to destroy themselves while attempting to land on Stalingrad's other bomb-pitted airfield of Gumrak. During their defence of Pitomnik, the German fighters had destroyed 130 Russian aircraft. Now, however, the transports would have to fly into Gumrak without even the benefit of their limited protection. To complicate matters still further, the Junkers 52s had been forced to evacuate their base at Ssalsk and were now operating from a makeshift airstrip at the extreme limit of their range. They had been there only a few hours when a whole regiment of Shturmoviks swept down on the airfield under a fighter umbrella and destroyed or badly damaged 50 of them in a strafing attack that lasted 20 minutes.

Despite everything, the surviving Junkers 52s, Condors and Heinkel 111s went on carrying supplies to Gumrak right up to the night of January 21st-22nd, when the airfield was finally overrun. The last few days of the airlift were a nightmare; in addition to the Russian fighters, which were on the prowl everywhere, Po-2s hovered around in the vicinity of the airfield by day and night, disrupting unloading operations with showers of fragmentation bombs and alerting the fighters when transports were leaving the pocket.

On January 31st, General Paulus received a personal signal from Adolf Hitler. It stated that, with immediate effect, he was promoted to the rank of Field Marshal. Two days later, Josef Stalin also received a message, from Lieutenant-Colonel Rokossovsky and Lieutenant-General Malinin, the commander and chief of staff of the Don front. It read: "Carrying out your order, the troops of the Don front at 4 pm on February 2nd 1943 completed the rout and destruction of the encircled group of enemy forces at Stalingrad. Twenty-two divisions have been destroyed or taken prisoner."

During the two months of the airlift, as well as carrying supplies into the pocket, the Luftwaffe had also evacuated 42,000 wounded—many of whom survived to fight again. That fact is often forgotten in accounts of this decisive and disastrous battle. But the cost had been frightful; during the airlift operation, the Germans lost 500 aircraft—and this figure does not include bomber and fighter losses during operations over the whole front. The total Luftwaffe losses in the battle for Stalingrad were 1,249 aircraft, of which over 900 were claimed by fighters and flak. A further 542 German aircraft of all types, mostly badly damaged, were captured by Russian ground forces when they overran enemy airfields. The Red Air Force had flown 45,325 sorties during the siege and had dropped 15,000 tons of bombs; ten Air Divisions of the 10th Air Army were made Guards Divisions for their part in the battle. The Luftwaffe had flown 70,241 sorties, averaging 1,049 a day—nearly twice as many as the Russians. But it had made no difference; the Luftwaffe had been defeated, not in battle but by senseless orders and the worst operating conditions that aircrews had ever had to face.

For the German Army, Stalingrad was the most shattering defeat it had ever suffered. For the Soviet Air Force, the battle was the first step on the road that was to lead to the mastery of the eastern sky.

Chapter 8

The Tide Turns

For the Soviet Air Force, the last half of 1942 had been significant. It had seen not only the re-equipment of many first-line V-VS units with aircraft that were at least a match for any the Germans had in service on the Eastern Front, but also the creation of an embryo long-range strategic bombing force capable of striking at targets in Germany.

Formed in March 1942, the Soviet Long-Range Aviation (ADD) was built around a nucleus of about 80 four-engined Petlyakov Pe-8 bombers. The Pe-8, or TB-7 as it was designated in V-VS service, was designed by Vladimir Petlyakov under the direction of Andrei Tupolev's design bureau in 1934, the prototype flying on December 27th 1936. The bomber, which entered service with the Soviet Air Force in 1940, was powered by four Mikulin AM-35A engines, which gave it a maximum speed of 270 mph and an operational ceiling of 31,988 feet. It could carry up to 8,818 pounds of bombs and was armed with a 20-mm ShVAK cannon in its tail and dorsal turrets, a 12·7-mm BS machine gun in the rear of each inboard engine nacelle, and twin ShKAS machine guns in the nose turret.

On May 19th 1942, a Pe-8 piloted by Colonel Endel Puusepp took off from its base near Moscow and set course westwards, flying at 20,000 feet over enemy territory. It carried a VIP passenger: Soviet Foreign Minister V. M. Molotov. At 04.55 the following morning, after a flight of 10 hours 15 minutes, the bomber touched down on an RAF airfield at Dundee and Molotov went to London by rail for a conference with Winston Churchill. The Pe-8 took off again on the morning of May 27th, this time bound for Washington via Goose Bay and Montreal. After a meeting between Molotov and President Roosevelt, the Pe-8 returned to Moscow uneventfully via the same route, having completed the longest journey made by an Soviet aircraft during the war.

The Soviet strategic air offensive against Germany began

in earnest in July 1942, when 15 Pe-8s bombed Königsberg. During the following weeks, the Pe-8 squadrons also attacked Berlin, Stettin, and Königsberg a second time, as well as Warsaw, Gdansk and the Rumanian oil refineries at Ploesti. The results of these raids were not significant, and the Russian long-range bombing offensive remained tiny in comparison with the strategic attacks mounted by the RAF and USAAF. Nevertheless, the psychological impact on the hard-pressed Russian people, badly in need of a morale booster, was enormous; and for propaganda purposes, the raids enabled Stalin to state that the air offensive against the German homeland was not exclusively an Anglo-American venture.

In 1943, however, the Russians no longer needed to rely on the ADD's pinpricks against German targets to raise morale. On January 3rd 1943—as the steel ring closed relentlessly on the trapped 6th Army in Stalingrad—the Soviet Caucasus front launched a big offensive aimed at wresting control of the Kuban Valley from the Germans, who had been pouring troops and equipment into the area in readiness for a major summer offensive against the Caucasus. Each side possessed an approximately equal number of aircraft; on the Russian side, air support was provided by the 4th Air Army under General N. F. Naumenko.

During the Battle of Kuban, the Germans tried desperately to regain the air superiority which, for the first time since the war on the Eastern Front began, they had lost during the Battle of Stalingrad. In the event, the air battles over the fighting on the Kuban peninsula—which lasted seven weeks —did mark a decisive turning-point in the air war, but not in the way the Germans had hoped. It was during the Kuban battle that Alexander Pokryshkin—whose fighter regiment formed part of the 4th Air Army—won the first of his gold stars, and it was there too that the tactics he had evolved in previous months helped the Russian fighter pilots to gain mastery of the air. Pokryshkin's formula for successful air combat was simple: 'Altitude—Speed—Manoeuvre—Fire!' Altitude meant that a fighter pilot always had the initiative, giving him an opportunity to select his target with the added advantage that he was free to manoeuvre into the best position for attack from above; speed meant a gain in precious seconds —a vital factor when the outcome of an air fight could be decided in a second or two. It also meant that a pilot could close rapidly on an adversary, with less fear of being attacked from the rear himself.

Using these tactics, Pokryshkin and a number of other aces —Retchkalov, Klubov, Golubev, Mudrov, Bazanov and Semyenishin—added substantially to their scores over the Kuban. Pokryshkin himself downed three enemy aircraft in a single sortie, probably destroying a fourth. His fighter, distinctively painted with a large white number 100 on the fuselage, became well known to both sides, and on more than one occasion Luftwaffe formations were known to scatter and become disorganized when the pilots heard the warning shout over the R/T, 'Achtung! Pokryshkin is airborne in this sector!' before a Russian fighter had even been sighted.

The Kuban battle was characterized by clashes between large air formations. The Soviet fighters often operated at full regiment strength, flying in stepped-up battle formation. As usual, the fighters were employed mainly in escorting assault and light bomber aircraft—Il-2s and Pe-2s—and the ratio of fighters to bombers on these missions depended on the number of bombers engaged. For example, four bombers would be escorted by 10 fighters, 16-24 bombers by 20 fighters. Offensive fighter sweeps usually involved one 'Gruppa' (three or four pairs, a total of six to eight fighters) patrolling within a defined sector, with a second Gruppa in readiness. In this way a fighter regiment with four Gruppi could maintain a constant patrol over the combat area. In addition, ranger patrols (Svobodnaya Okhota) were frequently carried out by fighters operating in pairs.

When escorting ground attack aircraft, the fighter cover was usually split into two parts: the immediate escort and the assault group. The immediate escort remained constantly near the ground attack aircraft and flew between 300 and 1,000 feet higher. These fighters had the task of engaging any enemy fighters that managed to break through the forward assault group to present a direct threat to the ground attack formation. They normally broke away over the target and circled out of range of the enemy anti-aircraft defences, ready to take up their original position for the withdrawal flight. Often, if no enemy fighters showed up, the immediate escort would themselves dive down to strafe targets on the ground.

The fighters of the assault group flew between 1,500 and 3,000 feet higher than the immediate escort, and either directly above or half a mile ahead of the assault formation. One pair was usually sent out in advance to scout for enemy fighters, while a second pair cruised at high altitude, up-sun of the assault formation, ready to dive out of the sun to surprise attacking enemy fighters. Over the target, the assault group normally went up to 10,000 feet or so—clear of most of the light flak—and patrolled the sky over a fixed area until they were required to cover the withdrawal of the ground attack aircraft. Changes in the strength of the escort—which was dependent on such factors as the distance to the target, weather and expected enemy fighter opposition as well as the size of the bomber formation—did not influence these tactics. When a reduction in strength had to be made, an equal number of fighters was withdrawn from both the immediate escort and the assault group. If it was felt necessary to increase the size of the escort, this was done by slotting in additional formations of fighters ahead of, behind or below the ground attack aircraft.

These tactics were pioneered by Pokryshkin and other veteran pilots—including Major-General I. S. Polbin, who was the leading Soviet bomber tactician in the close-support field and who twice became a Hero of the Soviet Union—during the Kuban battle, and remained in force for the rest of the war. In fact they became standard throughout the post-war Russian satellite air forces, and were encountered by United Nations pilots over Korea.

The Kuban offensive ended on February 14th with the recapture of Rostov by the Russians, which effectively removed the threat to the oil-rich Caucasus. Elsewhere, however, an attempt by the Soviet south-western and Voronezh fronts to encircle the German armies in the eastern Ukraine had failed, mainly because the Russian leaders believed that large quantities of armour which had been poured into the area between the rivers Dnieper and Donets were there to cover the German retreat—not to spearhead a German counter-attack, as was actually the case. The Russians took Kharkov on February 16th and raced on towards the strategic town of Dnepropetrovsk; and it was then that the Germans hit the offensive with everything they had. The 4th Panzer Army attacked savagely on both flanks of the south-western front and in a matter of days the Russians—battle-weary and badly over-extended—found themselves digging in along the line of the Don once more, back where they had started. The Germans recaptured Kharkov and Belgorod, but the Russians quickly strengthened the Donets line with fresh reinforcements and the enemy counter-offensive was halted. The Russian failure was almost entirely due to bad planning; in addition, the redeployment of several air divisions to the Stalingrad and Caucasus fronts had left the Luftwaffe with an air superiority of three to one in the Donets area, and the Soviet Air Force had found itself incapable of providing adequate support for the harassed troops.

With the coming of the spring thaw, large-scale operations along the whole front came to a standstill. As they had done a year earlier, both sides took the opportunity to strengthen their forces in preparation for a summer offensive. The Germans knew only too well that everything depended on the outcome of this summer of 1943; if they regained the initiative they would have a second chance to take Moscow; but if they lost it, the way would be open for a Russian advance into Central Europe.

The spring lull in the fighting had left the Soviet central and Voronezh fronts in a potentially dangerous situation, with two German salients at Orel and Kharkov flanking a deep bulge to the west of Kursk. In this bulge the Russians had concentrated twelve armies, including two crack Guards and two tank armies. If the Germans could smash their way through the Russian defences to the north and south of Kursk, they would split the Soviet front in two, cutting off all the Russian forces within the Kursk salient and destroying them. If the German plan succeeded, the Red Army would have little hope of recovering from such a shattering defeat.

There was no denying that the German chances of success were good; for the Kursk offensive the Germans had assembled 70 divisions and nearly 1,000,000 men, and several of the panzer divisions had re-equipped with the new Tiger and Panther medium tanks and with heavily armoured Ferdinand self-propelled guns. To support the land offensive, the Luftwaffe had 1,700 aircraft; many ground attack units were now equipped with the twin-engined Henschel Hs 129 tank-buster, which had made its operational debut over the Crimea the previous autumn, and the fighter Geschwader had begun to receive the Focke-Wulf Fw 190A-4. One thousand of the German aircraft were earmarked to support the southern arm of the projected German pincer movement, which was to be provided by the 4th Panzer Army under General Hoth, while the remaining 700 machines were detailed to support the northern thrust by General Model's 9th Army.

The Russian High Command, meanwhile, was well aware of the German intention and was making its own plans to forestall it by striking first. Within the salient, each army had constructed three formidable lines of defence 25 miles deep, and even if the Germans succeeded in breaking through them they would still have to cope with a reserve line of defences. Six of the Soviet armies were assigned to the northern part of the salient, with General Rudyenko's 16th Air Army in support, while the other six—supported by the 2nd Air Army under General Krasovski—were responsible for the defence of the southern part. There were, in addition, five more Soviet armies in reserve, together with the 5th Air Army commanded by General Goryunov and the 17th Air Army. The 1st and 15th Air Armies were earmarked to support the armies in the Orel sector.

The Russian plan envisaged a massive air strike on the Luftwaffe's airfields, effectively denuding the German panzer divisions of their all-important air support. The German offensive would be allowed to get under way, and the Russian commanders were confident that they could meet and defeat it. Then, once the enemy had been weakened, the Russians would hit back with all the forces at their disposal. There was, however, still one fact the Russians did not know: the time of the enemy offensive. Then, on July 4th, came an unexpected windfall; a Yugoslav conscript deserted to the Russians and told them that the German offensive was scheduled to begin at dawn on July 5th. Soviet intelligence officers were dubious as to whether the man was telling the truth; but when Soviet patrols observed German sappers clearing a path through the Russian minefields on the night of the 4th, there was no longer any doubt that the German attack was only a matter of hours away. The commanders of the two fronts defending the salient, generals Vatutin and Rokossovsky, immediately ordered their own artillery to put down a heavy barrage on the German artillery positions. This timely order, which came a matter of minutes before the Germans were due to open up with their own weapons, resulted in many German batteries being knocked out, reducing the firepower available to support the offensive.

At 03.15 on the morning of July 5th, 15 minutes before the offensive was due to begin, the calm summer air resounded to the thunder of engines as the 1,000 German fighters, bombers and ground attack aircraft that were crammed into five airfields around Kharkov started up and taxied out, ready to take off and blast the forward Soviet positions as the panzer spearheads rolled forward. Suddenly, the carefully planned take-off dissolved into chaos as the alarm went up. First of all, German radio monitors reported a large volume of R/T chatter between Russian pilots; then, a few minutes later, a radar station near Kharkov detected what appeared to be a whole air armada coming in from the north-east. Another minute or two, and there was no longer any doubt: the Russians were coming! There were over 400 of them, Shturmoviks, Pe-2s, Yak-9s, MiG-3s, La-5s and Airacobras, bearing down in waves on the overcrowded airfields around Kharkov. On these airfields, the German bombers and ground attack aircraft now got out of the way as rapidly as possible, making way for the Messerschmitts and Focke-Wulfs of JGs 3 and 52; only their intervention could save the Luftwaffe from disaster. By some miracle all the fighters got airborne without incident and climbed rapidly to meet the threat. It was an incredible sight that met the eyes of the German pilots; ahead of them, wave upon stepped-up wave of Russian aircraft was strung out across the sky.

Seconds later, the R/T was jammed with a gabble of yells in both Russian and German as the first fighters made contact. The Russian formations broke up as the German fighters tore through their ranks, and a mighty air battle—the biggest of the war, with over 500 aircraft involved—covered the sky for miles. The German fighters had taken off in time to gain the advantage of height and speed—ironically, Pokryshkin's well-tried formula—and now they exacted a fearful toll of the Soviet assault aircraft, claiming the destruction of 120 enemy machines for the loss of 20 of their own number. In fact, the actual total of Soviet aircraft destroyed was nearer 70; but the raid was broken up, and although some of the bombers did get through to the German airfields they did little damage.

With the danger over the Luftwaffe's own bombers were now able to take off, heading into a dawn sky that was still stained with the smoke of burning aircraft. As usual, the function of the Stukas and Henschels was to blast a way through for the panzers, and the morning of July 5th developed into a slogging match, with Stukas and Shturmoviks heavily committed against the armour of the opposing sides. During the first three days of the fighting, the German 4th Panzer Army succeeded in driving a wedge 25 miles deep northwards into the Russian salient. The tanks were under continual air attack, but several of the Il-2m3 regiments found that their 23-mm cannon shells simply bounced off the heavy armour of the Tigers and Panthers. Later production Il-2s, fitted with long-barrelled 37-mm cannon, were hurriedly rushed to the forward air elements, and from then on the Russian successes began to mount steadily. On one occasion, Il-2s equipped with these formidable weapons swept down on the

Line-up of Yak-1 fighters *(above)* and the Petlyakov Pe-8 heavy bomber, carrying M. Molotov, taxies in after arriving at Dundee in 1942 *(below) (Photos: Imperial War Museum)*

Two types that symbolize the Soviet Air Force's capability for rapid movement of troops and equipment during the 1970s: the Mil Mi-6 helicopter *(above)* and the massive Antonov An-22 transport *(below) (Photos: Armand Agababian)*

German 9th Panzer Division and reduced 70 tanks to burning wreckage in the space of 20 minutes. The success, however, was not all one-sided; on the morning of July 8th, German reconnaissance aircraft spotted 50 Russian tanks and masses of infantry advancing towards the exposed left flank of the 4th Panzer Army. The Soviet concentration was quickly attacked and thrown into confusion by 40 Henschel 129s armed with 30-mm cannon.

On the second day of the battle, Soviet fighters appeared over the battle area in strength and fierce dogfights once again flared up over the salient. This day saw the return to combat of Alexei Maresyev, now flying with artificial legs, after an absence of 15 months. His return was welcomed by the Luftwaffe; not only was he machine-gunned by a stray Messerschmitt while on his way to join his regiment near Kursk, but he also spent the next few nights crouching miserably in a slit-trench while German bombers attacked his airfield.

Maresyev's regiment—flying La-5s—was held in reserve during the first day of the Kursk offensive, and it was not until the following morning that the pilots were ordered into action. Their task was to provide an air umbrella over the Russian armoured units which were advancing to meet the enemy's 4th Panzer Army. The battlefield was wreathed in smoke, and Maresyev could see a number of T-34s burning on the ground. Then his squadron-leader's voice crackled over the R/T: 'Stukas below, to the right. Attack, Falcons, attack!'

There they were: 20 Junkers 87s, flying serenely through a maze of light anti-aircraft bursts. The Russian pilots manoeuvred until the sun was behind them, then, in line astern, they ripped through the enemy formation. A Junkers staggered drunkenly and fell away, one wing wrapped in flames. Another spun down, leaving a twisting spiral of black smoke. Maresyev picked out a Stuka and closed in on its tail. The distance narrowed rapidly until he could see every detail of the enemy: the olive-green camouflage, with the white-edged black crosses standing out boldly, and the rear-gunner, crouched over his weapon. Maresyev pressed the firing-button and the long glasshouse cockpit flew to pieces. A dull flicker of flame appeared at the Stuka's wing-root and suddenly the aircraft was a ball of fire, turning slowly over and over as it fell.

Maresyev broke away and went after another Junkers. This German pilot was no easy game; he twisted and turned in an effort to shake off the determined Russian clinging to his tail. It was no use; a long burst of cannon and machine gun fire, and it was all over. The Ju-87 went down vertically and hit the ground in a tremendous explosion. Looking around, Maresyev found himself alone in the sky; there was not an aircraft to be seen. Nothing except three columns of smoke from burning machines, one of them Maresyev's last kill, rising straight up towards the scattered clouds.

The following day, Maresyev's squadron was on patrol over the front with a squadron of Yak-9s providing top cover when a shoal of blunt-nosed fighters slid by to starboard, at a lower altitude. They were quickly identified as Focke-Wulf 190s. The Russians dived flat out towards the enemy, who had either not seen them or had mistaken the radial-engined La-5s for their own kind. As they got closer, Maresyev saw that the Focke-Wulfs bore yellow-painted engine cowlings. The Messerschmitts that had shot Maresyev down over a year earlier had also had yellow cowlings, and even though there may have been no connection between the two enemy units the Russian pilot felt a fierce exultation rise within him; he had a score to settle.

When the La-5s were almost within range the 190s suddenly scattered in all directions, and the sky became filled with individual dogfights. A Yak-9 shot past with a 190 in hot pursuit, and Maresyev went after them, getting off a solid burst that tore off the German's tail unit. The 190 went over on its back and disappeared. Maresyev looked round and saw another Focke-Wulf, flying along straight and level, apparently unconcerned by the aircraft twisting and diving all around. A short burst from Maresyev's guns and the German went into a spin, streaming a long ribbon of flame. As the Russian pilot turned away steeply, a black dot on the centre of his windscreen grew rapidly larger. It was a 190, cannon twinkling, heading straight for him. Maresyev levelled out and grimly held the La-5 steady. Tracer flashed over his cockpit. One of them would have to break, or there would be a collision. At the last instant, the German pulled up and Maresyev fired a burst into his pale blue, oil-streaked belly. The Russian hauled back the stick, pulled his fighter up into a loop and half rolled off the top, looking down as he did so. The Focke-Wulf had vanished. Then he saw it, already merging with the ground, fluttering down like a dead leaf. It was his fifth kill in two days. Once again he found himself alone in the sky.

Like Maresyev, another young Russian fighter pilot—Ivan Kozhedub—also had to wait until the second day of the offensive before his chance came to get to grips with the enemy. Kozhedub had spent the first year of the war as a flying instructor, and he was supremely confident of both his flying skill and his ability to fight. He had been through a good school; the CO of the operational training unit where he had converted to the La-5 was a man named Major Soldatyenko, a veteran of the Spanish Civil War.

He arrived on the Kursk front in March 1942, and took part in several of the air skirmishes that occurred prior to the main battle, when both sides were testing each other's strength. His first combat was very nearly his last; while attacking a flight of enemy bombers, he was himself attacked from the rear by a 109, which put a number of cannon shells into his fuselage. As shell splinters rattled against the armour-plating behind his seat, Kozhedub flung his fighter away from the danger—only to run slap into a string of Russian anti-aircraft shells that tore away one of the La-5's wingtips. More cannon shells peppered his fuselage and tail as four more 109s pounced on his aircraft, which went into a vicious spin. He managed to pull out at 1,000 feet and headed for home at full throttle; fortunately, the Messerschmitt pilots had decided to go home too, and he landed without further incident.

Second Lieutenant Kozhedub had still to shoot down his first aircraft when the Battle of Kursk began. At dawn on

July 5th, he and the other pilots of his regiment were awakened by the sound of artillery fire; a few minutes later they were assembled and addressed by their CO, who told them what was happening. He also told them that the regiment would not go into action that day, but would be held in reserve. The pilots fumed impotently as reports of big air battles began to come in; there was nothing they could do but wait.

Their chance came the following morning, when Kozhedub's squadron, led by Captain Semyenov, took off on a dawn fighter sweep. As they flew over the front line, the whole earth seemed to be in flames. Tongues of fire from burning vehicles licked hungrily across the dry ground, and the smell of burning penetrated the cockpits. Suddenly the R/T came alive; elsewhere other Russian fighters were already engaging the enemy.

A minute later they spotted the enemy: 20 Ju 87s, crossing the front line under strong fighter escort. The Russians dived down to the attack, led by Semyenov. The first victory was his; a Stuka plummeted earthwards in flames, one wing torn off by a hail of 23-mm shells. Then it was Kozhedub's turn. Throwing a quick glance behind to make sure that his wingman, Vassily Mukhin, was in position, he closed in on a Stuka and opened fire. The enemy aircraft obstinately refused either to catch fire or go down. Over the R/T, Kozhedub dimly heard Mukhin yelling words of encouragement. He had almost made up his mind to ram the Stuka when the aircraft began to trail a thin streamer of smoke. The smoke soon became shot with flame and the Stuka went down at last, cartwheeling over the ground in a cloud of blazing wreckage. As Kozhedub pulled up sharply a Messerschmitt shot past, frighteningly close. He had not seen it boring in from astern; but Mukhin had, and had driven it off just in time.

The remaining Stukas, thrown into confusion by the Russian fighters' surprise attack, jettisoned their bombs haphazardly over their own territory and flew away westwards. They were still in sight when a second formation of Stukas appeared. This time the Germans quickly formed a defensive circle and fought back hard, the gunners pouring accurate fire into the fighters that zoomed across their sights. Kozhedub selected a Stuka and closed in behind it, his thumb pressed on the firing button. Nothing happened; he had used up all his ammunition on his first kill. Cursing his own inexperience, he had no alternative but to break off the fight and return to base, together with Mukhin.

The following day he destroyed another Junkers 87, and two Messerschmitt 109s the day after. He had opened his score: a score that was to end with 62 enemy aircraft destroyed, making him Russia's top-ranking air ace. His part in the Battle of Kursk later earned him the award of the Order of the Red Banner; he was also appointed to command his own fighter squadron.

As with the air fighting around Stalingrad several months earlier, the Kursk battle produced its quota of Soviet Air Force heroes. The exploit of Guards Lieutenant A. K. Gorovetz was one good example; during a lone patrol, he came upon a formation of 20 Junkers 87s and immediately went into the attack. His skill in handling his Yak-9D was such that he succeeded, single-handed, in shooting down no fewer than nine of the Stukas before his ammunition ran out. In the early months of the war against Russia, several German pilots had scored similar massive successes in the course of a single sortie; now, in the summer of 1943, the tables had been turned with a vengeance.

On July 12th, at first light, the Russians launched a counter-offensive against the 4th Panzer Army towards Prokhorovka. The attack was carried out by the Soviet 5th Guards Army and the 5th Guards Tank Army, and was preceded by a short but heavy night bombardment of the German positions by medium bombers of the 1st Air Army under Lieutenant-General Mikhail M. Granov—which had been held in reserve —and by aircraft of the ADD, operating from bases well to the rear. In the strong morning sunshine, a fierce battle involving 1,500 tanks developed, with assault aircraft of both sides strafing incessantly. The pilots' task was not an easy one; in the swirling dust, it was often impossible to distinguish between friend and foe. By nightfall, the German 4th Panzer

Army had begun to fall back towards Prokhorovka, having lost 300 tanks and over 10,000 men. A second Soviet thrust, to the north and east of Orel, threatened Model's 9th and 2nd Panzer Armies with encirclement, and within a week Russian tanks were almost in a position to cut off the only supply route for Model's forces.

The situation was saved by the Luftwaffe; operating from Karachev, almost under the noses of the Russian tanks, the Stukas and Henschels launched attack after attack on the enemy armour, checking the onslaught long enough to allow the 9th and 2nd Panzer Armies to clear the Orel salient. Thanks to the Luftwaffe's intervention, a German defeat on a scale even more terrible than Stalingrad had been averted; but there was no escaping the fact that the Battle of Kursk had ended in an overwhelming Soviet victory.

The Russians were not slow in exploiting their success. In August 1943, supported by 100 air divisions totalling 10,000 aircraft, the whole Soviet battlefront began to roll relentlessly westwards. Kharkov was recaptured on August 23rd, and the decimated German armies—their reserves exhausted—fell back towards the Dnieper. By mid September the Soviet southern and south-western fronts had driven the enemy from the Donets Basin, and on the 22nd of that month the Dnieper had been reached by the 3rd Guards Tank Army. Three days later, two Soviet armies had succeeded in establishing a bridgehead 16 miles long and up to 20 miles deep on the west bank of the river, north of Kiev. The Germans counter-attacked savagely, but the Russian troops managed to hold on until the main body of their forces arrived. The Luftwaffe made a series of desperate attacks on the bridgehead, but the Soviet Air Force enjoyed air superiority and inflicted severe losses on the German aircraft. Kozhedub's squadron took part in these air battles, having hopped from airstrip to airstrip in the wake of the Russian offensive, and in the space of 10 days Kozhedub alone destroyed 11 enemy aircraft. On October 12th, his squadron—whose pilots had already flown several sorties that day—was ordered to take off and cover the crossing of the river by the 3rd Guards Tank Army, which was being transferred to the west bank to spearhead the coming assault on Kiev.

Patrolling the bridgehead on the south bank of the river, the Russian pilots soon spotted a formation of Junkers 87s heading for the crossing-point. Kozhedub dived on one of them and shot it down, coming under heavy and accurate fire from the Stuka's rear-gunner as he did so. As Kozhedub climbed away, a lurid streamer of flame shot back from his Lavochkin's starboard wing; the German's bullets had hit a fuel tank. Glancing down, the pilot saw that the fight had carried him well behind the enemy lines; he had little hope of reaching Russian-held territory before the flames ate their way through the wing's main spar. At that moment a German flak battery opened up on him and he went down in a shallow dive towards it, intent on crashing his aircraft on top of the battery and pulverizing the guns and their crews. It was then, miraculously, that the flames went out, extinguished by the powerful slipstream. At the last moment, Kozhedub hauled back the stick with both hands and the Lavochkin swept over the battery like a whirlwind. Ten minutes later he crossed the Dnieper, and soon afterwards landed safely at his base. It was only then that he realized how lucky he had been: the damaged tank was filled with highly explosive gases which might have ignited at any second during the flight back, tearing the aircraft apart.

On November 6th, the Russians recaptured Kiev after bitter fighting, and Soviet forces crossed the Dnieper at a number of other points. Further north, the central front under General Rokossovsky smashed across the river and reached the Pripet marshes, while the western front recaptured Smolensk and drove on towards Vitebsk.

One of the air divisions that supported the central front's assault—the 36th, equipped with DB-7 Bostons—particularly distinguished itself in the fighting and became known by the honorary title of the 'Smolensk Air Division'. Immediately after the capture of Smolensk, this air division was ordered to the Murmansk front to begin a series of intensive air attacks on German bases in northern Norway. The division had served in the far north for a time during 1942, and there were still a good many crews who were experienced in Arctic operations. The fighter defences of the Murmansk front were also strengthened by the addition of 20 Airacobras. By the end of the year, the Soviet Air Force on this front had the numerical air superiority that was necessary for the Soviet offensive that was scheduled to begin early in 1944.

During the summer and autumn offensives of 1943, one Yak-9 fighter regiment had achieved considerable success. Although they bore the same camouflage and red star markings as any other V-VS fighter unit, the aircraft carried distinctive squadron emblems: a white Cross of Lorraine stamped on their tail-fins, and red, white and blue bands painted round their spinners. The unit was known as the 'Regiment Normandie', and most of its pilots were Frenchmen. Its official designation was Groupe de Chasse 3, and it had been formed initially at Rayak in Syria on September 1st 1942, with British aid. Two months later, the entire complement of 72 officers and men had been transferred to Russia, where the unit reformed with Yak-1 fighters.

The Regiment Normandie went into action on the Orel front on February 22nd, 1943, under the leadership of Commandant Tulasne, and on April 5th Captain Albert Preziosi destroyed the unit's first enemy aircraft. The regiment was stationed less than 15 miles from the front line, which enabled the pilots to fly a large number of tactical support missions. By the end of the Kursk battle, the regiment's score had risen to 40 enemy aircraft destroyed, and the French pilots subsequently took part in the bitter air fighting over Smolensk, Yelnya and Vitebsk. During the last months of 1943, they accounted for a further 77 German aircraft for the loss of 25 of their own number. It was a good beginning; but for the Regiment Normandie, and indeed for all the first-line Soviet Air Force units, some of the most hectic air fighting was yet to come. For, although the Russians now held definite air superiority, the Luftwaffe was by no means finished; and during the long retreat from the east of 1944, the German Air Force was to fight back with a courage born of desperation.

Chapter 9

On the Offensive

The Soviet High Command lost no time in striking the first of the giant hammer-blows which, during 1944, were planned to drive the Germans from the soil of the Soviet Union. On January 14th, the Soviet 2nd Shock Army and the 42nd and 59th Armies struck hard at the German defences in the Baltic sector, driving back the German Army Group North and capturing Novgorod by a huge pincer movement. At the same time, the armies massed on the Leningrad and Volkhov fronts smashed their way through to the Estonian border, where they halted and prepared for the big summer offensive that was scheduled to follow the spring thaw. To the south, a massive offensive that would end with the expulsion of the Germans from the Ukraine was getting under way, while further south still three Soviet armies gathered their strength for a big push that would liberate the Crimea. During the preliminaries to this last offensive, the Soviet Air Force and Naval Air Arm played a major part in strangling the Germans' lifelines by attacking enemy transport vessels in the Black Sea. Shturmoviks were the principal type used, armed with torpedoes as well as with bombs and rockets. The Il-2 in fact continued to be the most widely used Russian combat aircraft along the whole Soviet-German front, and went on adding to a list of battle honours that was already impressively long.

Alexander Pokryshkin's fighter squadron was also operating on the Crimean front, where it became known as the 'Mariupol Squadron' in honour of the part it played in the liberation of the town of that name. His pilots also ranged over the Black Sea on frequent patrols, adding several Junkers 52 transports to their score. Pokryshkin's squadron, in fact, helped to pioneer the use of Soviet radar during this period; the first sets produced by the Russians were primitive enough, but Pokryshkin reported enthusiastically that even limited radar control made the fighter pilot's task easier by half, and during the early months of 1944 a network of mobile radar units was set up along the most important areas of the front.

At the beginning of 1944, Pokryshkin—now a Guards colonel and twice a Hero of the Soviet Union—took command of the 16th Guards Air Regiment, which—as part of the 9th Guards Air Division—supported Marshal Koniev's drive through Bessarabia in March. On the 26th of that month, when Koniev's forces entered Rumania, Pokryskhin's regiment was operating from an airfield on the banks of the River Prut —the very airfield on which Pokryshkin had been stationed when the Luftwaffe smashed the Soviet Air Force on June 22nd 1941. The wheel had turned full circle.

In a bid to throw the Russian forces off Rumanian soil, the Germans launched a strong counter-offensive at Yassy, a few miles inside the frontier. To provide air cover, the Luftwaffe had assembled some of its finest fighter squadrons, opposed on the Russian side by a number of Guards fighter regiments. Many of the Russian aces were there, including Pokryshkin, Kozhedub, Klubov and Retchkalov; the list of names of the pilots on both sides read like a 'who's who' of Heroes of the Soviet Union and holders of the Knight's Cross. Inevitably, as they met in combat, the Battle of Yassy was marked by air fighting of a savagery unmatched since Kursk. From dawn until dusk, the air thundered with the sound of engines as the Germans hurled wave after wave of bombers, escorted by Messerschmitts and Focke-Wulfs, against the Soviet ground forces.

The Luftwaffe had adopted the stepped-up attack formation developed by the Russians during the Kuban battle, and initially the Russian fighter pilots were taken completely by surprise when confronted with their own tactics; on the first day of the offensive, most of the enemy bombers reached their objectives because the Soviet pilots made the mistake of tangling with the massive German fighter escort. Pokryshkin's solution to this problem was simple; he increased the number of attacking fighters, leaving plenty to engage the bombers even after the Messerschmitts and Focke-Wulfs had been taken on. The success of this move became apparent on the second day of the fighting, when the pilots of Pokryshkin's regiment destroyed 30 enemy aircraft for no loss to themselves.

After several days of bitter fighting, the Battle of Yassy ended in failure for the Germans. It was the last time that the Luftwaffe would make a serious attempt to gain air superiority over a battlefield on the Eastern Front; after Yassy, the German squadrons were shared out piecemeal along the front, and although the pilots still fought gallantly their operations lacked any pretence at cohesion. Of the Soviet fighter pilots who shattered the Luftwaffe's last hopes over Yassy, the most successful was Alexander Klubov; he shot down nine enemy aircraft in five days. They had been hard-won victories, scored against men who possessed a high degree of skill; pilots who were among the last of the Luftwaffe's elité. There were very few of them left now; many had survived three years of fighting in the east only to give their lives in a hopeless attempt to stem the Allied air onslaught from the west. A few of the men who replaced them were good enough, but most were overwhelmed before they had a chance to prove their worth. From the beginning of 1944, the calibre of the Luftwaffe aircrews showed a general decline that was to continue until the final collapse.

In April and May 1944, the Russians liberated the Crimea. This was the last major operation before the main Soviet offensive of 1944, the object of which was the destruction of the German Army Group Centre. Centred on Minsk, this Army Group, which was under the command of Field Marshal Model, comprised the 2nd, 4th and 9th Armies and the 3rd Panzer Army—a total of 50 divisions, with 1,000 tanks and 1,200,000 men. For air support, the Luftwaffe had managed to scrape together about 1,400 combat aircraft.

The destruction of Army Group Centre would not only result in the expulsion of German forces from the Soviet Union; the Army Group was defending what amounted to a broad highway that led into the heart of Central Europe, and if Model's forces were smashed that highway would be left wide open. In readiness for the offensive, the Russians assembled over two and a half million men on four fronts, stretching in a huge shield from north to south. The most

northerly of the four was the first Baltic front, which extended
from Velikiye Luki on the River Dvina to Vitebsk, commanded
by General Bagramyan, a redoubtable Armenian who had
shown distinguished leadership at Orel; then came the third
Byelorussian front, lying between Vitebsk and the Dnieper,
and commanded by General Chernyakhovski; this linked up
with the second Byelorussian front under General Zakharov,
whose forces were concentrated on the Dnieper at Mogilev;
while the fourth front and the biggest of all, the first Byelorussian under General Rokossovsky, stretched from the Dnieper
across the Pripet Marshes to Kovel, where its flank was
guarded by the 8th Guards Army under General Chuikov
—the defender of Stalingrad. Air support along the four
fronts was provided by the 1st, 2nd, 3rd, 4th, 6th, 8th and
16th Air Armies of the Soviet Frontal Aviation; a total of
over 70 air divisions.

Early in June—a matter of days after the Allied landings in
Normandy—the Russians struck their first blow, in effect a
preliminary to the main offensive. The attack was launched
against the Russians' old adversary, Finland, now an ally
of Germany. At this time, the Finnish Air Force operated
an agglomeration of German, British, French, American,
Swedish and even Russian aircraft, the last having been
captured during and after the Winter War; types in service
included Messerschmitt Bf 109Gs, Brewster Buffaloes, Morane
406s, Curtiss Hawks, Blenheims, Junkers 88s, Dornier 17s and
22s, Gladiators, Fokker D 21s, SB-2s, DB-3s, I-153s and Pe-2s.
Fierce air fighting took place during the Russian advance,
and between June 1st and August 31st one of the Finnish
Bf 109G squadrons—HLeLv 24, which had enjoyed so much
success with its Fokker D 21s in the Winter War—claimed
the destruction of 70 La-5s, 62 Shturmoviks, 35 Yak-9s, 23
Pe-2s and a similar number of Airacobras, six LaGG-3s, six
DB-3Fs and five Mustangs.

These successes, however, could not slow down the Russian
advance; neither could the sacrifice of the small Finnish
bomber force, which was almost entirely shot out of the sky
during a series of desperate attacks on the enemy. On

September 4th 1944, the Finns were forced into an armistice with the Russians for the second time in five years, and under the terms of this armistice they turned their weapons on their former allies, who were now withdrawing into Norway, blowing up anything of importance as they went.

The main Soviet offensive in Byelorussia was scheduled to begin at dawn on June 22nd—three years to the day, and almost to the minute, after the victorious Wehrmacht had first smashed its way into the Soviet Union. A matter of hours before the assault got under way, however, the Luftwaffe demonstrated in a dramatic way that it was still capable of dealing a knock-out punch when a force of Junkers 88s and Heinkel 111s attacked the Russian airfield of Poltava, deep inside Russian territory between Kiev and Kharkov, in the Ukraine.

Poltava was one of three Soviet airfields which, since June 2nd 1944, had somewhat reluctantly been made available to the Americans to enable them to extend the range of their bomber operations over enemy territory. The idea was that the bombers, flying from bases in Britain or Italy, would land at the Soviet airfields after bombing targets in Germany or in one of Germany's 'satellite' countries such as Rumania or Hungary. Then, after refuelling and rearming, they would fly back to their home bases—bombing more objectives on the way. For this operation—code-named FRANTIC—the Russians allowed the USAAF the use of Poltava, Mirgorod and Piryatin. The first two were suitable for the big B-17 Flying Fortresses, but Piryatin could handle only the fighters of the American long-range escort.

On June 21st, 2,500 bombers and fighters of the England-based US 8th Air Force attacked several targets in Germany, including Berlin. Before the massed bomber formations reached the German capital, 114 Fortresses and 70 Mustang long-range fighters broke away and went on to their own objective, a synthetic oil plant 75 miles south of Berlin. After a successful attack, they then droned on across eastern Germany and Poland, heading for the Ukraine and the airfields of Poltava and Mirgorod. They arrived shortly before sunset and landed without incident, while the Mustangs touched down at Piryatin. Seventy-three of the Fortresses were dispersed on Poltava, most of them parked in a long line beside the main runway.

What neither the Americans nor the Russians knew was that the bomber and fighter force had been shadowed all the way by high-flying German reconnaissance aircraft. The first indication of trouble came when, shortly after 23.30, a large formation of German aircraft was reported crossing into Soviet territory. As more reports indicated that the enemy bombers were heading for Poltava, the alarm went up and the personnel on the airfield—including the Americans—took shelter in slit trenches.

The minutes ticked by slowly; it began to look as though the alarm had been false. Then, at five minutes past midnight, there was a sudden roar of engines and seconds later the night sky burst into brilliance as a shower of flares cascaded down on the airfield, lighting the way for the Heinkels and Junkers—80 of them. The Heinkels came in first, dropping fragmentation bombs that exploded among the lined-up Fortresses. Then it was the turn of the Ju 88s, which dropped high explosives and incendiaries. Flashes twinkled across the sky as a dozen Russian anti-aircraft batteries opened up, but the gunners were wildly off target. There was no respite from the attacks; for 50 minutes the German bombers droned over the airfield in ones and twos, dropping their clusters of bombs. One after the other, the Fortresses went up in flames. Incendiaries touched off a fuel dump, which exploded in a great ball of flame.

The distinctive sound of VK-105 engines was suddenly added to the uneven beat of the German motors as a squadron of Pe-2 night-fighters arrived on the scene. Soon after their arrival, the bombing ceased abruptly and the German bombers droned away; because of the small formations used by the enemy the Pe-2 crews—lacking any form of AI radar—failed to make contact and returned to base, believing that the raid was over.

They were wrong. Fifteen minutes later, as Russian firefighters were beginning a desperate attempt to salvage something from the wreckage, half a dozen Junkers 88s swept across the airfield at low altitude, pouring machine-gun fire into aircraft that were still intact and sending them up in flames too. They were followed by two reconnaissance Heinkels, which circled the area for several minutes taking photographs. Then they too droned away; the attack was finally over.

Behind them, the bombers left 47 B-17s totally destroyed, together with another 26 severely damaged. Two C-47 Dakotas—the transports that had brought the American ground crews to Poltava—and two Russian aircraft had also been destroyed, and 400,000 gallons of petrol in the fuel dump were still burning the following day.

The destruction of the B-17s at Poltava brought the 8th Air Force's bomber losses for that one day to 91 aircraft. It was to be the biggest single disaster suffered by the 8th AAF in three years of operations over Europe, and it was also to be the last and most devastating major raid launched by the Luftwaffe's bomber squadrons against a target on Russian soil. The Heinkels and Junkers returned the following night, this time with Mirgorod as their objective, but there was nothing left for them to bomb. The airfield had been evacuated.

While the fires still raged at Poltava, the Byelorussian front exploded as the Russians at last opened their offensive. The first attacks were directed against three key German strongpoints: Vitebsk, Mogilev and Bobruisk. For several hours, waves of Soviet bombers—Il-2s, Pe-2s, Tu-2s and DB-7s—subjected these bastions to a merciless pounding from the air. After the bombers had gone, the Russians moved up their heavy artillery and Katyusha rocket batteries and continued the onslaught for another two or three hours. In spite of the fearful battering they had received, however, the German defenders were still capable of fighting back hard, as the Soviet infantry discovered when their turn came to move in. Their casualties were terrible; nevertheless, two Soviet armies succeeded in linking up west of Vitebsk on June 25th, inflicting heavy casualties on the 3rd Panzer Army, and the fortress itself fell two days later. The following day Mogilev was also captured, but at such appalling cost to the Russians that the second Byelorussian front was unable to continue the offensive until strong reinforcements arrived.

The greatest initial success came on the first Byelorussian front, where—under the brilliant leadership of General Rokossovsky—the Russians managed to isolate part of the German 9th Army around Bobruisk. The trapped German forces were then systematically torn to ribbons by the 16th Air Army, and on June 29th they were finally overwhelmed by Rokossovsky's troops.

By July 13th, the Russian High Command had achieved its primary aim: the German Army Group Centre had virtually ceased to exist. The German retreat continued throughout August, by which time the Russians had forced their way to the borders of East Prussia. The first and second Byelorussian fronts had already reached the River Bug in July and captured Lublin, subsequently launching a new thrust towards the Vistula and Warsaw. As this drive got under way, the strength of the 16th Air Army was increased by the arrival of three recently formed air regiments manned by Polish personnel. They were the 1st Polish 'Warsaw' Fighter Regiment equipped with Yak-3s, the 2nd 'Krakow' Night Bomber Regiment with Pe-2s, and the 3rd Ground Attack Regiment with Il-2s. The three regiments were all commanded by Russians and together were known as the 1st Polish Composite Air Division. It was from this division that the nucleus of the post-war Polish Air Force was later to be formed under Russian control.

The aircraft that equipped the Polish Fighter Regiment, the Yak-3, was the latest Soviet fighter. Contrary to what might be supposed from its designation, it replaced the Yak-9 in several Russian fighter divisions in the summer of 1944. One of the units to receive the new type was the French Regiment Normandie, which at this time was attached to the third Byelorussian front as part of the 2nd Air Army. Between June 22nd and the end of August, while still flying their Yak-9s, the French pilots destroyed a further 30 German aircraft. In September and October, they were engaged in a bitter period of air fighting over the Niemen and East Prussia. Their main opponents were Focke-Wulf 190 fighter-bombers, mostly flown by inexperienced pilots who had hurriedly converted from Junkers 87s and who were incapable of getting the best out of the faster and more agile Focke-Wulfs. On one memorable day in October, the Frenchmen—led by Lieutenant-Colonel Pierre Pouyade—destroyed no fewer than 26 enemy aircraft for no loss to themselves. The exploit earned them the honorary title of the 'Normandie-Niemen Regiment', and they were cited in a special Red Army Order of the Day —an honour reserved for outstanding achievements in battle.

Another foreign air unit also appeared in combat alongside the Russians during the summer offensive of 1944: the Czechoslovak Fighter Regiment, equipped with Lavochkin La-5FN fighters. The regiment arrived at Proskurov airfield, near Lvov, in July 1944, and the following September moved to the Polish airfield of Stubno, a few miles behind the front. At this time the Czechs and Slovaks had risen in open revolt against the Germans and the Czech Fighter Regiment was at once earmarked to support the uprising. Its first task was to provide fighter cover for Russian Li-2 (Dakota) transports which were airlifting supplies to the airfield of Tri Duby, held by the insurgent forces in the face of strong German attacks. Then, on September 18th, the regiment—now operating from the Czech airfield of Zolna—made a daring low-level attack with eight La-5s on the German air base at Piestany, which was crowded with 50 aircraft of all types. The raid took the Germans completely by surprise and 30 aircraft were destroyed on the ground.

More surprise attacks were made during the next four weeks, although the regiment was forced to operate under extremely difficult conditions; at times there was a critical shortage of fuel and spares. Finally, under extreme pressure from the Germans, the Czechs were compelled to abandon Zolna and withdraw to another airfield in the Soviet-controlled part of Hungary. Their exile, however, was not destined to be a long one.

Meanwhile, on August 2nd, Rokossovsky's forces had crossed the Vistula and were now heading for Warsaw. A day earlier, the Polish Underground Army in Warsaw had received a signal from Radio Moscow, calling upon the resistance fighters to rise up and drive the Germans from the capital. Within five hours the Underground Army had seized three-quarters of the city after savage fighting and it held on grimly, waiting for the arrival of the first Soviet troops. It was then that the unexpected happened: Rokossovsky's forces suddenly broke off contact with the retreating Germans and withdrew several miles, and there they stayed while the enemy hurled tanks and men against Warsaw.

To their utter amazement, the commanders of the air regiments supporting Rokossovsky's offensive received strict orders from the highest level to the effect that their pilots were not to operate west of the Vistula under any circumstances until further notice. Patrolling the river, the Russian pilots could see the pall of smoke billowing over Warsaw; they watched helplessly as the minute black specks that were Stukas wheeled and dived over the city again and again. Pokryshkin's regiment was among those affected by the orders; its pilots had fought with particular distinction during the advance to the Vistula, and they found the apparently senseless situation galling in the extreme. Just a few days earlier, Pokryshkin had learned that he had been made a Hero of the Soviet Union for the third time.

The Germans, safe from Soviet intervention, went on with the systematic destruction of the Underground Army. On August 24th, in response to a desperate appeal from the Poles, President Roosevelt asked Stalin for the use of airfields to enable the USAAF to fly in supplies to the dying city: Stalin did not even bother to reply. For two months the RAF, USAAF and the South African Air Force did their best to keep the Polish capital supplied from air bases in Italy, but the trip involved a long daylight flight over enemy territory and losses were appalling. In six weeks the RAF's No. 138 Squadron—manned by Polish crews—lost 32 aircraft and 234 men, while the South Africans lost 24 Liberators.

As the airlift continued during September, the transport crews reported that they had encountered Russian Pe-2 night-fighters in the Warsaw area, and that they had actually been fired on by these aircraft. It is hard to believe that such attacks could have been the result of faulty recognition on the part of the Russian pilots; the Germans had no large four-engined aircraft that resembled the Halifaxes and Liberators. The Soviet Air Force finally received orders to continue its offensive operations in the Warsaw sector towards the end of September, but by then it was too late; Warsaw lay in ruins and the Underground Army had been annihilated.

While the Russians advanced to the Vistula and established a series of bridgeheads on the west bank of the river, Soviet forces were pushing the Germans steadily back through Latvia and Estonia. By the end of the year, Estonia had been liberated completely and the German forces that remained in Latvia were penned up in the north-west corner of the country. They were still there when the Germans surrendered in May 1945. Ivan Kozhedub, now a member of a Guards Fighter Regiment, operated on this front during the autumn of 1944. His regiment was in fact a special duties unit, and was liable to be sent from one end of the front to the other wherever there was a prospect of tough air fighting. It was equipped with the new Lavochkin La-7, basically similar to the La-5FN but with aerodynamic improvements that gave it a better combat performance.

In September, the Russians occupied Rumania and Bulgaria. The following month, they captured Belgrade and moved north-westwards into Hungary to begin a winter offensive against the German and Hungarian armies which were still putting up a stiff resistance. By mid December, 180,000 German and Hungarian troops were besieged in Budapest. At the turn of the year, the front ran from Yugoslavia to the Baltic, cutting across Poland and Czechoslovakia and running along the border of East Prussia. The stage was now set for the vast offensive of 1945. For the final thrust that would take them into the heart of Germany, the Russians had assembled nearly 5,000,000 men—twice as many as the opposing Germans—divided among 45 field armies, 11 Guards armies, five shock armies and six tank armies. A vast air umbrella over the offensive would be provided by the 17,000 combat aircraft of 13 air armies; they outnumbered the Luftwaffe on the Eastern Front by 10 to one.

In the Far North, too, the last months of 1944 had seen the expulsion of the last Germans from Russian soil. The Russians recaptured Petsamo in October and afterwards set about destroying the German 19th Mountain Corps. On October 15th, the enemy attempted to evacuate the remnants of their forces by sea from Bekfjord, and it was during the subsequent attack on the enemy convoy by DB-7s of the 36th Air Division that one Russian crew gave an example of the type of courage that had been displayed so many times by Soviet airmen in the course of the war.

The German convoy's progress was reported constantly by reconnaissance aircraft during the night of October 14th/15th, and at first light the following morning it was dive-bombed by 12 Il-2s—two flights of six aircraft, led by Captain Yevdokimov and Lieutenant Suvorov. They sank one small escort and damaged two other vessels. A second attack was made an hour later, also by 12 Il-2s, led by Major Pavlov and Lieutenant Smorodinov; this time a German destroyer received a direct hit and sank, and two MTBs were set on fire. During this attack, the Ilyushins were bounced by seven Messerschmitt 109Gs and one Il-2 was shot down over Varanger Fjord. The score was evened when a 109 flew into a cone of fire from the rear guns of the remaining bombers and spun down in flames.

A third attack was made by 10 torpedo-carrying DB-7s, led by Guards Major Voloshin; they sank one freighter and three smaller craft, but three of the bombers were shot down by the convoy's extremely accurate anti-aircraft fire. Another 10 DB-7s went into the attack almost immediately, this time escorted by 15 Airacobras. This attack was led by Guards Lieutenant-Colonel Boris P. Syromyatnikov, the CO of the DB-7 air regiment; his two-man crew consisted of the navigator, Alexander I. Sknarev, and the wireless operator/air gunner,

Guards Sergeant Grigory S. Aseyev. While the fighters tangled with the 109s—shooting down five of them—the DB-7s made their torpedo-run through heavy flak. With a mile and a half to go, Syromyatnikov's aircraft was hit by a shell in its port engine, setting it on fire. As though on a signal, every anti-aircraft gun in the convoy now opened up on the stricken aircraft; more shells ripped into it and both wings burst into flames as fuel poured from ruptured tanks. Yet still Syromyatnikov held the aircraft steady, holding on until the last moment before releasing his torpedo.

As the torpedo exploded against the side of a German transport, the DB-7 went into a sudden steep climb. Then it stalled and plunged into the sea, a fiery ball shedding burning fragments. There had been no chance for the crew to bale out. For their courage all three were posthumously made Heroes of the Soviet Union.

The German convoy was shattered. All three of the freighters had been sunk, together with 10 escort vessels. Eight Russian and six German aircraft had been shot down.

During the three-week northern offensive by the troops of the Soviet Karelian front, supported by the Northern Fleet and the Soviet Air Force, the enemy lost 156 ships of all sizes and 56 aircraft. Here, as elsewhere, the last German forces were driven from Russian soil by the end of the year.

The Third Reich was entering its last 100 days.

Chapter 10

Battle over Germany

February 15th 1945.

The morning was clear and crisp, and Kozhedub found it difficult to fight off the pleasant feeling of drowsiness brought about by the sun beating down strongly through the cockpit canopy. From 10,000 feet there was no sign of the scars of war that cut across the land on both sides of the Oder. Down there, the Soviet armies under Marshals Zhukov and Koniev were preparing to smash their way through eight lines of German defences on the final drive that would take them to Berlin; they had already established a bridgehead on the west bank of the river, and the Luftwaffe—still far from being totally destroyed—had made a series of attacks on the Russian positions during the past week.

The attacks were of the hit-and-run type, carried out by Focke-Wulf 190s which came in low and fast, dropping their bombs and then rocketing up into the nearest cloud cover before the Russian fighters had a chance to catch them. Three days earlier, on February 12th, Kozhedub had been leading three pairs of La-7s on a patrol over the front line when 30 bomb-carrying Focke-Wulfs suddenly dropped down out of a layer of cloud, diving towards the Russian positions. Kozhedub attacked at once, covered by his wing-man, Lieutenant Gromakovsky; torn apart by his cannon-shells, a 190 dived into the ground with a tremendous explosion. It was followed by another an instant later, one wing ripped off by a long burst of fire from Gromakovsky.

As Kozhedub and his wing-man broke away, the second pair of La-7s attacked in turn. The leader, Sasha Kumanitchkin, closed with a 190 in a head-on pass and opened fire at 200 yards; the enemy aircraft blew up in mid air and Kumanitchkin sped through the spreading cloud of smoke and debris. Then it was the turn of the third pair, Captain Orlov and Lieutenant Stetsenko. Orlov's shells shattered the cockpit of a 190 and it went into a spin, the pilot slumped over the controls. Elated, the Russian pilot turned away steeply, looking for another victim; he never saw the Focke-Wulf that came diving vertically on him. The Lavochkin burst into flames and went straight down, hitting the snow-covered ground in a mushroom of smoke.

The remaining five Russian pilots turned furiously on the Focke-Wulfs, which were now heading for the clouds. Kozhedub went after the last of them: the German pilot jettisoned his bombs over his own territory and tried every trick in the book to get away. He had almost reached the sheltering clouds when Kozhedub's shells found their target; the Focke-Wulf hung in mid air for a long moment, its propeller windmilling, then went over on its back and crashed. The Russian fighters formed up and headed for home at low altitude, running the gauntlet of a barrage of German 20-mm flak. They had destroyed seven enemy aircraft for the loss of Orlov.

Now, on this brilliant morning of February 15th, Kozhedub was on a lone reconnaissance patrol. He had been airborne for 30 minutes without sighting any enemy aircraft when suddenly, far below, his eye caught a flicker of movement against the snow-covered ground. It was an aircraft, skimming across dark patches of woodland, its presence betrayed by the flash of sunlight on a wing. Kozhedub immediately dived towards it. At 450 mph the Lavochkin plummeted earthwards like a rocket and the distance between it and the strange aircraft narrowed rapidly. The Russian pilot could make out its shape now; it was like a glittering arrowhead, with a slender shark-like fuselage, swept-back wings and a pair of long, low-slung engines that trailed thin streams of smoke. Kozhedub felt a sudden thrill of exultation as he realized what the aircraft was: a Messerschmitt 262 jet fighter. Although British and American fighter pilots had been encountering 262s in combat for some time now, it was the first time to Kozhedub's knowledge that one had turned up on the Eastern Front.

With 400 yards still to go the pilot of the 262 at last woke up to the danger and opened his throttles, the streams of smoke from his turbines growing denser as the jet began to draw away from its pursuer. It was now or never; the Lavochkin, still travelling at high speed, shuddered violently as Kozhedub fired. It was a lucky shot: strikes danced and sparkled over the 262's port wing and a long ribbon of flame shot back from its engine. The Russian fired again and the 262 went down, cutting a great swathe through a wood and exploding in a sheet of blazing fuel.

A few days later two more Russian fighter pilots, Lieutenant-General E. Savitsky—an ace with 22 victories—and Major Okolelov, also caught and destroyed a pair of 262s.

While Zhukov and Koniev were preparing for the thrust to Berlin, the Soviet forces in East Prussia were engaged in bitter fighting as they systematically destroyed each centre of German resistance. In March, the exceptionally strong German defensive position at Heilsberg was eliminated and the Russians now turned their attention to Königsberg, where 130,000 Germans were holding one of the mightiest fortresses in Europe. For two weeks, 2,000 Soviet bombers hammered the bastion from end to end, and early in April four Soviet armies hurled themselves against the enemy defences, suffering staggering casualties before the garrison was finally overwhelmed.

During the last week of March, the Russian forces in the south broke through to the Austrian border, and on April 7th they were fighting for Vienna. Soon afterwards they joined up with the Americans at Linz, completing the Allied ring around southern Germany. The focus now shifted to the Oder-Neisse Line, where Zhukov and Koniev had completed their preparations. Along the two rivers, a massive force of 1,600,000 men, 41,000 guns and 6,300 tanks stood ready for the final assault. On the front-line Soviet airfields, the 2nd, 4th, 8th and 16th Air Armies under generals Krasovsky, Vershinin, Khryukin and Rudyenko had assembled 8,400 combat aircraft. In spite of the crippling losses it suffered, the Luftwaffe continued to attack the Soviet build-up with a wide variety of aircraft. Among the types that fell to the guns of the Russian fighters was the 'Mistel' (Mistletoe), a pick-a-back combination of a Focke-Wulf 190 or a Messerschmitt 109 and a Junkers 88 or Dornier 217 bomber. Packed with explosives, the unmanned bomber would be released by the pilot of the fighter, to be guided to the target by remote control. The combination—the forerunner of the stand-off bomb—was ingenious enough, but its cumbersome nature made it an easy target and it had little more than a nuisance value.

At dawn on April 16th, the four Air Force generals launched the whole of their available bomber strength in a massive air onslaught against the German positions west of the Oder and Neisse. For hours successive waves of Shturmoviks, Pe-2s, Tu-2s and many other types roved over enemy territory, diving down to attack anything that moved. Above, the few German fighters that tried to intervene were massacred by the avalanche of Yaks and Lavochkins. Then, in the wake of one of the biggest artillery barrages in history, masses of Soviet shock troops stormed the first line of German defences. The Germans fought back fanatically, but they were overwhelmed by sheer weight of numbers. Nevertheless, it took the Russians two days to advance over the five miles to the second defensive line. German resistance was less fierce both here and at the third line of defence, and within a week Zhukov's forces had broken through and smashed the German 9th Army. Then, on April 21st, came the news that the crack 8th Guards Army under General Chuikov was fighting in the suburbs of Berlin; a fitting triumph for the old campaigner who had withstood the German onslaught against Stalingrad. It had been a long and bitter road from the city on the Volga to the capital of Hitler's Reich.

As the Russian advance rolled forward, the supporting air units went with it—and found themselves in possession of ready-made airstrips in the shape of the straight, broad German autobahns. The time involved in repairing the damage to these was far less than it took to construct new forward airfields, and the woods that ran along either side of the roads provided excellent camouflage for dispersed aircraft. The idea was not new; for some months now, the Luftwaffe—bombed out of its main airfields—had been operating combat aircraft, including jets, from this ready-made network of emergency runways.

From these autobahn airstrips, the Russian fighter units roved freely over Berlin, escorting the Ilyushins and Pe-2s that were bombing German strongpoints in the shattered streets or challenging the Luftwaffe's remaining fighters to join combat. All the surviving aces had assembled for the last battle; Kozhedub, Pokryskhin, Retchkalov, Golubev, Klubov, Sukhov, Vorozheikin and Dmitri Glinka—all of whom were in Pokryshkin's 16th Guards Air Regiment, with the exception of Kozhedub—added to their already impressive scores in the burning sky over the German capital.

The Luftwaffe went on fighting hard to the last, the German pilots hurling themselves on the great air armada with suicidal courage. Scraping together their last reserves, they flew an average of 1,000 sorties a day during the month-long battle for Berlin. It was a mere drop in the ocean; in one day alone, during the final assault on the capital, the Soviet air armies flew nearly 17,000 missions. The daily average in April was 15,000.

Ivan Kozhedub scored his last two victories during a memorable fight over Berlin on April 17th, the day after the Russian offensive began. The sun was going down as he took off and headed westwards with his wing-man, Lieutenant Dmitri Titorenko. Beneath their wings, the whole earth seemed to be on fire; the sun shone blood-red through a curtain of smoke. Over the city's north-west suburbs, the two Lavochkins described a lazy circle in the sky as the Russian pilots scanned the horizon for enemy aircraft. They had not encountered any so far that day, and Kozhedub was playing a hunch that the German fighter-bombers would attack as it was getting dusk; in this way they might stand a chance of avoiding the Russian day-fighters.

Kozhedub was right. A few minutes later, a cluster of dots appeared in the western sky; they grew rapidly until the Russians identified them as a mixed formation of Focke-Wulf 190s and 'long-nose' Focke-Wulf Ta 152s, the former carrying bombs and the latter presumably acting as their escort. The

Ta-152 was the last of the German piston-engined fighters to go into production; it was extremely fast, as well as retaining all the excellent characteristics of the redoubtable 190.

There were 40 aircraft in the enemy formation; this time the odds were too long even for Kozhedub. There was some scattered cloud a few thousand feet above, and the two Russian pilots climbed towards it. The Focke-Wulfs slid past below and the Russians began to shadow them, alerting base of their approach by radio. Kozhedub had no idea if the German pilots had spotted them or not; if they had, they made no move in the direction of the two Lavochkins. Studying the enemy formation carefully, Kozhedub made up his mind; he would take the biggest gamble of his life and attack. Altitude—speed—manoeuvre—fire! Pokryshkin's formula ran through his mind. He had the advantage of altitude and speed, but it was still two against 40. His plan might work; if not, then the careers of himself and Dmitri Titorenko would end here, in the sky of Berlin.

Kozhedub gave a curt order to his wing-man and the two La-7s went into a long, powerful dive on the upper echelon of Focke-Wulfs, which was bringing up the rear. A 190 loomed in his sights and he fired at almost point-blank range; the German aircraft exploded and went down to crash among the ruined streets below, tracing a vertical streamer of smoke down the sky. The other Focke-Wulfs scattered in all directions as the Russian fighters dived headlong through their ranks towards the lower echelon. Kozhedub opened fire again and saw pieces fly off a second 190, which flicked sharply away out of trouble. Then, out of the corner of his eye, the Russian pilot saw a Ta 152 turning steeply, level with him; in a fleeting instant he knew that the German intended to ram him and that there was nothing he could do to get out of the way in time. Suddenly the 152 literally fell apart and spun down in a cloud of debris, the victim of a well-aimed burst from Titorenko.

The enemy formation had become completely dislocated. The enemy pilots, no doubt believing that they were being attacked by a far superior force of Russian fighters, dropped their bombs haphazardly and sped back the way they had come. All except one. Of sterner stuff than the rest, he headed towards the front line at maximum speed, still carrying his bomb, and hotly pursued by the two Russians. Over Russian-held territory, the 190's pilot went into a dive and let go his bomb on whatever objective he had selected, afterwards pulling up into a steep climb. He flew straight into Kozhedub's cannon-shells. One wing broke away and the 190 went into a fast roll, still carried upwards by its speed. Then, rolling all the time, the fighter-bomber reached the top of its crazy arc and plunged into the ground. The pilot, Kozhedub's sixty-second victim, had not bailed out.

The end came quickly now. On April 25th, the Soviet 4th Guards Tank Army and the 2nd Tank Army linked up at Potsdam; Berlin was now encircled by a ring of fire and steel. On that day, too, Russian and American soldiers clasped hands at Torgau on the River Elbe. On April 30th Hitler committed suicide, and the following day the German forces that were still resisting in Berlin were penned up in three pockets, under constant attack by artillery and flights of rocket-carrying Shturmoviks. The Russian assault pilots carried out their last operation of the war with considerable daring, often flying between ruined buildings to get a good shot at their target. When the Germans still refused to surrender, the Russians brought up all their available artillery and opened up with a tremendous barrage; finally, at noon on May 2nd, the few surviving defenders—dazed with the fury that had descended on them—crawled out of their holes and gave themselves up.

Ironically, neither Kozhedub nor Pokryshkin was there to see the final surrender of Berlin. Kozhedub had flown to Moscow a couple of days earlier to represent the air units of the first Byelorussian front at the traditional May-Day Parade, while Pokryshkin's regiment had moved south to an airfield near Prague. The Czech capital was the last pocket of German resistance in the east; the garrison held out for a week after the fall of Berlin. On May 9th, the day of the final German surrender in Prague, Major V. Golubev—one of

Pokryshkin's pilots, and the sixteenth-ranking Soviet ace—shot down a Messerschmitt 109 over the city. It was the last aircraft to be destroyed in air combat during the European war.

On May 1st 1945, a flight of three Yak-3 fighters flew low over the outskirts of Berlin. At 100 feet they roared along the Spree, the broad road on its bank lined with the tanks of the 1st Guards Army. Turning steeply over the shattered cathedral, they levelled out again and swept over the Reichstag. From the cockpit of the leading fighter something fluttered down, unfurling slowly: a red banner. The Guards Fighter Regiment to which the Yak-3s belonged had carried that banner for three years, throughout the long hunt across eastern Europe which had followed the German defeat at the gates of Moscow. On it, in gold, was embroidered a single Russian word: Pobyeda.

Victory.

Chapter 11

The New Enemy

In the early evening of July 30th 1944, a squadron of Yak-9 fighters based on the Far Eastern airfield of Spassk was ordered to scramble in response to a sudden alert. An unidentified aircraft had been detected approaching Vladivostok from the direction of Manchuria, and although the Soviet Union was not at war with Japan the Russian air defence commanders in the Far East had been ordered to intercept any Japanese aircraft that infringed Soviet air space.

This aircraft, however, was not Japanese. It was a large and very streamlined four-engined bomber; an American B-29 Superfortress. In fact, the aircraft belonged to the USAAF's 58th Bomber Wing, the first unit to equip with the new type; operating out of Chengtu Air Base in southern China, it had been part of a force of 100 B-29s which, a couple of hours earlier, had attacked a Japanese steel mill at Anshan in Manchuria.

The B-29 was hit by an anti-aircraft shell over the target and number three engine was put out of action. The pilot knew that the aircraft could not reach its base on three engines, so he decided to head for Soviet territory—following the standard emergency procedure. As the bomber circled over Vladivostok, the Russian fighters arrived on the scene and took it in turns to buzz the American aircraft, flying dangerously close and sending short bursts of fire across its nose. Then the Russian squadron commander came up alongside and indicated by signs that he wished the B-29 pilot to land at a small airfield near Tavrichanka, at the northern tip of Vladivostok Bay. The airfield was very small, but the American pilot had no choice but to obey; he brought the big aircraft in as slowly as possible, scraping over the airfield boundary. The B-29 came to a stop a matter of yards from where the end of the runway fell away into the sea. Thirty minutes later, the members of the crew were being interrogated by Soviet Air Force officers; it was to be several months before they finally left the Soviet Union on their way home to the United States. They never saw their B-29 again.

The unexpected arrival of the B-29—which was followed by three more under similar circumstances during the remaining months of 1944—was the answer to the Russians' prayer. As the war drew to a close, the Chief Administration of the Soviet Air Force already had plans in hand for the updating of the V-VS, and these included the formation of a modern strategic bombing force. In 1944, the only Soviet long-range bomber was the obsolescent Pe-8, which, together with the twin-engined Tu-2, formed the main equipment of the Long-Range Aviation. But the ADD had ceased to exist as an independent force; early in 1944, it had been redesignated the 18th Air Army and turned over to tactical duties in support of the Soviet ground forces.

With the wartime emphasis very much on the development of tactical bombers, assault aircraft and fighters, Soviet designers had had little time to study long-range bomber projects, and it was obvious that even if work on such projects began in 1944 there would still be a dangerous gap before a Soviet long-range bomber could be produced in series. Then, suddenly, a ready-made answer literally fell out of the Russian sky: the B-29.

By copying the B-29 in every detail, the Russians hoped to avoid all the technological problems associated with the development of an aircraft of this kind at one blow. The designer chosen for the formidable task was Andrei Tupolev, while the job of copying the B-29's Wright R-3350 engines went to A. D. Shvetsov. The work was not easy; big snags cropped up frequently, particularly in connection with electronically operated equipment such as the B-29's gun turrets. Despite everything, however, construction of the prototype Russian B-29—designated Tu-4—was begun in March 1945, and the first three prototypes were ready for flight-testing at the beginning of 1947. The following year these three aircraft were publicly revealed at the big Soviet air display at Tushino, near Moscow—by which time series production of the Tu-4 was well under way, the first examples having already been delivered to operational V-VS squadrons.

Meanwhile, the years 1946 and 1947 had seen the substantial reorganization of the Soviet Air Force under the direction of its new C-in-C, Marshal of Aviation Konstantin A. Vershinin, who succeeded the wartime V-VS commander, Alexander A. Nivikov, after the latter fell out with Stalin and was imprisoned in 1946. Vershinin's deputy was Marshal V. A. Sudyets, who was succeeded by the extremely able Marshal Sergei I. Rudyenko—the former C-in-C of the 16th Air Army—in 1949.

Under Vershinin's leadership, the Soviet Air Force was welded into five commands: the Long-Range Aviation (DA), built around the nucleus of Tu-4 bombers and commanded by Marshal Sudyets; the Fighter Aviation of the Air Defence Forces (IA-PVO); the Frontal Aviation (FA); the Naval Aviation (A-VMF); and the Aviation of the Airborne Troops (A-VDV). This structure remains basically the same today.

At the end of the war, the Soviet aircraft industry lagged far behind those of Germany, Britain and the United States in the development of jet aircraft. By May 1945, substantial numbers of jet combat aircraft had reached the Luftwaffe's squadrons, and many more advanced types were projected; the Gloster Meteor had been in service with the RAF for nearly two years, and the first squadron of F-80 Shooting Stars had just become operational with the USAF; whereas the last word in Russian fighters was the Lavochkin La-9— a progressive piston-engined development of the La-7. The failure of the Russians to keep pace with the leading western nations in jet aircraft development was surprising, for Russian engineers had been among the first in the world to build experimental reaction motors in the early 1930s, and in fact had established a considerable lead over the rest of the world in the development of rocket motors for use in aircraft.

Research was accelerated immediately before the outbreak of war, and in July 1941 two designers—Berezniak and Isayev —submitted details of a proposed rocket interceptor, the BI-1, to the State Defence Committee. The latter approved the design and ordered the construction of five prototypes, the first of which was completed exactly 40 days later. The BI-1 was a single-seat cantilever mid-wing monoplane of mixed construction, featuring a retractable undercarriage and an armament of two 20-mm cannon. It made its first unpowered flight on September 10th 1941, gliding to earth after being towed to altitude behind a Pe-2, and on May 15th 1942 it finally flew under the power of its rocket motor. Several more prototypes were built and delivered to an experimental squadron, but after a number of serious snags—including one fatal crash—the project was abandoned.

The designs of two other experimental rocket fighters—the Polikarpov 'Malyutka' (Baby) and the Tikhonravov 302 —also made their appearance at the same time as the BI-1, although neither showed as much promise as Berezniak's and Isayev's aircraft, and neither was completed. All three types were to have been powered by a Dushkin rocket motor which gave them an estimated flight duration of between eight and 15 minutes—insufficient for operational use. Apart from these types, only two other experimental Soviet aircraft incorporated reaction engines during the war, and both were 'mixed-power' aircraft, using a combination of conventional piston engines and small turbojets. The first was the Mikoyan-designed I-205 (N), which—powered by a VK-107R piston engine coupled with a turbo-jet mounted in the rear fuselage—reached a speed of 514 mph at 26,000 feet in May 1945. The second aircraft was the similarly powered Sukhoi I-107; it was slightly slower, with a maximum speed of 503 mph.

It was the German surrender that provided the Russians with the opportunity to break through into the modern jet aircraft field. To escape Allied bombing, the Germans had concentrated their main centres of jet aircraft production in the eastern half of the country, and in 1945 vast quantities of material fell into the hands of the advancing Russians, who lost no time in transferring it to the Soviet Union—together with most of the engineers and technicians who were unable or unwilling to make their escape to the west. With the help of these men, the Russians not only tested to exhaustion every type of jet aircraft flown by the Germans—Messerschmitt 262s and 163s, Heinkel 162s, Arado 234s and Junkers 287s—but they also completed a number of half-finished prototypes and tested them too. They included the Focke-Wulf Ta-183, an advanced jet interceptor with sharply swept wings, a high tail and a stubby barrel-shaped fuselage; and the DFS-346 research aircraft, powered by a Walter HWK 509B-1 rocket motor, which had been under construction at the Siebel Aircraft Factory at Halle when the war ended. The factory was initially captured by the Americans, who handed everything over to the Russians when Halle became part of the Soviet Zone of Occupation. The Russians immediately rounded up the entire Siebel staff and ordered them to resume work on the DFS-346 project; then, in October 1946, both factory and personnel were moved to Podberesye, east of Moscow.

Two 346s were built; one was used for structural testing and the other was flight-tested at Toplistan airfield near Moscow early in 1948 by Herr Ziese, Siebel's former chief test pilot. The aircraft was released from a B-25 Mitchell and also from one of the B-29s that force-landed in Siberia during 1944. The DFS-346 was destroyed during a high-speed run in 1951, when it went out of control shortly after its rocket motor ignited. Ziese ejected safely and was only slightly injured.

The most important haul seized by the Russians early in 1945, however, was a large quantity of BMW 003A and Junkers Jumo 004A turbojets, which were shared out among various Soviet designers for experimental use while the engine manufacturers geared up to produce them in series. One of the designers involved was Alexander S. Yakovlev, who set about adapting a standard Yak-3 airframe to accommodate a Jumo 004B. The resulting aircraft—designated Yak-15—made its first flight on April 24th 1946, and early the following year the first production aircraft were being delivered to selected IA-PVO squadrons. The Yak-15—Russia's first jet fighter—was essentially a 'stop-gap' aircraft and looked it, but its light weight and manoeuvrability gave it a performance that compared well with that of Western jet types of the period. In 1948 it was replaced by the Yak-17, a modified version featuring a tricycle undercarriage.

Meanwhile, in February 1945, Artem Mikoyan had also begun work on a jet aircraft, the I-300, built around two BMW 003A engines. The prototype I-300 flew on the same day as the prototype Yak-15, and the production version—designated MiG-9—entered service in small numbers in mid 1947, after a spate of teething troubles which had included the crash of the prototype, killing test pilot Alexei Grinchik. Three other Soviet jet fighter designs, the Sukhoi Su-9—based on the Messerschmitt 262—and the Lavochkin La-150 and 152, were test-flown, but failed to meet the necessary requirements and did not enter service.

In March 1947, while the first Soviet Air Force pilots were converting to their new jets, Mikoyan's team was already working on the prototype of an aircraft that was later to become world-famous, serving with the air forces of many nations: the MiG-15. From the outset, this aircraft owed much of its success to its engine: the RD-45F, the Russian version of the British Rolls-Royce Nene, a batch of which had recently been delivered to the Soviet Union. The RD-45F developed twice the power of the modified German turbojets which equipped the Yak-15 and MiG-9, and it took the Russians exactly one year to copy the Nene and produce it in quantity.

The MiG-15 made its first flight on December 30th 1947. Three months earlier, another revolutionary aircraft had also taken off on its maiden flight: the North American F-86 Sabre. Within four years, the two were destined to meet in the skies of Korea, locked in the first ever jet-versus-jet battles over the Yalu River.

Throughout the late 1940s, Soviet aircraft development was characterized by bold strides forward such as the designing of the MiG-15, and by a spate of 'one-off' prototypes that probably confused the Russians as much as they did Western observers when the aircraft—mostly bearing the hallmark of German influence—shot briefly across the sky at Tushino and their blurred images appeared in Western aviation publications, often accompanied by sensational pronouncements that were utterly remote from the truth. What is true is that the Russians plunged whole-heartedly into every possible line of aeronautical research during the early post-war years, and their success was evident in the fact that by 1950 the Soviet Air Force—for the first time in its history—possessed aircraft that compared favourably with any produced in the West.

Although the late forties saw the reorganization of the Soviet Air Force and its unification under one ministry as a separate service—instead of being portioned out piecemeal to the Army and Navy—there was little reduction in its combat strength after the end of hostilities. Aircraft production fell from its wartime peak of 40,000 a year to 10,000, but the V-VS remained the second largest air force in the world (after the USAF) with a strength of 19,000 aircraft, over 75 per cent of which were based in the western USSR or in the newly acquired Soviet satellite countries. Conflict had given way to confrontation, and although the Russian airmen were no longer required to fire their guns and drop their bombs in anger they were active in other spheres, providing transport facilities for the renewed Chinese Communist offensive against Chiang Kai-shek and dropping supplies to the ELAS communist guerrillas in Greece immediately after the war.

Then, in June 1948, the East-West tension reached a new peak when the Russians closed rail and road access to West Berlin through their zone: the culmination of a long series of provocations. On June 26th, USAF Dakotas made 32 trips to the city, carrying 80 tons of supplies; they were joined by British transport aircraft two days later. The Berlin airlift, which was to become the most massive operation of its kind in history, had begun.

The airlift presented the Russians with a dilemma from which there was no way out. They had not believed it possible that the Allies could mount an operation of this size, let alone sustain it for several months in all kinds of weather, and once it was under way there was nothing they could do about it short of shooting down the Allied transport aircraft, which— since the Allies had legal access to Berlin via the three air corridors—would have constituted an act of war. They could, however, do everything in their power to harass the airlift without resorting to force, and this was their policy until the blockade was eventually lifted in May 1949. During the weeks that followed the start of the airlift, British and American intelligence sources indicated that additional Soviet Air Force fighter and bomber units were arriving on airfields in the Russian Zone, and a few days later the Russians began what to all appearances was a large-scale air exercise. Aircrews flying along the corridors reported that the Russians appeared to be constructing air-to-ground firing ranges directly below, and that in fact was precisely what they were doing. Before long the Allied crews began to encounter increasing numbers of Soviet aircraft in the corridors; the aircraft involved were mainly Yak-3s, La-9s and Il-2s, and the tactics employed by the Russian pilots were varied and often ingenious.

One of the favourite tactics was to fly at high speed along the corridors, usually in the opposite direction to the stream of transport aircraft, either singly or in formation. The fighters would make a fast head-on pass at a transport, pulling up sharply at the last minute. In the year from August 1948 to August 1949, American transport crews alone reported 77 'buzzing' incidents in the corridors by Soviet aircraft, together with another 96 incidents that were loosely described as 'close flying'. The Americans also stated that Russian fighters fired bursts of cannon and machine-gun fire in the vicinity of transport aircraft on 14 separate occasions, although no instance of a deliberate attack was recorded.

What the Russians called 'routine air-to-ground firing practices' were frightening enough, but seldom dangerous. The Soviet fighters would hang around the corridors in the vicinity of one of their firing-ranges, flying singly or in pairs at about 6,000 feet—above the main stream of traffic. They would then go into a shallow dive towards the range, passing right in front of the transports, guns blazing all the way down.

American pilots also reported Soviet anti-aircraft fire in the corridors on 54 occasions, although the Russian gunners were careful to place their shells well clear of the transport aircraft. Searchlights were the most common nuisance; the Russians lined the corridors with batteries of them and they made accurate night-flying—which was absolutely essential in such a high traffic density—very tiring work. The Russians also tried jamming the Allied radio frequencies, both by the use of primitive countermeasures equipment and by the simpler expedient of ordering their pilots to use the frequencies as much as possible, filling the already overcrowded ether with Russian chatter.

By the end of 1948, it was becoming obvious that the airlift had beaten the blockade; however, it was to be another five months before all access routes to the city were reopened. The Soviet Air Force—which could have destroyed the operation at any time, with the inevitable consequence of escalation into another war which the Soviet Union, because of America's monopoly in nuclear weapons, would have been in no position to fight—had done its best to carry out its orders to harass the airlift within the strict limitations imposed on it, but it had failed to disrupt the flow of air traffic in the slightest.

The blockade of Berlin had been the first battle, and the first Russian defeat, of the Cold War.

Chapter 12

Into Battle Again

At 13.15 hours in the afternoon of June 25th 1950, two strange aircraft flew low over the South Korean airfields of Seoul and Kimpo. They were Russian-built Yak-9s, and on their uncamouflaged wings they bore the red star and circle of the North Korean Air Force.

At first light on that June day, North Korean infantry—spearheaded by T-34 tanks—had launched an all-out offensive across the 38th Parallel into the Republic of Korea, and the South Korean and American personnel of Kimpo and Seoul airfields had been anticipating a possible communist air strike all morning. The first two enemy aircraft that appeared, however, made no attempt to attack; after taking a good look at the airfields, they flew off to the north. But the airfields were not destined to escape for long; at 15.00 hours the Yaks came back in force. Two of them raced over Kimpo, spraying the field with cannon and machine-gun fire. Shells tore through the control tower and found their mark in a fuel dump, which exploded with a tremendous roar. A USAF C-54 transport aircraft was also hit and damaged. Four more Yaks attacked Seoul, damaging seven T-6 trainer aircraft, and at 16.00 a second attack was made on Kimpo. This time the C-54 transport damaged in the earlier raid went up in flames.

On June 27th, with the North Koreans advancing rapidly and the situation deteriorating fast, the Americans ordered the evacuation of all their non-essential personnel—mostly servicemen's families—from Korea. A small armada of US transport aircraft immediately began a shuttle service between the two major South Korean airfields and Japan. Fighter cover for the airlift was provided by F-80 Shooting Stars, which patrolled to the north of Seoul, and by F-82 Twin Mustangs. It had been rightly expected that the North Korean Air Force would attempt to interfere with the transports, and at noon on the 27th five Yak-3s were sighted over Seoul, heading for Kimpo. They were intercepted by five F-82s, which shot down three out of the five Yaks in the first air battle of the Korean War. That afternoon the communists tried again, this time with eight Ilyushin Il-10s—the improved version of the famous Il-2 Shturmovik. Like the Yaks, the Il-10s never reached Kimpo; they were caught by the F-80 jets of the 35th Fighter-Bomber Squadron, and after a brief one-sided fight four of them were blazing on the ground. The other four turned and ran for their base at Heijo, near Pyongyang. There were no further attacks during the two remaining days of the airlift.

At the time of the offensive against South Korea, the North Korean Air Force possessed a total of 162 aircraft divided among a fighter regiment, a ground attack regiment and a training regiment. The aircraft in service were all of Soviet manufacture, and included 70 Yak-3s and Yak-9s, 62 Il-10s, eight Po-2s and 22 miscellaneous types. The small air force was trained entirely by Soviet Air Force instructors, who found the North Koreans to be capable pupils; they were keen and aggressive, extremely self-confident, although they lacked experience. This showed up plainly during the early combats with American pilots, mostly veterans of the Second World War, over Seoul.

Nevertheless, the North Korean pilots did score successes where American fighter opposition was lacking; while the F-80s and F-82s were committed to defending the airlift, for instance, four Yak-9s attacked Suwon airfield at 13.30 hours on June 28th, destroying an F-82 and a B-26 light bomber on the ground. Later that afternoon, three pairs of Yaks arrived over the same airfield and attacked a C-54 that was coming in to land; fortunately, the pilot managed to get away and returned to Japan, where he made an emergency landing with severe damage. The same Yaks then made a strafing pass over the airfield, setting another C-54 on fire. Six more attacks were made on Suwon the following day, but this time the American F-80s were up and two enemy aircraft were shot down. One was a Lavochkin La-7, a type not previously encountered. Also on the 29th, American B-26 bombers attacked the North Korean airfields around Pyongyang, destroying 25 aircraft on the ground; one Yak-3 made a gallant attempt to intercept the B-26s, but it was shot down.

The North Korean Air Force went to war with two main objectives: first, to knock out the small South Korean Air Force—which it was quite capable of doing—and second, to provide air support for the communist army. A North Korean pilot, captured during the first days of the war, revealed that the planning for the attack had been done by Soviet advisers who, apparently, had assumed that the United Nations would not intervene in strength. In view of the way in which some of the North Korean aircraft were handled in combat during the early air attacks, there is little doubt that the Soviet instructors acted in more than just an advisory capacity.

The communist plans were upset from the start by the rapid deployment of US combat aircraft to Korea, which resulted in the speedy establishment of United Nations air superiority. As American attacks on their main airfields mounted, the North Koreans fell back on the old Russian strategem of dispersing their aircraft on well-camouflaged temporary airstrips near the front, from which they carried out a series of low-level hit-and-run attacks in July. These attacks were carefully timed, the Yaks striking when any American fighters in the vicinity were nearing the end of their patrol and growing short of fuel. On two occasions, F-80 jets were caught in these circumstances by piston-engined Yaks and had to run for their lives, too low on fuel to join combat. The North Korean air offensive, however, was nearing its end; the USAF and US Navy mounted heavy strikes against the North Korean airfields, including those captured by the enemy in his drive south, and by July 20th they had destroyed 49 communist aircraft on the ground, eight in the air, and damaged 30 more. Early in August, a NKAF build-up on the captured air bases of Kimpo and Suwon was smashed by American fighter-bombers, which destroyed nine enemy aircraft and claimed a further nine 'probables'.

By the end of August, following an assessment of the photographs of communist airfields brought back by American PR aircraft, it was estimated that the combat strength of the North Korean Air Force had been reduced to not more than 20 machines. Deprived of their air cover, the North Korean forces were unable to withstand the massive onslaught by United Nations fighter-bombers, which turned their columns and lines of supply into a burning shambles; nor could they oppose the formations of B-29s that roved over the north, attacking targets of military importance. The North Korean troops began to fall back, still fighting hard, but unable to stem the tide of the American and South Korean counter-offensive. By mid October, the UN forces were advancing rapidly with the intention of occupying the whole of North Korea, and it was then that the whole situation began to change dramatically.

In the early morning and again in the late evening of October 14th, unidentified intruder aircraft bombed Kimpo airfield—now in UN hands once more—under cover of darkness. At dawn the following morning, four American Mustang aircraft on a reconnaissance flight along the Yalu River ran into heavy anti-aircraft fire from Chinese batteries on the opposite bank, in Manchuria; and three days later a reconnaissance B-29 reported a line-up of 75 Chinese communist aircraft on Antung airfield, just across the river.

On November 1st, a B-26 bomber was attacked by three Chinese Yak-9s south of the Yalu; all three were shot down, one by the B-26's gunners and the other two by Mustangs that arrived just in time. Later that day, nine F-80s attacked Sinuiju airfield, on the southern bank of the river, destroying or damaging seven out of 15 Yaks that had been seen there; one F-80 was shot down by Chinese A/A fire. Then, in the afternoon, a flight of Mustangs patrolling the river was attacked by six fast jet aircraft that came whistling up out of Manchuria; the Americans managed to escape, but they knew that from now on the air war would be no walkover. The MiG-15 had arrived in Korea.

On November 2nd the first Chinese 'volunteer' forces crossed in strength into North Korea, and during the week that followed air combats along the Yalu grew in intensity.

The communist tactics, based on the orders that forbade United Nations pilots to cross the Yalu, were simple; the MiGs and Yaks would climb to high altitude over Manchurian territory, then they would dive across the river at maximum speed, engaging in a short combat before crossing the river to safety once more, afterwards climbing to repeat the process all over again. In spite of these tactics the piston-engined Yaks suffered heavy punishment, and after a few days they were encountered only infrequently. The number of MiG-15s engaged, however, grew as the days went by, and on November 8th the first all-jet battle in history was fought between MiGs and F-80 Shooting Stars which were providing top cover for a force of B-29s. Although the F-80s were technically outclassed, the inexperience of the communist pilots resulted in one MiG being shot down by Lt. Russell J. Brown of the 51st Fighter Intercepter Wing. On that same day, RB-29 reconnaissance aircraft received such a severe mauling from the MiGs in the Yalu area that future missions were carried out by RF-80 jets.

For the first time, the United Nations pilots found themselves faced with a really dangerous challenge to their air superiority. The MiG-15s were superior on every count to the American aircraft opposing them, and only the greater skill of the UN pilots saved them from severe losses. By December 1950, the Chinese People's Air Force had received about 100 of the formidable Russian jets; the total strength of the CPAF had risen, with Soviet assistance, to something in the order of 650 aircraft, including—in addition to the MiGs—150 Yak-9s, La-9s and Yak-15s, 175 Il-2s and Il-10s, 150 Pe-2s and Tu-2s, and 75 transport aircraft, mostly Li-2s. The Russians saw the CPAF as a virtual extension of the Soviet Air Force, and at the end of 1950 this in effect was what it was. Its instructors were Russian, as were the leaders of its combat formations and its senior technical personnel. Early in 1951, Soviet radar specialists set up a fighter control network in Manchuria which subsequently allowed the MiGs to operate much more effectively.

In December 1950, the first step to combat the MiG threat

was taken when the North American F-86A Sabres of the 4th Intercepter Wing were hurriedly rushed out to Korea from the United States via Japan. During their first sweep along the Yalu on the afternoon of December 17th, the Sabre pilots shot down one MiG—one of a formation of four which mistook the F-86s for more vulnerable F-80s. The Sabre's biggest disadvantage was its limited radius of action; whereas the MiGs operated within sight of their own airfields, the Sabres had to make the long trip north from Kimpo or Taengu, which reduced the time they could spend in the combat area to a matter of minutes. To extend their 'combat loiter' period, the Sabre pilots were forced to patrol at relatively low airspeeds in order to conserve fuel, which placed them at a distinct disadvantage. The MiG pilots were quick to exploit the Sabres' weakness, attacking from above at near-sonic speed and making their getaway before the Sabre pilots could increase their own speed enough to react.

The Sabre pilots countered by reducing their time on patrol still further, and adopted new tactics which involved sending four flights of Sabres into the combat area at five-minute intervals and at high speed. The new plan worked; in an air battle over the Yalu on December 22nd between eight Sabres and 15 MiGs, six of the communist aircraft were shot down for the loss of one F-86. By the end of the year, the 4th Intercepter Wing had flown 234 combat missions, during which there had been 76 combats with MiGs resulting in the destruction of eight of the enemy fighters, with another two probably destroyed and seven damaged. In conditions where the communist pilots always enjoyed the initial advantage, it was not a bad record.

These combats, however, were merely preliminary skirmishes. The Chinese build-up on the Manchurian airfields went on steadily, with the aim of establishing air superiority over north-west Korea; this would enable the communists to repair existing airfields in North Korea and to set up new ones, from which a large-scale air offensive could subsequently be launched against the United Nations. During January and February 1951, the Sabres were pulled back to Japan for maintenance—a step made necessary by the lack of facilities in Korea—and for several weeks United Nations aircraft operating over north-west Korea had a difficult time. For the first time in the war, the communists enjoyed a definite measure of air superiority, and they retained it even when the Sabres returned and began operating out of Suwon.

Although several large air battles developed during March, the Sabres scored no kills. By this time there were 75 MiG-15s —a complete air division—based on Antung airfield across the Yalu, and the sight of the enemy fighters taking off in a cloud of dust, then climbing at their leisure to combat altitude, was galling in the extreme for the UN pilots—still restricted by their orders not to cross the Yalu under any circumstances. The biggest air fights took place in April, when strong formations of MiGs intercepted UN bombers attacking targets near the Yalu; F-84 Thunderjets acted as close escort for the bombers while Sabres provided top cover. It was not a satisfactory arrangement, for many MiGs invariably succeeded in diving through the Sabre screen on to the bomber formations below, where the slow Thunderjets were unable to cope. On April 12th, a huge dogfight flared up when 50 MiGs attacked a force of 39 B-29s, escorted by Sabres and Thunderjets; three bombers were shot down and six more badly damaged, while the Sabres claimed four MiGs destroyed and six damaged. The Thunderjets, fighting for their lives, got off a few shots but scored no kills, although their pilots—somewhat optimistically—claimed three probables.

The Americans emerged from the battle of April 12th severely shaken. The MiGs had pressed home their attacks with a skill and determination hitherto uncharacteristic of the average Chinese pilot. The reason was revealed later, by a Polish pilot defecting to the West: in March 1951—in addition to the Soviet personnel already acting as advisers to the Chinese—Soviet, Polish and Czech pilots began to arrive in Manchuria to serve a three-month tour of duty with CPAF combat units. There were reports that the Soviet fighter pilot contingent was commanded by the legendary Ivan Kozhedub, but they were never confirmed. It is known, however, that Kozhedub took up a senior command in the Far East about this time, after a ground tour at the Zhukovsky Military Academy. Whatever the truth, it was not just a case of Soviet pilots flying CPAF MiGs; whole Soviet fighter regiments were attached to CPAF air divisions, their Russian markings carefully replaced by Chinese ones.

The large-scale air activity in April was intended as a prelude to the planned communist air offensive. In the event, the communists' plans were forestalled by a series of timely attacks on their airfields in North Korea—which, towards the end of April, were almost ready to receive combat aircraft. The first major airfield strike took place on April 22nd, and on this occasion the MiGs received a severe trouncing at the hands of the Sabres, which were up in strength. From that moment on, the Sabre pilots began to establish a marked ascendancy over their opponents. During May, the communists went back to their earlier hit-and-run tactics, crossing the Yalu for a brief skirmish and then withdrawing at high speed. The only big air battle during this month occurred on the 20th, when 36 Sabres tangled with 50 MiGs and shot down three of them, damaging five more.

It was in June 1951 that the Soviet Air Force began to commit some of its fighter regiments to the Korean air war, and although the United Nations pilots were not aware of this at the time they did note an overall rise in the efficiency and flying discipline of the communist units. The Sabres continued to score a high rate of kills, but they began to lose some of their own number; so far, only one Sabre had been destroyed in air combat, but on June 18th and 19th two more were lost within 24 hours. The Russian MiG pilots showed no hesitation in operating south of the Yalu; carrying wing tanks, they ranged as far afield as Pyongyang and Chinnampo. For the most part they stayed upstairs at over 25,000 feet, where they enjoyed a slight advantage over the F-86, and for this reason they never interfered seriously with United Nations fighter-bombers. On the few occasions when they did make a low-level 'bounce', they could usually be outflown by F-80 and F-84 pilots, who managed to shoot a few MiGs down. On several occasions, MiGs were also destroyed by piston-engined fighters, notably Hawker Sea Furies of the British Fleet Air Arm, which were flying strikes against North Korean targets from carriers.

By the end of June 1951, over 300 MiG-15s were based on the three airfields of Antung, Ta-ku-shan and Ta-tung-kou, across the Yalu, and more airfields were rapidly being built. It was also estimated that the communists had another 150 MiGs in reserve in China, and against this formidable force the United Nations had only 44 Sabres in Korea, with a further 45 available in Japan. Nevertheless, the Sabres managed to hold their own, in spite of being outnumbered two to one in many dogfights. During this period, the UN pilots noted that the communists appeared to be experimenting with various types of tactics, including one which the Sabre pilots nicknamed the 'Yo-yo'. A large formation of MiGs would orbit over the battle area at maximum ceiling, breaking off in small sections to make high-speed passes on the UN aircraft below and then zooming up to altitude again. Many American pilots observed that some of the communist tactics seemed strangely familiar, and then they suddenly realized that they were exactly the same as those employed by the Luftwaffe's fighters against the big daylight bomber formations over Europe in 1944-5. The Russians had learned a lot in the half-decade since the war.

A series of big air battles was fought in September, when the MiGs operated in formations of up to 75 aircraft, and the odds against the Sabres suddenly shot up to three or four to one. During this month, the UN lost three Sabres, one F-51, one F-80 and an F-84, while the American pilots claimed the destruction of 14 MiGs. There was more fierce fighting in October, when the MiGs came up in strength to intercept formations of B-29s that had been detailed to attack new airfields which the communists were once again attempting to build in North Korea. In four weeks the MiGs flew over 2,500 missions and presented a dangerous challenge to the UN air superiority yet again. The Americans lost 15 aircraft, but 32 MiGs were claimed to have been shot down. The determined attacks pressed home by the MiGs, however, had prevented the bombers from neutralizing their targets, and at the end of the month—for the first time—25 MiGs began to operate from the North Korean base of Uiju.

The battles of October resulted in a tactical victory for the communists and it had a notable effect on the planners of the US Air Defense Command. Within a fortnight, an additional 75 Sabres were on their way out to Japan, earmarked for combat duty in Korea. These aircraft were new F-86Es, and—equipping the 51st Fighter Wing—they arrived in Korea early in January, affording a much-needed respite for the battered 4th Fighter Wing. During that month, the 51st Wing shot down 25 MiGs, and the situation now began to ease considerably.

Frequent air battles continued during February and March, but the communists had now ceased to appear in large formations and instead were operating in formations of 12 aircraft or less. Then, in May, came a new development; the MiGs, with the help of their recently completed radar control network, began a period of intensive night operations. On the night of June 10th, during their first successful radar-controlled interception, the MiGs destroyed three of a formation of four B-29s over North Korea; cover of darkness, formerly the bombers' main ally, had been brutally torn aside.

Despite their new techniques, however, the communists failed in their bid to wrest air superiority from the United Nations—although they had come perilously close to achieving it in the autumn of 1951. Even so, while the UN pilots retained superiority over North Korea during 1952, the communist air build-up in Manchuria went on; by the beginning of December they had 1,500 combat aircraft north of the Yalu, including 950 MiGs. It was then that reconnaissance revealed a new threat: 100 new jet bombers, lined up on two Manchurian bases. They were twin-jet Ilyushin Il-28s, Russia's first operational jet bombers, and if the communists decided to use them offensively they could range as far afield as Japan with impunity at night, although they would be vulnerable in daylight operations. But they never were used; their presence in Manchuria was purely a show of strength, and although they were sighted several times by UN pilots they always kept well to the north of the river.

It was in November 1952 that the Soviet Air Force made its only open attempt to interfere with UN air operations over Korea. On November 18th, while Task Force 77's Navy jets were attacking the town of Hoeryong, close to North Korea's border with the Soviet Union, a large formation of MiGs was sighted assembling over the Russian airfields around Vladivostok. A few minutes later a number of MiGs were seen approaching the Task Force from the north; they bore no national markings, but there was no doubt as to their identity. They were intercepted by the Task Force's Grumman Panthers, who shot one down and drove the rest off. Details of this fight were not made public until years later, because of the political implications.

In January 1953, the MiG squadrons entered combat with an aggressiveness such as they had not shown before. An improved version of the Russian fighter, the MiG-15bis, had by this time arrived in Manchuria and the Sabre pilots found it a formidable opponent. For the first time, the communist pilots often stayed to fight even when the odds were against them, but by the end of the month the UN fighters had claimed the destruction of 37 MiGs for the loss of a single Sabre. Many of the MiGs encountered during the air battles of early 1953 bore the plain red star of the Soviet Air Force instead of CPAF insignia.

Although the UN pilots ruled the daylight skies over Korea, it was a different story at night. From November 1952 onwards, the effectiveness of the communist night-fighters increased considerably and the B-29 squadrons suffered heavy losses. The Americans sent F3D-2 Skynight and F-94 Starfire all-weather fighters on intruder missions over the north to cover the bomber stream at night, and the Skynights shot down a MiG-15 and a Yak-15 in November, but these operations presented no solution to the night-fighter menace. Their biggest value was as a morale-booster for the bomber crews; it was comforting to know that friendly fighters were in the vicinity over hostile territory, even though they could not be seen. The main drawback for the communists was that they had no true all-weather radar-equipped interceptors; if they had possessed aircraft of the same calibre as the Skynight and Starfire, they could have smashed the UN night bombing offensive.

In the spring of 1953, the F-94s were also in action against communist intruder aircraft; these were mainly Po-2 biplanes, La-11s and Yak-18s, with a few Tu-2 light bombers. Because of the low speed at which the Russian-built aircraft operated, the jet night-fighters registered few kills; one F-94 crew did manage to shoot down a Po-2 after throttling right back and lowering gear and flaps, but the fighter stalled and spun in immediately afterwards. The 'Bedcheck Charlies', as the Americans nicknamed the communist night raiders, did little damage, but they had an adverse psychological effect on the UN forces. The lessons of the Spanish Civil War had not been forgotten.

The Korean War, in general, ended with a victory for neither side. It had been a slogging match in which the opposing forces had fought each other to a standstill. But there had been a victory: a victory in the air for the United Nations pilots. When the last shots were fired, the UN airmen claimed to have destroyed 900 enemy aircraft in three years of fighting, a total that included 792 MiG-15s claimed by the Sabre pilots for the loss of 78 of their own number. There is no reason to doubt these claims; the great majority were recorded accurately on film. The reason for the Sabres' ten-to-one kill ratio over aircraft that were technically their match was a combination of many factors, not the least of which was the higher overall standard of training among the UN pilots. The Sabre, too, was the better weapon system; in other words, a better amalgamation of airframe, engine, guns and pilot. Its six 0·5 machine guns proved to be more effective than the MiGs' heavy 23-mm and 37-mm cannon, which—although ideal for knocking down bombers—had a rate of fire that was too slow for air combat at near-sonic speeds. The big 37-mm cannon, for example, fired so slowly that its shells could be seen in flight.

The communists learned a lot from the air war over Korea, as the constant evolution of their air tactics showed, and the Russians were not slow in embodying the technical lessons in their latest combat aircraft designs. They had developed their teamwork to a high degree, but—with the exception of a few veteran Soviet 'advisers'—they had proved consistently unable to get the best out of what was basically a very fine fighter aircraft. The communists were too regimented; they lacked the individuality that is necessary in the making of a good fighter pilot.

One thing they did learn, as did the Americans, was that most of the air fighting rules drawn up in combat during the second world war were still suited to the fast pace of jet warfare. Height—speed—manoeuvre—fire! The formulae worked out by Pokryskhin and the aces of many nations in the heat of battle 10 years earlier still held good, even in the jet age.

Chapter 13

The Years of Crisis

On April 4th 1949, the Foreign Ministers of 12 Western nations met in Washington to sign a charter that resulted in the formation of the most powerful defensive alliance in history: the North Atlantic Treaty Organization. The signing of the Atlantic Charter had two immediate effects; it broke the Soviet stranglehold on Berlin by convincing the Russians that the Western allies would fight rather than give in to their demands, and it led to a complete revision of the Soviet Union's own defensive system in Eastern Europe.

Between 1949 and 1951, the embryo armed forces of Poland, Rumania, Hungary and Czechoslovakia were rapidly expanded. Two years later they began to receive some of the latest Soviet military equipment, including MiG-15 fighters, and senior command posts—previously filled by Soviet personnel—were now taken over by carefully selected officers from the satellite countries themselves, all of whom had received thorough ideological training in the Soviet Union. Nevertheless, the Russians took no chances; there was no substantial reduction of their own military commitment in the satellite states, and Soviet advisers retained a firm grip on the satellite forces at all levels of command. Neither did they make any pretence of disguising the real function of the satellite forces in the event of a war with NATO; their task was to absorb the first shock of a possible invasion from the west. While Poles, Rumanians, Czechs and Hungarians sacrificed themselves, the Russians would have time to regroup their own forces for a counter-offensive against the NATO thrust, which would have blunted itself against the satellite defences. Also, the buffer states provided a convenient springboard for a possible Soviet offensive into the heart of Europe. In either event, the Russians had made sure that the first and most devastating battles of a war between East and West would not be fought on Russian soil; there would be no repetition of 1941.

In the early 1950s, one of the largest satellite air forces was that of Hungary, with a strength of 280 aircraft by the beginning of 1953. Three years later, the Hungarian fighter regiments had exchanged all their elderly Yak-9s for MiG-15s, and by the spring of 1956 there were some 240 MiGs in service with four fighter regiments, with plans under way to manufacture the type under licence. Some of the regiments had also begun to receive small numbers of the new MiG-17 fighter. In addition, there were four assault and attack bomber regiments equipped with Ilyushin Il-10s and Tupolev Tu-2s, and a few Hungarian pilots had converted to Il-28 jet bombers in preparation for the planned re-equipment of the bomber regiments with this type.

The Russians, however, showed no inclination to leave the air defence of Hungary to the Hungarians. There were two Soviet Air Force divisions in the country, equipped with MiG-17s and Il-28s, and they occupied seven major air bases. The Russians also had six squadrons of ground attack MiG-15s in Hungary—a total of 120 aircraft—for the support of ground forces. Nevertheless, the Hungarian Air Force personnel were regarded by the Russians as being among the most co-operative and politically conscious of any in the satellite countries. All were carefully screened, and for acceptance into the Air Force even their parents had to be Party members. Great attention was paid to political instruction during training, and if a trainee showed the slightest lack of enthusiasm for communist doctrines he was immediately dismissed. At a time when defections to the West by personnel of other satellite air forces were frequent, there was only one recorded instance of an attempted defection by Hungarian airmen; it happened in February 1956, when the crew of a Tu-2 bomber tried to fly to Austria. They were shot down in flames by Russian MiG-17s almost within sight of the frontier.

Then, suddenly, things began to go wrong with what the Russians looked upon as the well-ordered communist way of life in Hungary. In the summer of 1956, they began to sense a rebellious undercurrent, particularly among the youth of the country, but they were not certain about how to react to it. The situation became even more tense when, in a radio broadcast to the nation, the First Secretary of the Hungarian Communist Party told the people in harsh terms that there would be no reforms.

In the quiet autumn evening of October 23rd, the storm finally broke. In Budapest, workers on their way home found the city's transport at a standstill and the streets thronged with marchers. Students, carrying Hungarian flags, moved on the headquarters of the AVO, the Hungarian Secret Police. The AVO hurled tear gas, and then opened fire; the students seized weapons and began to shoot back. The Hungarian Revolution, one of the most heroic and most tragic acts of the twentieth century, had begun.

The revolution had started spontaneously, without leaders, and above all without any promise or indication of support from the Hungarian armed forces. For the first 48 hours, the loyalty of the Hungarian soldiers and airmen hung in the balance. Then the C-in-C of the Hungarian Army visited the Hungarian War Minister with a demand that the government should order the police and security services to stop firing on students and other demonstrators; but he was shot dead by security men. As soon as they heard the news, patriotic Hungarian officers and men quickly overpowered the dissenters in their ranks and turned their weapons over to the freedom fighters. By nightfall on October 26th, heavy fighting had broken out between Hungarian revolutionaries, including elements of the armed forces, and the Soviet forces stationed in the country.

On October 28th, the Hungarian Air Force intervened for the first time. The Hungarian personnel had already seized control of two air bases near Budapest, and three Soviet Mi-4 helicopters that tried to land assault troops were shot down in flames by anti-aircraft fire. Then Hungarian MiGs appeared over the capital, their red stars daubed out and replaced by hurriedly painted green, white and red bands, the national colours of Hungary. For half an hour they whistled across the sky, diving on Soviet artillery and tanks around Budapest and in the city's suburbs, attacking them with cannon fire. The MiGs reappeared over the capital the following day, and on October 30th it was the Hungarian Air Force that delivered the final ultimatum to the Russians, demanding the complete withdrawal of all Soviet troops and armour from Budapest by four o'clock in the morning of the 31st. The 2nd and 17th Guards Mechanized Divisions, which now found themselves trapped in the Budapest area and almost completely cut off by patriotic Hungarian forces, had little choice but to obey, and when dawn broke on October 31st the guns in Budapest were silent and the tanks had gone.

The Russians announced that they would negotiate the withdrawal of Soviet forces from Hungary with the newly formed independent government headed by Imre Nagy, released from prison by the Hungarian Army. Ostensibly to cover the planned withdrawal, eight Soviet divisions under the command of General P. I. Batov were sent into Hungary from the Carpathians while the negotiations got under way, and the Soviet Air Force units still in possession of Hungarian airfields were quietly strengthened.

Then, at dawn on Sunday, November 4th, the Russians struck. MiGs swept over the outskirts of Budapest, bombing and strafing, and then long files of tanks rumbled into the city, firing haphazardly as they went. Hungarian Army units were quickly surrounded and disarmed, their leaders rounded up and bundled off for interrogation. Russian fighters orbited the Hungarian Air Force bases, ready to shoot down any aircraft that attempted to take off. A few Hungarian flak batteries turned their guns on the heavy T-54s that poured on to the bases, but they were quickly overwhelmed. Within a week the revolution had been crushed.

With the Russians once again in complete occupation of the country, the Hungarian armed forces ceased to exist. The effective strength of the army was reduced to one regiment —the only one out of 11 Hungarian divisions which had given active support to the Russians—and the air force was temporarily disbanded. It was later reconstituted, but the Russians made certain that it could never again present a threat to their security. Even today, its combat strength stands at only

150 aircraft, compared with East Germany's 400, Poland's 950 and Czechoslovakia's 750, and the size of the Soviet land forces in Hungary remains double what it was before October 1956.

During the summer of 1955, while deliveries of modern Russian combat aircraft continued to the seven countries which at that time formed the Soviet bloc (Poland, Hungary, Czechoslovakia, Rumania, Bulgaria, North Korea and Communist China), determined efforts were being made to extend sales to countries which did not come directly within the sphere of Soviet influence. Attempts to persuade Yugoslavia to buy Russian aircraft had failed, in spite of considerable Soviet pressure; the Yugoslav Air Force continued to operate American types, received under the terms of the Mutual Assistance Pact.

The eagerly awaited breakthrough came on September 27th 1955, when Egypt and Czechoslovakia concluded a three-year trade pact, under the terms of which the Czechs undertook to supply the Egyptians with substantial quantities of MiG-15s, MiG-17s and Il-28s, as well as tanks, artillery and other weapons, to the total value of £80 million. The reaction of the western nations to this agreement—which upset the whole balance of power in the super-tense Middle East—was not long in coming. The United States, Britain and the International Bank refused to finance the building of the Aswan High Dam, and in July 1956 President Nasser hit back by nationalizing the Suez Canal Company.

The first batch of MiGs and Ilyushins was delivered by the end of 1955, the aircraft being assembled by Egyptian technicians who had undergone a three-month training course in Czechoslovakia. On January 15th 1956, 12 MiG-15s—flown by Czech pilots—made a 'prestige' flight over Cairo. While the first Egyptian MiG squadron was being formed at Almaza, near Cairo, Czech and Soviet instructors were helping Egyptian pilots to convert to the new jets from their old de Havilland Vampires at Kabrit air base, in the Canal Zone. It was not an easy task; the Egyptians showed complete ineptitude in handling the MiGs. They were not only poor pilots; they also lacked the necessary intelligence to master their advanced aircraft adequately, and the accident rate was high.

At the end of October 1956, when the British and French governments decided on joint intervention to protect their interests in the Canal Zone, most of the 60 MiGs that were by this time operational with the Egyptian Air Force were still being flown by Czech and Russian pilots. About half the total force was held in storage at Abu Sueir until sufficient numbers of Egyptian pilots became available to form new squadrons, but the MiGs were flown frequently and checked out by Central European pilots to keep them in good condition. The remaining MiGs were divided between Almaza and Kabrit. Twenty Ilyushin 28s were also based on Kabrit, and there were 10 more at Cairo West. Like the MiGs, the great majority of the Il-28s were in storage, waiting for Egyptian crews to be formed. A further 20 Il-28s in Egypt at this time were destined for the Syrian Air Force, which had also begun to receive Russian aircraft within the framework of Syria's Mutual Defence Pact with Egypt.

The British and French plans to invade Suez were influenced from the start by the belief that the invasion would be opposed by MiGs and Ilyushins flown by Russian or Czech pilots. It was for this reason that although the Egyptians rejected the Anglo-French ultimatum (which called for the Egyptian and Israeli governments to stop all warlike acts, to withdraw 10 miles either side of the Suez Canal and to allow British and French forces temporarily to occupy key positions in the Canal Zone) in the early hours of October 31st, the first attacks on Egyptian airfields by RAF bombers were not made until the following night.

When the attacks did take place, the damage inflicted was not significant—for the simple reason that the MiGs and Il-28s had gone. Every serviceable aircraft—and this by no means accounted for the total force—was hastily flown out of the danger area by the Russian and Czech crews. From Kabrit, 20 MiGs and 20 Il-28s destined for the Syrian Air Force flew to Riyadh, in Saudi Arabia, accompanied by 10

Egyptian MiG-15s and followed up by 10 Ilyushin 14 twin-engined transports; after refuelling, they went on to Syrian bases. Twenty Egyptian Il-28s were evacuated south to Luxor, on the Red Sea coast, but they were unlucky; they had been there less than 48 hours when a squadron of French Air Force Mystere IVA jets, based on an Israeli airfield, swept over the Gulf of Suez and pulverized them with rocket and cannon-fire. Eight more Il-28s were destroyed and six damaged by British carrier-borne aircraft in the course of attacks on other Egyptian airfields, resulting in the total loss of Nasser's entire jet bomber force.

The Egyptian Air Force did appear to oppose the Israeli advance through Sinai, but the aircraft involved were mainly Vampires and Meteors. The few MiGs that entered combat did not succeed in establishing air superiority over the Israelis, who shot down two MiG-15s and a MiG-17. The MiGs never appeared to challenge the Allied bombers over Egypt, although the two squadrons at Almaza and Inchass remained virtually intact until the afternoon of November 1st, when they were knocked out by strike aircraft. The reason, perhaps, was that every available Russian and Czech pilot was engaged in ferrying combat aircraft to safety, and the Egyptian pilots who were qualified to fly the MiGs had no experience in combat techniques. Apart from that, the initial raids took place under cover of darkness, and, as Western instructors who had served in Egypt before the arrival of the Czechs and Russians had observed on many occasions, the Egyptians had an instinctive and totally irrational fear of night flying. If the Egyptians had been of a different calibre, the RAF night bombers might have suffered considerable losses, for there was a Russian-manned GCI (Ground Controlled Interception) station north-west of Deversoir.

As it was, only one RAF aircraft was destroyed in air combat during the entire operation, and that was a Canberra of No. 13 Squadron which was shot down by a MiG-15 while on a photo-reconnaissance mission over Syria, gathering evidence of the build-up of MiGs and Il-28s on Syrian airfields. It is almost certain that the MiG was flown by a Russian or Czech pilot, for at the time of the Suez operation no Syrians had been fully trained to fly the Russian fighter. The MiG must also have been an evacuated Egyptian aircraft, for all the jet fighters earmarked for delivery to Syria had in fact been based on the Egyptian airfields of Almaza and Abu Sueir while their pilots underwent conversion, and only four—all MiG-15UTI two-seat trainers—escaped the Anglo-French air strikes.

As soon as the Anglo-French invasion force withdrew from Suez, Egypt and Syria began negotiations with the communist bloc with a view to making good the losses suffered during the week of Allied air strikes. During the first week of March 1957, 15 crated MiG-17s and 10 Il-28s were unloaded from Rumanian freighters at Alexandria and assembled at Almaza. Fifty MiGs had been supplied by the beginning of April, and on July 23rd—when a big flypast was held over Cairo—the total number of Russian aircraft on the Egyptian Air Force inventory included 100 MiG-17s and 40 Il-28s: almost double what it had been before November 1956. Twelve MiG-17s, the first of a batch of 60, were also delivered to the Syrian Air Force early in 1957, and both Syrian and Egyptian pilots and technicians were now being trained in Czechoslovakia and Poland. As well as the hundreds of Soviet and Czech personnel in Egypt, there was also an 'advisory group' of 60 Soviet Air Force officers in Syria, including one general and 10 top flying instructors.

With the amalgamation of Egypt and Syria into the United Arab Republic on February 1st 1958, the structure of the air forces of both countries was substantially revised and organized more on Soviet lines. Great efforts were made to improve the standard of training, and by the middle of 1958 instructors from every Soviet satellite country, as well as from the USSR itself, were serving in Egypt and Syria. This enormous influx of European instructors and advisers had the desired effect: both the flying and the technical standards of the UAR Air Forces improved tremendously. It was a very favourable reflection on both the capability of the Soviet bloc pilots and their system of training. Egypt, in fact, became a training centre for the pilots of several nations that eventually purchased Soviet aircraft, including Indonesia, Cuba, Iraq and Afghanistan—the last being the Soviet Union's oldest customer, having formed its little air force with Russian types in 1924.

By the mid 1960s, Soviet help had turned the Egyptian Air Force into the best equipped and largest on the African continent. It possessed 500 aircraft, including 60 Tupolev Tu-16 twin-jet medium bombers, 80 MiG-17s, 80 MiG-19s—Russia's first supersonic jet fighter—and 50 MiG-21 supersonic interceptors, capable of twice the speed of sound. There were also a number of MiG-15s and Il-28s for tactical support duties, although most of the older Russian types had now been phased out.

In the decade since Suez, the Russians had boosted Nasser to a position of strength from which, as their ally, he could assume leadership over the Arab nations. With the Egyptian armed forces serving as a model, they had turned Egypt into an impressive 'arms agency', the centre of a network of Soviet influence and power in a vital strategic area. But the Russians made one big mistake; they believed that because Nasser was dependent on them for his armed might, they could firmly control his policies. They were wrong. When Nasser's troops and armour concentrated in the Sinai Desert to fulfil the Arab dream of the destruction of Israel, there was nothing the Russians could do to turn him from his intention. And even Egypt's ultra-modern air defence system, with its supersonic interceptors and its Soviet SAM-2 ground-to-air missiles, could not prevent the holocaust that engulfed the Egyptian forces when an armada of Israeli jets swept low over the Suez Canal on that morning of June 5th 1967.

Chapter 14

Battle in the Stratosphere

On the morning of September 2nd 1958, a Lockheed C-130 Hercules transport of the United States Air Force took off from the NATO air base at Adana, in southern Turkey, and set course north-eastwards. Ninety minutes later the aircraft was over Trabzon, on the southern shores of the Black Sea, and the pilot, Captain Paul E. Duncan, brought it round in a wide turn on to the second leg of its flight, skirting the borders of Soviet Armenia and heading for Lake Van, 200 miles to the south.

The C-130 was attached to the 7406th Support Squadron and was normally based at Rhein-Main Air Base in West Germany, but it was no ordinary transport. It was packed with the latest electronic equipment and carried a crew of 17, 13 of them radio and radar specialists. On this September day in 1958, their mission was to intercept and identify signals from the Soviet radar network to the north of the Black Sea and in Armenia and Georgia; signals that would tell them not only what type of radar was being used, but also reveal its range.

The Hercules never reached Lake Van, and an extensive search for it over western Turkey revealed nothing. There could be only one possible conclusion: the aircraft had come down in Soviet territory. Then, on September 13th, the American chargé d'affaires in Moscow delivered a note to the Soviet Foreign Minister, claiming that the USAF had proof that the Hercules had been intercepted and shot down by Soviet fighters several miles inside the Soviet border. Eyewitnesses on the Turkish side of the frontier had seen the aircraft pass overhead; a few minutes later they had heard an explosion and observed a column of smoke on the horizon. At the same time, a US radio station engaged in monitoring the Soviet Air Force frequencies had made a tape-recording of the following R/T conversation between four Russian pilots:

'I see the target, to the right!'

'I see the target.'
'Roger.'
'The target is a big one.'
'Attack by four-fourths.'
'Roger.'
'The target is a four-engined transport.'
'Target speed is three zero zero. I am going along with it. It is turning towards the "fence".'
'The target is burning.'
'There's a hit.'
'The target is burning, 582.'
'281, are you attacking?'
'Yes, yes, I . . .'
'The target is burning . . . the tail assembly is falling off the target. 82, can you see me? I am in front of the target.'
'Look! Look at him, he will not get away. He is already falling.'
'Yes, he is falling. I will finish him off, boys. I will finish him off on this run.'
'The target has lost control. It is going down.'
'The target has turned over. . . . Aha, you see, it is falling!'
'All right . . . form up, head for home.'
'The target started burning after my third pass. . . .'

A month after the incident, the official Soviet Air Force newspaper *Sovietskaya Aviatsiya* published an article purporting to describe an attack by four MiG-17 fighters on an aerial target during the course of an 'air exercise'. The call-signs of two of the fighters in the article were the same as those picked up by the American listening-post; courses, altitudes and speeds were all identical. In the article, the Russian pilots responsible for destroying the 'aerial target' were named as senior lieutenants Gavrilov, Lopatkov, Ivanov and Kucherayev.

On September 24th, meanwhile, the Russians handed over the bodies of six of the C-130's crew after admitting that the aircraft had crashed 30 miles north-west of Yerevan in Soviet Armenia. They claimed that the Hercules had deliberately violated Soviet air space, and refused to allow the Americans to examine the wreckage. The Americans, in turn, claimed that the C-130 had been lured over the border by a false radio homing beam and then deliberately destroyed.

Whatever the real truth behind the events that led up to the destruction of the ill-fated Hercules by Soviet fighters, the aircraft had become one more victim of a form of secret warfare between the air forces of East and West. It was a war that had begun almost as soon as the echoes of the Second World War had died away, and it is still being waged today. Between 1945 and the end of 1960, it cost the lives of 69 American airmen and caused the loss of 15 US aircraft.

Electronic Countermeasures—the ability to confuse and disrupt an enemy's radar defences, allowing attacking aircraft to slip through—was first used extensively by the British and Germans during the Second World War. On June 5th 1944, for example, two squadrons of RAF Lancasters flew backwards and forwards over the Channel, dropping bundles of 'window'—strips of tinfoil cut exactly to the wavelength of the German radar—and succeeded in making the enemy believe that the D-Day invasion was taking place miles from the actual landing-zones. Two years earlier, in February 1942, the Germans had jammed British radar stations along the south coast, making possible the escape of the German battle-cruisers *Scharnhorst*, *Gneisenau* and *Prinz Eugen* from the French port of Brest.

The probing of the other side's radar defences by both the Russians and Americans subsequently became a vital aspect of the cold war, with the Americans initially using RB-29s and RB-50s and the Russians using the Tu-4. Unlike the Americans, the Russians showed no scruples in attacking reconnaissance aircraft well outside their own territory, but as there were never any survivors from American reconnaissance aircraft that went missing during flights around the fringes of the Soviet Union, it was difficult for the US Government to lodge a formal protest to the effect that the aircraft had been destroyed by Soviet fighters in international airspace. The first concrete evidence that this is what had been happening came on July 29th 1953, when an RB-50 operating out of

Yokota Air Force Base in Japan was attacked by Soviet MiG-15s at 06.15 hours while cruising at 21,000 feet 40 miles from the Russian coast over the Sea of Japan—28 miles outside the territorial limit. The RB-50's gunners opened fire in return, but with one wing torn off by a hail of 23-mm shells the big bomber went into a slow spin towards the sea three miles below, breaking up as it fell. One crew member escaped by parachute and was picked up by an American destroyer after drifting in his liferaft for several hours.

The growing efficiency of the Soviet air defence system, coupled with the quick-reaction time of the MiG-15 and MiG-17 interceptors, made 'ferret' missions by piston-engined US reconnaissance aircraft prohibitively dangerous, and the reconnaissance units were progressively re-equipped with RB-45 Tornados and RB-57s—the American licence-built version of the highly successful British Canberra—during the mid 1950s. For long-range reconnaissance at high altitude there was the RB-47, the reconnaissance version of the six-jet Stratojet which by that time had re-equipped the bulk of the Strategic Air Command Wings. On the Russian side, after the phasing out of the Tu-4, electronic reconnaissance was undertaken by specially adapted versions of the Ilyushin 28 and the Tupolev Tu-14, the latter a twin-jet bomber in service with the Soviet Naval Air Arm, and subsequently by reconnaissance versions of the Myasishchev Mya-4, Tu-16 and Tu-20 long-range strategic bombers.

In the spring of 1956, a USAF unit known as the 1st Provisional Weather Squadron, based at Watertown Strip in Nevada, received the first examples of a radical new aircraft that was to change the whole concept of air reconnaissance: the Lockheed U-2. Virtually a powered glider, with a wingspan of 80 feet and fitted with a modified version of the well-tried J-57 jet engine, the U-2 was the answer to an urgent USAF requirement for an aircraft capable of flying deep inside Soviet territory at an altitude that would make it immune from interception by the Russian fighters then in service.

The initial production batch of 10 U-2s was in fact used

for high-altitude weather reconnaissance and radioactive sampling in the upper atmosphere, but subsequent aircraft were assigned to the 4028th and 4080th Strategic Reconnaissance Squadrons of Strategic Air Command. These squadrons were based on Laughlin AFB in Texas and Ramey AFB in Puerto Rico, but detachments were sent to Lakenheath in Britain, Wiesbaden in Germany and Incirlik in Turkey, and during the autumn of 1956 a series of probing flights was carried out over the fringes of Soviet territory from these bases. When these preliminary flights ended without incident, the U-2 squadrons then began to undertake deep penetration missions into the heart of the Soviet Union, photographing air bases, missile sites under construction, factories, industrial complexes, radar sites and other objectives of interest to Strategic Air Command's target planners.

Throughout 1957, the U-2s cruised singly over the Soviet Union at altitudes of 80,000 feet and sometimes more, apparently undetected by the Soviet defences. By 1958, however, the Russians had woken up to what was going on, and fighters were sent up to intercept the elusive American aircraft. U-2 pilots began to report attempted interceptions by MiG-19s and the latest MiG-21s, but the Soviet fighters simply could not reach the altitude at which the U-2s operated. They would zoom-climb up to 70,000 feet, fire their cannon at the top of their trajectory, and then stall in the thin air and fall away in a spin. Yet, because of the severe loss of prestige that would have resulted from an open admission that American aircraft were roving over the Soviet Union at will, the Russians never made any form of protest; the first indication that they knew exactly what was happening came by way of an article in *Sovietskaya Aviatsiya*, which admitted that Russian intelligence officers were seriously worried about the threat to Soviet security presented by the American aircraft.

In 1959 and the early months of 1960, the black-painted U-2s turned their attention to the IRBM and ICBM bases that were springing up all over the Soviet Union. In April 1960, the Central Intelligence Agency received information that the Russians had completed a very advanced missile site near Sverdlovsk, and a U-2 of the special CIA 10-10 Squadron was detailed to photograph it, along with the rocket site at Tyura Tam and the air and naval bases at Archangel and Murmansk. In the early hours of May 1st, with Captain Gary Powers at the controls, the U-2 took off from Peshawar in Pakistan on the first leg of a 3,000-mile flight across the breadth of the Soviet Union to the NATO air base at Bodo, in northern Norway.

What happened on that flight is history. Tracked all the way from the Pakistan border by Soviet radar, the U-2 was allowed to penetrate 2,000 miles inside the Soviet Union, and was then shot down by an anti-aircraft missile battery near Sverdlovsk. Powers was unlucky; this battery was among the relatively few that had recently re-equipped with an improved version of the standard SA-2 surface-to-air missile, and this weapon gave the Soviet defences a high 'kill' probability at altitudes of up to 70,000 feet. Soviet missile technology had at last caught up with Lockheed's 'Black Lady'. Two months after the U-2 incident, an RB-47E reconnaissance aircraft was shot down over the Barents Sea—well outside Soviet air space—by a missile fired from a MiG-19. Two crew members survived and were later repatriated.

Several weeks before Powers and the U-2 burst into the world headlines, the prototype of the aircraft that was Russia's answer to the U-2 made its first flight. The Russians had not attempted to design an aircraft specifically for high-altitude reconnaissance from the outset; instead, they had taken the fuselage of one of the standard Soviet Air Force all-weather fighters, the Yakovlev Yak-25, and fitted it with an extended-span high-aspect ratio wing. In this way a good performance at high altitude was made possible without a great deal of redesign; the Americans had followed the same technique a few years earlier, when they turned the B-57 into a high-altitude reconnaissance aircraft by extending its wingspan.

The Russian aircraft, known as Mandrake under the NATO code-name system, became operational with several Soviet medium-range reconnaissance squadrons in April 1963. A single-seater with a wingspan of 70 feet, it is powered by two modified Klimov VK-9 engines and has an operational ceiling of 70,000 feet. Aircraft of this type have been known to make short penetration flights at high altitude into Greek and Turkish air space and over the eastern Mediterranean, and it is believed that they are also used to keep the Chinese nuclear production centres and testing grounds in the Sinkiang Desert under surveillance.

The use of flight refuelling enabled the Soviet Air Force to extend its long-range strategic reconnaissance considerably during the early 1960s, and since then Tu-16s and Tu-20s have been sighted ranging far afield over the Atlantic and Pacific. Soviet 'shadowers' have appeared in the area whenever a NATO sea exercise has been held in recent years, and on one occasion a Tu-16 crashed into the sea while making a low flight over NATO warships in the North Atlantic. Tu-16s and Tu-20s are intercepted frequently by US fighters on the fringes of American air space around Alaska, and Lightning fighters of the Royal Air Force rendezvous from time to time with Myasischev Mya-4s over the North Sea and escort them 'off the premises'. The Mya-4s—known by the NATO code-name of Bison and as 'Molyot' in Russian service—are Naval Air Arm aircraft and are based on the Murmansk Peninsula. The majority of these and other Soviet long-range reconnaissance aircraft bear no unit markings or serial numbers, but simply carry a two-figure individual aircraft code in addition to the red star insignia.

In the summer of 1962, the Russians believed that they had found a chink in the electronic armour of the United States when they began to ship IRBMs, Ilyushin 28 bombers and surface-to-air missiles to Cuba, right on America's doorstep. The Il-28s were intended to be flown by Cuban Air Force personnel, but the SA-2 anti-aircraft missile and IRBM sites were to be manned by Russians. Although the CIA were aware that modern Soviet weapons were arriving in Cuba, they did not know that they included strategic missiles until a U-2 aircraft revealed the secret on October 14th. Early reconnaissance flights, on August 29th and September 5th, had revealed nothing unusual except for a few vague patterns on the ground near Guanajay. They looked like earthworks, but it was impossible to identify them positively. Another reconnaissance flight was proposed on October 4th and approved on the 9th; the aircraft was all ready to go the next day, but poor weather conditions prevented the sortie. The mission was finally accomplished, without incident, on Sunday October 14th. As soon as the U-2 landed its cameras were rushed to a special laboratory, and on Monday morning the films were taken to an intelligence centre where interpreters set about examining each photograph. This time the photographs taken over San Cristobal, near the western tip of Cuba, clearly showed the presence of four Soviet-made ballistic missiles.

The story of the Cuban crisis is well known. What is not so well known is that on Saturday, October 27th, when the crisis was at its height, two separate incidents occurred thousands of miles apart, and each one of them might have brought about an exchange of nuclear blows between the United States and the Soviet Union.

Early that morning, a Lockheed U-2 was on a routine high-altitude reconnaissance mission over Cuba when it was shot down by an SA-2 missile. The missile was fired by a Russian crew. A few hours later a second U-2, genuinely engaged in a routine scientific flight to measure radiation in the upper atmosphere between Alaska and the North Pole, inadvertently strayed into Soviet air space over Russia's north-eastern tip. There was no question of this being a spy flight: the pilot had simply made a navigational error. But a few miles farther south was the Red Army's important missile complex at Anadyr, and to the radar controllers of the IA-PVO—the Soviet Air Defence Force—the U-2's flight looked very much like a last-minute reconnaissance before an imminent nuclear strike.

Within minutes, MiG-21s were climbing towards the freezing reaches of the stratosphere where, 14 miles above the earth, the U-2 spun its thread-like contrail. Its pilot heard the R/T chatter on the Russian frequency, realized his mistake and swung the aircraft round in a 45-degree turn over the coast, breaking radio silence to send out a frantic call for help. A US controller in Alaska vectored a flight of F-104 Starfighters to the pilot's assistance, with orders to infringe Soviet air space if necessary. They rendezvoused with the U-2 over the Bering Strait and escorted it safely back to Alaska. There was no sign of the Russian fighters; they had failed to intercept.

As a result of the U-2's intrusion, the Soviet air and rocket forces were brought up to a red alert, and there was a temporary worsening of the Cuban situation. It had been the closest the USAF and the Soviet Air Force had come to an all-out clash since the Korean War; fortunately for the world, it never happened.

Chapter 15

Invasion 1968

On February 28th 1968, the Commander-in-Chief of the Warsaw Pact forces—57-year old Marshal Ivan Ignatievitch Yakubovsky—arrived in Czechoslovakia with an entourage of 13 high-ranking Soviet officers. Ostensibly, the purpose of the visit was to liaise with Czech military commanders in the preparations for the series of vast military manoeuvres that was to take place around the borders of Czechoslovakia. The real reason was to ferret out the state of readiness of the Czech armed forces, to establish whether they would remain loyal to the Warsaw Pact, and to make an up-to-date assessment of their weak points on the assumption that an armed conflict might develop out of Czechoslovakia's growing 'liberal' attitude.

During the third week in March, NATO Intelligence began to assemble information on the large-scale movements of troops and armour that had begun to take place in the German Democratic Republic. Both of East Germany's armoured and two of her four mechanized infantry divisions appeared to be involved. Agents reported that the 11th Mechanized Infantry Division and the 7th Armoured Division had left their bases in Erfurt and Dresden and were moving south along roads that were congested with all types of military traffic. In East Germany, the Russians had 10 armoured divisions and a similar number of mechanized infantry divisions; about half this total strength was on the move. Two Soviet armoured divisions were reported to have left East German territory and to have crossed over the border into Poland, presumably to reinforce the solitary Russian armoured division that was there already.

On May 10th, an exercise involving two tank armies—one Russian and one Polish, a total of 2,800 tanks of all types and some 84,000 men—began in southern Poland. Primarily, it was designed to test mobility and the effectiveness of co-operation between large Russian and Polish formations.

About 150 Russian and Polish combat aircraft—mainly ground-attack types such as the Yakovlev Yak-28 and the Sukhoi Su-7B—were also involved in this exercise, together with an unspecified number of large assault helicopters. The manoeuvres ended on May 22nd.

On June 10th, the manoeuvres entered a second phase with an exercise on East German territory. Once again co-operation was the keyword; five Soviet armoured divisions operated in concert with two East German mechanized infantry divisions, and two East German MiG-21 regiments flew top cover for Soviet Yak-28s in a simulated ground attack exercise. This exercise lasted a week, ending on June 17th.

Three days later, it was learned that Warsaw Pact C-in-C Yakubovsky had set up a temporary headquarters in Prague, from where the third phase of the manoeuvres was to be controlled. This third exercise, known as 'Bohemian Forest', began on June 20th. Involving some 40,000 men, its purpose —based on the results of the two previous exercises—was to co-ordinate the mobility of the Warsaw Pact land and air forces in Poland, East Germany and Czechoslovakia. The exercise ended on June 30th and all foreign units departed from Czech territory without any fuss. Soon afterwards, however, the West German Intelligence Service—the BND— reported that the exercise had been a brilliant rehearsal for a planned invasion of Czechoslovakia; significantly, most of the Soviet, Polish and East German units that had taken part in 'Bohemian Forest' stayed just across the border in Poland and the GDR.

Then came a new and alarming development. In the early hours of July 6th, a line of sleek warships slipped quietly and unobtrusively through the narrow straits that separate Denmark from Sweden. A few hours later, a Norwegian maritime patrol aircraft sighted them leaving the Skagerrak and heading north-westwards into the Atlantic. The vessels—a unit of the Soviet Baltic Fleet—included four guided missile cruisers of the Krupny class, armed with advanced surface-to-surface cruise missiles with an estimated range of between 50 and 100 miles. The cruisers were escorted by a screen of

Kotlin and Kresta class destroyers, armed with surface-to-air missile systems.

Shackleton aircraft of Royal Air Force Coastal Command, operating out of Kinloss in Scotland and Ballykelly in Northern Ireland, kept a discreet watch on the Soviet warships as they headed out into the North Atlantic. On July 8th, they rendez-voused with units of the Soviet Arctic Fleet off Iceland. A week later, the strong Soviet naval force was in position within striking distance of the transatlantic shipping routes, with Tu-16 and Tu-20 maritime reconnaissance aircraft maintaining standing patrols overhead.

Meanwhile, on July 11th, other units of the Soviet, Polish and East German navies had begun a large-scale fleet manoeuvre (Exercise North) in the Baltic. The exercise, which was under the command of the Soviet Navy C-in-C Admiral Gorshkov, involved the landing of troops and armour on an 'enemy-held coast'. Soviet assault helicopters of all types took part, as did formations of the Soviet Naval Air Arm's latest combat aircraft: the supersonic Tupolev Tu-22 medium bomber. It ended on July 19th, and five days later it was the Soviet Air Force's turn with a massive air exercise known as 'Skyshield'. This covered a triangular area between the Baltic, Moscow and the Black Sea and was under the direction of air defence chief Marshal Batitsky. The whole of the Soviet air defences, including early warning systems on a line between Kaliningrad in the north and Odessa in the south were to remain on full alert for over a month, the state of readiness being eventually downgraded only on August 25th.

Three principal commands of the Soviet Air Force were involved in this exercise: the IA-PVO, Russia's fighter force, the DA (Dalnaya Aviatsiya, known as SUSAC by the Americans and the equivalent of their own Strategic Air Command) and the Frontal Aviation (Frontovaia Aviatsiya). By July 31st, an estimated force of 200 MiG-19 and MiG-21 interceptors, together with about 50 Su-7B ground attack jets, had been dispersed on the forward military airfields of Legnica, Wroclaw, Opole, Katowice and Krakow in southern

Poland. Transport aircraft had flown in full supporting equipment and the Russian combat units showed no signs of leaving in the near future. Three of Poland's nine fighter regiments (MiG-17s and MiG-21s) and one fighter/ground attack regiment (MiG-17s and Su-7s) were also placed on readiness, involving about 160 first-line Polish combat aircraft.

On July 28th, while the vapour trails of Exercise Skyshield still criss-crossed the sky over the cornfields of the Ukraine, the Warsaw Pact manoeuvres entered what appeared to be their final phase with Exercise Niemen—a gigantic support operation in which the aim was to establish how rapidly the forces in the 'front line' on the frontiers of NATO could be reinforced and supplied. The logistics problem was enormous; later, NATO experts assessed that if 'Niemen' had really been the type of operation the Russians would mount to support nearly a quarter of a million men, then it had turned out a sorry failure. To carry out the exercise, the Russians had to call out thousands of reservists; they even requisitioned large numbers of civilian lorries from all over the Ukraine—right in the middle of the harvest. It is not known how much Soviet agriculture in the Ukraine suffered as a result of the ill-timed demands made on it by 'Niemen', but the conclusions drawn by NATO Intelligence were that the Russians would be unable to launch a successful conventional attack on the West unless their supply organization was completely reorganized and the logistics aspect planned in minute detail months in advance.

Forty-eight hours after the start of Exercise Niemen, the American Military Intelligence Service requested the United States Defense Department to authorize the USAF to undertake high-level reconnaissance missions along the East German and Czech frontiers. These missions were to be flown principally by a flight of Lockheed SR-71 aircraft of Strategic Air Command's 4200th Strategic Reconnaissance Wing, on detachment in West Germany. The SR-71 was the powerful, ultra-secret successor to the famous U-2; able to operate at an altitude of between 70,000 and 90,000 feet and with a maximum speed of more than three times the speed of sound, it could fly operational missions on the fringes of hostile territory with impunity. At a height of 80,000 feet, the horizon stretches away for more than 300 miles—which meant that while flying over the West German border, the SR-71's advanced electronic reconnaissance equipment could pick up radar signals originating deep inside Poland and Czechoslovakia. In addition, the aircraft could obtain high-resolution photographic coverage of a large area of East Germany and the western part of Czechoslovakia.

By the end of July, the SR-71s' reconnaissance sorties had confirmed reports from the West German BND (the Intelligence Service) that massive concentrations of Warsaw Pact troops, armour and aircraft were in position along the frontier of Czechoslovakia. On July 30th, the BND reported to the German Government that the strategic aim of the Warsaw Pact manoeuvres was to prepare for a thrust into Czechoslovakia that would effectively cut the country in half. That same day, the Bundeswehr High Command apprised its senior officers, down to brigade level, of the situation and its dangers.

Meanwhile, as last-minute talks between the Czech and Soviet Governments continued, the Russians made no attempt to ease the tension by halting, even temporarily, the massive Warsaw Pact manoeuvres. On the day the talks began, a vast convoy of Soviet and East German troops was moving southwards towards the Czech border along the autobahn leading from Dresden; while columns of Soviet armour were converging on an assembly point south of Warsaw. At the same time, units of the Bulgarian Army—having disembarked from transport ships at the Black Sea port of Odessa—were making their way through Soviet territory towards Hungary, skirting the frontier of 'unsympathetic' Rumania. A week later, Bulgarian and Hungarian forces were scheduled to begin a series of joint exercises involving 67,000 men and 2,000 tanks.

On Monday, August 5th, came the sudden and unexpected resignation of the Russian Chief of Staff of the Warsaw Pact forces, General Kazakov. Kazakov was replaced by a tougher and more inflexible commander, General Shtemenko, who had been Deputy Defence Minister and Chief of the Soviet General Staff under Stalin. This was regarded as a clear indication that the Warsaw Pact leaders had committed themselves to an invasion of Czechoslovakia if the talks broke down.

In spite of the months of manoeuvres, in spite of the fact that plans for the subjugation of Czechoslovakia had existed for a considerable time, the Warsaw Pact forces were far from ready for such an undertaking. No one knew this better than Marshal Ivan Yakubovsky, the C-in-C, as he sent out the necessary orders from the headquarters of Army Group A in Legnica, Poland, in the early hours of Tuesday August 20th. The success of the whole operation depended on three principal factors: lack of Czech resistance, the speed with which the land forces could capture their objectives, and a rapid follow-up by Soviet political units. Yakubovsky's supply organization was chaotic after the manoeuvres of July and August, and he knew that in the likely event of the Czechs refusing to co-operate, supplies could be kept flowing to the occupation forces for only three or four days at the very outside.

The invasion plan itself was simple enough. The Warsaw Pact forces, under the command of General Pavlovsky—the former C-in-C of the Soviet Far Eastern Military Area—would advance across the Czech border towards 10 major objectives. H-Hour was fixed for 23.00 on August 20th. Everything depended on good timing; the plan called for the capture of major military and civil airfields by airborne troops at the same time as the land forces reached their first objectives. The order of battle was as follows:

To the north, in Poland, Army Group A, with its HQ at Legnica. Strength: three Soviet armoured divisions, one Soviet mechanized infantry division and one Soviet airborne division; one Polish mechanized infantry division, one Polish airborne division and one Polish Air Force division, whose MiG-21s and Antonov An-12s would provide fighter cover and follow-up logistics support. These land forces totalled some 61,000 men and 1,600 tanks.

To the north-west, in East Germany, Army Group B, with its HQ in Leipzig. Strength: three Soviet armoured divisions and one East German mechanized infantry division, with no supporting artillery, but with air cover provided by one East German MiG-19 regiment and one Soviet Air Force Yak-28 regiment. In all, 37,000 men and 1,400 tanks.

To the south, in Hungary, Army Group C, with its HQ at Györ. This Army Group, which had the task of advancing northwards across a 240-mile front into Slovakia, was split up into four separate units. The first, on the left flank, consisted of two Soviet armoured divisions backed up by supply units; on its right stood one Hungarian mechanized infantry division, backed up by two Soviet armoured regiments from the 3rd Soviet Armoured Division and two Russian artillery regiments; the third unit, to the east of Budapest, consisted of one Soviet armoured regiment, one Bulgarian mechanized infantry regiment and four Soviet rocket batteries; and finally, on the right flank, came two Soviet pioneer battalions, an armoured reconnaissance battalion from the 3rd Soviet Armoured Division, one Bulgarian armoured regiment and four Bulgarian mechanized infantry companies accompanied by maintenance units. The total strength of Army Group C was in the order of 40,000 men and 1,500 tanks.

On the afternoon of August 20th, therefore, an overwhelming force of nearly 140,000 men and 4,500 tanks stood poised to fall on Czechoslovakia. Behind them, on five airfields in Poland, 250 huge Antonov An-12 transports and 100 smaller An-24s were lined up in readiness for their part in the invasion. Top cover would be provided, if necessary, by a mixed Soviet and Polish force of 200 MiG-19s, MiG-21s and Su-7s, and about 150 helicopters and small aircraft were being held in reserve until the airborne forces captured their objectives. The indications were that the Czech Army would not resist, but just in case there was some opposition the Russians and their allies laboured throughout Tuesday afternoon to paint white identification crosses on the turrets of their tanks. At night, or from the air and at long range, there was no other way of distinguishing between Czech and Soviet T-54s and T-55s.

As dusk fell on the evening of August 20th, thousands of Russian, East German, Polish, Hungarian and Bulgarian troops crouched beside the tanks and trucks that were drawn up in the forests around Czechoslovakia's borders and ate their evening meal. For many of them, it was to be the last proper meal they would eat for days. Most of the soldiers—mere boys of 19 and 20—were apprehensive. Propaganda had done its work well; they had been told that NATO forces were massing inside West Germany, on the Czecho-slovak border, and that the Czechs were calling in their allies to help defend their homeland. It could mean only one thing: war was imminent.

Slowly the minutes ticked away towards H-Hour. At 22.45, the tank crews climbed into their steel juggernauts; five minutes later, 5,000 powerful diesel engines burst into thunderous life and the earth trembled under grinding, clattering tracks as the first units began to move forward.

At 21.52, an hour before the land offensive got under way, the control tower staff at Ruzyne, Prague's international airport, were thankfully coming to the end of a routine but tiring day. Away to the east of the field, landing lights flared brightly in the darkness; an aircraft was on the approach to Runway 25. It was a twin-engined Antonov An-24 turboprop transport belonging to Aeroflot, the Soviet airline, on an unscheduled flight from Moscow. Engines whining shrilly, the Antonov slid over the threshold and touched down smoothly. It came to a stop briefly while the pilot obtained taxi instructions, then turned off the runway and taxied towards the concrete pan on the eastern side of the airport buildings. A handful of passengers disembarked and made their way into the terminal.

Meanwhile, in the tower, the duty controllers were stretch-ing their tired limbs. They could afford to relax a little now; the next scheduled aircraft movement was not until 23.10, when a Polish Airlines Tupolev 104 jet airliner was due to depart for Teheran. After that they could go off duty; the next watch was due to take over at 03.00, in time for the early-morning departure of a Yugoslav Ilyushin 18 for Belgrade.

Suddenly, at exactly 22.03, the pilot of a second Russian aircraft—another Antonov—contacted Ruzyne tower and requested landing clearance. The controllers were puzzled; they had had no prior warning of this arrival. Over the radio, the Russian pilot informed them that he was inbound from Lvov with 25 passengers on board. His intention was to land and discharge them, and then take off again.

The Antonov touched down and taxied to a stop outside the terminal building. A small group of Russians was waiting for the passengers and greeted them warmly; then they boarded an airport bus which moved off towards Prague. A few minutes later, the Antonov taxied back on to the runway and took off again, quickly disappearing in the darkness. It was then that the tower staff noticed something strange; the first Antonov had vanished from its position on the apron. They spotted it a minute later, parked by the side of the main runway and showing no lights. The senior controller tried to make contact with it over the R/T, meaning to ask the pilot what his intentions were. There was no answer. After the fourth attempt, the controller gave up. He felt tense and uneasy, and soon afterwards he had even more cause for apprehension when a top-priority signal came clattering over the teleprinter. It was from the Department of the Interior and it read simply: 'QGO. Immediate effect.' The code-letters QGO meant that all landings and take-offs were to be prohibited at once until further notice.

The controllers went into action quickly, shutting down the airfield and runway lighting and all radio equipment except the R/T. Then they waited, nervously smoking, as the minutes ticked by. Suddenly the R/T came to life again. A distorted Russian voice crackled over the air, calling Ruzyne tower. A flight of three Soviet transport aircraft, approximately 10 miles north-east of the airfield, was running low on fuel and requested an emergency landing. The senior controller thought quickly; it was his decision alone. It did not take him long to make up his mind. He told the Russian flight leader that the airport was inoperative and that facilities had been closed down for the night, suggesting that the

Russians contacted Kbely military air base. He waited for an acknowledgement, but none came. The suspense was on again.

Then things began to happen quickly. A huge dark shape slid down out of the eastern sky and rolled along the main runway, its landing-lights ablaze. The shocked controllers recognized the bulky contours of an Antonov An-12 transport. A giant's roar split the night as its four powerful Ivchenko turboprops were slammed into reverse pitch, bringing it to a stop quickly. The loading-ramp that fitted snugly under the big upswept tail unit came down slowly and a host of shadowy figures came running out of the transport's massive belly, jumping down on to the concrete surface of the runway. There were 40 or 50 of them: Russian paratroops, wearing camouflaged smocks and full battle order. Now, as the huge An-12 thundered off down the runway and climbed away into the night once more, they fanned out in an extended line and advanced rapidly towards the airport buildings. A second aircraft roared in from the darkness, followed quickly by a third. With near-incredible speed, they discharged their cargoes of men and equipment before taking off again to make room for more. The Russian transports had not needed the assistance of Ruzyne control tower for their rapid landing; they already had their own mobile control tower and Ground Controlled Approach on the airfield in the shape of the Antonov 24 that was parked by the side of the main runway. The aircraft was crammed with electronic equipment of all shapes and sizes, and it carried a small crew of Soviet Air Force radar specialists. The passengers who had disembarked when the aircraft first landed had successfully camouflaged its real purpose.

Within minutes, the Russian paratroops had secured the control tower, the airport switchboard and other strategic points on Ruzyne. The night now reverberated with the roar of engines as a constant stream of Soviet transport aircraft thundered out of the darkness, touching down at the rate of one every 50 seconds. They were mostly An-12s and An-24s, with an occasional gigantic Antonov 22—the biggest transport aircraft in service anywhere in the world. Each transport disgorged its load of men and material; the tanks came first, mostly ASU-57s but with a smaller number of the newer ASU-85s, their long 85-mm guns poking like accusing fingers from the squat silhouettes of their turrets. Then came the BTRs, the armoured personnel carriers into which the troops piled with well-rehearsed efficiency. Within minutes, the column was rumbling on its way towards Prague. Bringing up the rear were light and medium artillery, jeeps and radio vehicles.

Thirty minutes after the first of the Soviet transports touched down at Ruzyne, the controllers at Brno Airport—120 miles to the south-east—also picked up a 'distress' signal from what was thought to be a Russian charter aircraft. The pilot requested an emergency landing on the grounds that he was short of fuel, and this was approved immediately. The airport's ambulance and fire services were alerted and stood by alongside the runway. A few minutes later the aircraft landed safely—but instead of taxying to the airport buildings it rolled straight on to the end of the runway, where it stopped. It was another Antonov 24 'flying control tower'. Before the airport authorities had time to take any action, the wheels of the first giant freighter that followed it were hitting the tarmac and seconds later Soviet paratroops were fanning out across the airfield. The major airports at Bratislava and Ostrava were taken completely by surprise in a similar way.

The Russians also tried the same tactics in an effort to capture the Czech Air Force Headquarters at Kbely, near Prague. It was a vital objective; if the Czech armed forces chose to resist the invasion, air operations would be directed from here. But the base commander already knew that Soviet and other Warsaw Pact forces were crossing Czechoslovakia's frontiers, and he had taken precautions to prevent Soviet aircraft landing on the airfield. The precautions were simple enough; he had merely ordered his men to park every available vehicle, from fire tenders to private cars, in long lines right down the middle of all three runways. When the Soviet transports arrived overhead at 01.50 hours on August

21st, the pilots found that they were unable to land and had to divert to the already congested airport at Ruzyne. It was not until four hours later that Kbely was finally overrun—by ground forces.

The capture of the Czech airfields by airborne troops—although the operation added nothing to the laurels of the Soviet Air Force—had been a masterpiece of planning. By concentrating on civil airports, the planners had successfully avoided any danger of opposition from anti-aircraft defences, and the whole operation had unfolded with a speed and efficiency that astounded NATO observers. It was true, as some NATO experts pointed out, that the unserviceability rate among the Soviet transport aircraft was high after several days of flying in supplies and equipment to the forces of occupation, but this did not disguise the fact that the A-VDV, the Soviet Air Support Command, had ably demonstrated its capability to mount a successful assault from the air. The invasion of Czechoslovakia, tragic and distasteful though it was, proved once and for all that in terms of planning, strategy and equipment the Soviet Air Force was well prepared for the type of challenge it might have to face in the 1970s.

Chapter 16

The Challenge

At the end of 1969, the total strength of the Soviet Air Forces stood at some 10,000 aircraft; 5,000 fewer than the active inventory of the United States Air Forces, but a formidable force none the less. Moreover, the new types of combat aircraft revealed during the past three or four years show that the Soviet Union is keeping pace with, and in some cases may even have surpassed, the West in combat aircraft and weapon systems technology.

As is the case with the United States and Britain, Russia's strategic nuclear capability has now been mainly handed over to the Strategic Rocket Forces, which are under Army command, and to the Navy's nuclear-missile-carrying submarines. Large numbers of the aircraft that were the backbone of Russia's long-range striking force 10 years ago, however, are still in service, and in some cases have been adapted to perform other roles. Some of the 60 remaining Mya-4s and 75 Tu-20s, for example, have been adapted as flight refuelling tankers, and as we have seen they are also used for long-range maritime reconnaissance. The spearhead of the Soviet long-range striking force is now the supersonic twin-jet Tu-22, which carries an advanced 36-foot air-to-surface missile, known by the NATO code-name of 'Kitchen' and presumably fitted with a one-megaton hydrogen warhead, partially recessed in its bomb-bay. Some 300 Tu-22s are in service, having replaced the elderly Tu-16 medium bomber in many Dalnaya Aviatsiya units. Nevertheless, about 600 Tu-16s are still active, many of them with the A-VMF, the Naval Air Arm. The Tu-16s of the A-VMF's long-range patrol squadrons carry two anti-shipping missiles under their wings. Two different types of missile are in service: the first, code-named 'Kennel', is a turbojet-powered cruise missile looking rather like a scaled-down pilotless MiG-15, which has also been supplied to Indonesia and Egypt; the second—code-named 'Kelt'—appears to be a larger rocket-powered development

The Challenge

of 'Kennel'. An earlier type of anti-shipping missile, the 31-foot 'Kipper' with an underslung turbojet, is now thought to have been phased out.

Since the appearance of the Tu-22 at the Tushino air display in 1961, there have been no dramatic revelations of new Soviet strategic bombers. Vladimir M. Myasishchev, designer of the Mya-4, produced a supersonic heavy bomber—code-named 'Bounder'—a few years ago, but the type never attained service status and the prototypes were used as research aircraft in connection with Russia's supersonic airliner programme, which culminated in the Tupolev Tu-144.

As always, the Frontovaia Aviatsiya—the Soviet Tactical Air Force—is the largest Soviet air command, with some 4,000 first-line aircraft. The MiG-15 and the Il-28, once the mainstay of the post-war FA, have now been phased out completely from the tactical units, although they still serve with some reserve formations and equip operational training units. Ground-attack versions of the MiG-17 and MiG-19 are still very much in evidence, but they are being progressively replaced by the supersonic Sukhoi Su-7. Medium-range tactical reconnaissance and strike squadrons are equipped with versions of the twin-engined Yak-25 and the more advanced Yak-28. One of the latest types to enter service is the Sukhoi Su-11, a Mach 2·5 tactical fighter with a Short Take-Off and Landing capability, and a STOL version of the MiG-21 interceptor is also believed to have gone into service. A Mikoyan-designed variable geometry tactical fighter was revealed at the 1967 Domodedovo air display, as was a variable geometry version of the Sukhoi Su-7, but neither of these types is operational. The Russians have not yet succeeded in developing an operational VTOL strike aircraft like Britain's Harrier, although an experimental Yakovlev VTOL aircraft appeared at Domodedovo carrying a variety of underwing weapon loads.

Operationally, the MiG-21 and the Su-7 enjoy one big advantage over equivalent American tactical aircraft: their extremely robust construction and relative lack of complexity enable them to operate from semi-prepared front-line airfields, and take-off performance is increased by the use of jettisonable rocket bottles. Vulnerable runways are not needed, and by operating from emergency strips immediately behind the front line the Soviet tactical formations would be able to establish rapid air superiority. This was one of the lessons learned by the Soviet Air Force during the Second World War, and it has not been forgotten.

Coming a close second behind the FA in terms of numerical strength is the IA-PVO, Russia's air defence force, with some 3,900 first-line aircraft. Standard equipment of the IA-PVO's short range day-fighter squadrons is the MiG-21, and all-weather fighter units are equipped with the Sukhoi Su-9 single-seat and the Yak-28 two-seat all-weather interceptors. The IA-PVO has, in addition, an important long-range all-weather fighter capability in the shape of a very powerful supersonic twin-jet interceptor designed by Tupolev and code-named 'Fiddler'. This aircraft, which can carry four 'Ash' air-to-air missiles, was designed as an answer to the threat from long-range strategic bombers, having sufficient range and endurance to effect an interception before the attackers reach the frontiers of the Soviet Union.

The latest aircraft to enter service with the IA-PVO is the MiG-23 high-altitude all-weather interceptor, which—under the designation Ye-266—established a payload-to-height record by carrying a 2,000-kg payload to 98,349 feet and a speed record by flying over a 500-km closed circuit at a speed of 1,852·61 mph, both in October 1967. The MiG-23 is Russia's answer to high-flying reconnaissance aircraft and to the Mach Two-plus strike aircraft; it has an estimated maximum speed of Mach 3 and can carry four underwing missiles of an unspecified type—possibly a developed version of 'Ash'.

The missile known by the NATO code-name of 'Ash' is one of four types of air-to-air weapons in use by the IA-PVO. The others are 'Alkali', which still equips some of the SovAF's MiG-19s and is in widespread use among the satellite air forces; 'Anab', which is carried by both the Yak-28P and the Su-9; and 'Atoll', which equips the MiG-21. Surface-to-air missiles in service with the IA-PVO include the V750-VK, more commonly known as the SA-2 'Guideline', which is also used by several countries outside the Soviet Union; a developed version of the V750-K known as 'Guild'; a two-stage short-range missile for defence against fast low-flying aircraft code-named 'Goa', and an even more advanced and compact missile system designed for the same purpose and known as 'Gainful'; the ramjet-powered 'Ganef', which can also be used as a surface-to-surface tactical weapon; 'Griffon' and 'Galosh', the former a long-range missile primarily for use against aircraft, but with the capability of destroying air-launched missiles, and the latter a first-generation anti-missile missile system. 'Galosh' is believed to be operational on a limited scale.

One of the most important commands in the Soviet Air Force is the A-VDV, the Air Support Command (or, more correctly, the Aviation of the Airborne Troops), and its importance is likely to grow still further. With the threat to the Soviet Union's Far Eastern frontiers likely to increase in proportion to the growing military strength of Communist China, the ability to move large quantities of men and material from one end of the USSR to the other will be vital, and only a massive military air transport organization can assure this. The present strength of the A-VDV stands at about 1,000 aircraft, some 200 fewer than the US Air Support Command possesses, but it should not be forgotten that in a time of national emergency the Soviet Air Force has provision to requisition the entire Aeroflot fleet, which at the present time amounts to some 500 aircraft.

The Soviet Air Force has the distinction of being the only air arm in the world (apart from the satellite countries) to use a transport biplane, the Antonov An-2. This versatile aircraft, over 5,000 of which were built between 1950 and 1960, is a true general-purpose machine, being used for almost everything from passenger and freight transport to navigation training and paratrooping. It shares the A-VDV's 'sundry duties' in company with another Antonov design, the An-14 Pchelka ('Little Bee'). The standard medium transport is the An-24, with the bulk of the transport force made up by the 'heavies'—the An-12 and the massive An-22 Antheus. Some turboprop-powered Il-18s are also in use, as are small numbers of Tu-104, Tu-124 and Tu-134 jet transports. Quite a number of elderly Il-12s and Il-14s, as well as Li-2s (Dakotas), also continue to soldier on.

The A-VDV's standard heavy general-purpose transport helicopter is the Mil Mi-6, which, when it first made its appearance in 1957, was the largest helicopter in the world. The Mi-10, a flying crane development of the Mi-6, is also in use. Other helicopters that serve with the A-VDV in large numbers include the Mil Mi-1 and Mi-4, the Yak-24 tandem-rotor helicopter and the Kamov Ka-15.

Nikolai I. Kamov is also the producer of tactical and anti-submarine warfare helicopters for the Soviet Army and Navy. The two principal types used in both roles are the Kamov Ka-20 and Ka-25, which can carry two air-to-surface missiles and machine guns. Kamov is reported to have produced a fast helicopter gunship for service with the Soviet Army, but no aircraft of this kind is as yet in service. The Russians, however, are learning as much from the war in Vietnam as the Americans—and at far less cost—and it is certain that the effectiveness of the helicopter gunship has not escaped their notice.

The Vietnam War has, in fact, provided the Russians with an unparalleled opportunity to examine the latest types of combat aircraft and equipment in service with the USAF and US Navy at their leisure. One of the stipulations of the agreement to supply Soviet arms to Vietnam was that the wreckage of any US aircraft shot down over Vietnam should immediately be turned over to Russian Air Force specialists, and since every type of fighter-bomber on the American inventory has been lost over North Vietnam at one time or another, the Russians have reaped a rich harvest of technical intelligence. They have also been able to test some of their latest weapons, including the MiG-21 and the V750-VK surface-to-air missile; they found that the MiG was definitely superior to the American F-105 Thunderchief and A-4 Sky-hawk and that in the hands of a capable pilot it could meet the redoubtable F-4 Phantom on more or less equal terms; but with the V750-VK it was a different story. The missile's performance was found to be woefully inadequate against fast jet aircraft; its acceleration was so slow that American pilots could see it coming in plenty of time to take avoiding action. Cannon, too, were found to be far more effective in a dogfight than air-to-air missiles; the latter were too susceptible to various influences such as temperature changes and cloud layers, and in the whirl of an air battle they were as big a danger to friendly as to enemy aircraft.

Although Russian advisers are present in large numbers in North Vietnam, there is no evidence to show that Soviet pilots have flown MiGs in combat against the Americans so far during the conflict.

For the Soviet Air Force—and indeed for the whole world —the big question-mark during the coming decade will be Communist China: a China trained by Soviet personnel and still equipped mainly with Soviet weapons, but now rattling a nuclear sabre of her own forging. Although the Soviet Air Force is five times the size of the CPAF and infinitely superior in technical terms, the Chinese aircraft industry is producing modern combat aircraft such as the MiG-19— some of which it has sold to Pakistan—and its own version of the supersonic MiG-21, both without the permission of the Soviet Union. The bulk of the CPAF is still equipped with old MiG-15s and MiG-17s, and apart from 100 or so Il-28s it has no bombers; but a nation that has a sufficiently advanced technology to produce a hydrogen bomb is quite capable of producing its own military aircraft, and China may be expected to make great strides in this direction over the next few years. Missile development is already well under way, but missiles could strike only the first blows in an all-out war; the hard slogging that came after would be done by manned aircraft.

Soviet airmen have already been in action—albeit on a small scale—against Chinese troops infiltrating the disputed border territory along the Ussuri River, and with the eyes of China turned covetously to the great Siberian plains it seems almost inevitable that they will be in action again. Talks aimed at reaching a settlement have done little to still the tongues of many Soviet military leaders, who have been advocating a pre-emptive strike on China's nuclear centres. Such a drastic step may never be taken; but the indications are that it is in the remote Far East that the Soviet Air Force may be called upon to fight its next and possibly its greatest battle.

NATO Classification of Soviet Aircraft since 1949

NATO code-name	Soviet designation	Remarks
Backfin*	Tupolev Tu-98	Supersonic light bomber
Badger	Tupolev Tu-16	Medium bomber
Bank	B-25	Lease-lend Mitchell
Barge*	Tupolev Tu-85	Development of Tu-4
Bark	Il-2	Shturmovik
Bat	Tupolev Tu-2	Twin-engined light bomber
Beagle	Ilyushin Il-28	Twin-jet light bomber
Bear	Tupolev Tu-20	Long-range bomber/reconnaissance/maritime patrol aircraft
Beast	Ilyushin Il-10	Last Shturmovik variant
Bison	Myasishchev Mya-4	Long-range bomber/reconnaissance aircraft
Blinder (originally Beauty)	Tupolev Tu-22	Supersonic medium bomber
Blowlamp*	Ilyushin Il-54	Supersonic light bomber
Bob	Ilyushin Il-4	DB-3F medium bomber
Boot*	Tupolev Tu-91	Turboprop-powered anti-submarine aircraft
Bosun	Tupolev Tu-14	Twin-jet light bomber
Bounder*	Myasishchev M-52	Supersonic heavy bomber prototype
Box	DB-7B	Lease-lend A-20 Havoc
Brawny*	Ilyushin Il-40	Tactical fighter-bomber
Brewer (originally Brassard)	Yakovlev Yak-28	Supersonic tactical multi-purpose aircraft
Buck	Petlyakov Pe-2	Light bomber and night fighter
Bull	Tupolev Tu-4	Russian copy of B-29
Butcher*	Tupolev Tu-82	Swept-wing Il-28 development
Cab	Li-2	Russian version of C-47 Dakota
Camel	Tupolev Tu-104	First Russian jet airliner
Camp	Antonov An-8	Twin-turboprop transport
Cart	Tupolev Tu-70	Transport version of Tu-4
Cat	Antonov An-10	Four-engined turboprop passenger and freight transport
Charger	Tupolev Tu-144	Prototype Russian supersonic airliner
Clam*	Ilyushin Il-18 (1947)	Prototype heavy transport

NATO code-name	Soviet designation	Remarks
Classic	Ilyushin Il-62	Four-jet airliner
Cleat	Tupolev Tu-114	Turboprop airliner
Clod	Antonov An-14	Light multi-purpose transport
Coach	Ilyushin Il-12	Twin piston-engined medium transport
Cock	Antonov An-22	Largest Soviet transport
Codling	Yakovlev Yak-40	Short-haul jet transport
Coke	Antonov An-24	Medium-haul transport
Colt	Antonov An-2	General-purpose biplane
Cooker*	Tupolev Tu-110	Four-jet development of Tu-104
Cookpot	Tupolev Tu-124	Medium-range transport
Coot	Ilyushin Il-18 'Moskva'	Medium-range transport
Cork	Yakovlev Yak-16	Twin-engined light transport
Crate	Ilyushin Il-14	Development of Il-12
Creek (also Crow)	Yakovlev Yak-12	Light single-engined general-purpose aircraft
Crib	Yakovlev Yak-8	Twin-engined light transport and general-purpose aircraft
Crusty	Tupolev Tu-134	Medium-range jet transport
Cub	Antonov An-12	Standard A-VDV transport
Cuff	Beriev Be-30	Light commercial feeder-liner
Fagot	MiG-15	First Soviet jet fighter produced in large numbers
Faithless	MiG-?	STOL tactical fighter
Fang	Lavochkin La-11	Last Soviet piston-engined fighter
Fantail	Lavochkin La-15	Contender with MiG-15. Small number only served for short time with SovAF
Fargo	MiG-9	Mikoyan's first jet fighter
Farmer	MiG-19	First Soviet supersonic fighter
Feather	Yak-17	First Russian jet fighter to serve in quantity
Fiddler	Yak-?	Long-range all-weather fighter
Fin	Lavochkin La-7	One of standard Soviet fighters at end of WW2
Firebar	Yakovlev Yak-28P	All-weather fighter
Fishbed (originally Faceplate)	MiG-21	Standard Soviet day fighter
Fishpot	Sukhoi Su-9	All-weather fighter

NATO code-name	*Soviet designation*	*Remarks*
Fitter	Sukhoi Su-7	Ground-attack fighter
Flagon	Sukhoi Su-11	Tactical fighter
Flashlight	Yakovlev Yak-25	All-weather fighter
Flipper*	MiG-?	Experimental development of MiG-21
Flogger	MiG-?	Variable-geometry tactical fighter. Not yet in service
Flora	Yakovlev Yak-23	Development of Yak-17. Russia's first 'export fighter'
Foxbat	MiG-23 (Ye-266)	High-altitude, Mach 3 + interceptor
Frank	Yakovlev Yak-9	One of standard Soviet fighters at end of WW2
Fred	P-63 Kingcobra	Assault aircraft acquired under lease-lend
Freehand	Yak-?	Experimental VTOL tactical fighter. Not yet ready for service
Fresco	MiG-17	Replaced MiG-15 in service. Still exported in large numbers
Fritz	Lavochkin La-9	Development of La-7
Hare	Mil Mi-1	General-purpose helicopter
Harke	Mil Mi-10	'Flying Crane' development of Mi-6
Harp	Kamov Ka-20	General purpose and ASW helicopter
Hat	Kamov Ka-10	Utility helicopter
Hen	Kamov Ka-15	General purpose helicopter
Hip	Mil Mi-8	Commercial transport helicopter
Hog	Kamov Ka-18	Four-seat utility helicopter
Hoodlum	Kamov Ka-26	Light utility helicopter
Hook	Mil Mi-6	Heavy transport helicopter
Hoop*	Kamov Ka-22	Transport convertiplane
Hoplite	Mil Mi-2	Turbine-powered version of Mi-1
Horse	Yakovlev Yak-24	Twin-rotor transport and assault helicopter
Hound	Mil Mi-4	General-purpose helicopter
Madge	Beriev Be-6	Twin-engined reconnaissance and transport flying-boat

The Red Falcons

* Denotes aircraft did not attain service status.

Soviet Air Aces of the Second World War

The following is a list of leading Soviet fighter pilots and the number of enemy aircraft destroyed by these pilots.

KOZHEDUB, Ivan Nikitich (3HSU)	62
POKRYSHKIN, Aleksandr Ivanovich (3HSU)	59
RECHKALOV, Grigorii Andreevich (2HSU)	58
GULAEV, Nikolai Dmitrievich (2HSU)	57
YEVSTIGNEEV, Kirill Alekseevich (2HSU)	52
GLINKA, Dmitrii Borisovich (2HSU)	50
KLUBOV, Aleksandr Fedorovich (2HSU)	50
PILIPENKO, Ivan Markovich (HSU)	48
VOROZHEIKIN, Arsenii Vasil'evich (2HSU) (+6 at Khalkhin-Gol)	46
KUBAREV, Vasilii Nikolaevich (HSU)	46
SKOMOROKHOV, Nikolai Mikhailovich (2HSU)	46
KOSTILEV, Georgii Dmitrievich (HSU)	43
MORGUNOV, Sergei N. (HSU)	42
POPKOV, Vitalii Ivanovich (2HSU)	41
ALELIUKHIN, Aleksei Vasil'evich (2HSU)	40
GOLUBEV, Viktor Fedorovich	39
GULUBEV, Vasilii Fedorovich	38
LUGANSKII, Sergei Danilovich (2HSU)	37
PIVOVAROV, Mikhail Yevdokimovich (HSU)	37
GUL'TYAEV, Grigorii Kapitanovich (HSU)	36
DOLGIKH, Anatolii Gavrilovich	36
KUZNETSOV, Nikolai Fedorovich (HSU)	36
KOLDUNOV, Aleksandr Ivanovich (2HSU)	36
BABAK, Ivan Il'ich (HSU)	35
KAMOZIN, Pavel Mikhailovich (2HSU)	35
LAVRINENKOV, Vladimir Dmitrievich (2HSU)	35
PAVLUSHKIN, Nikolai Sazonovich	35
GNIDO, Petr Andreevich (HSU)	34
KOTCHEKOV, Aleksandr Vasil'evich (HSU)	34
LUK'YANOV, Sergei Ivanovich (HSU)	34
SYTOV, Ivan Nikitich (HSU)	34
CHISLOV, Aleksandr Mikhailovich (HSU)	34
CHUBUKOV, Fedor Mikhailovich (HSU)	34
BOROVYKH, Andreii Yegorovich (2HSU)	32
ZELENKIN, Mikhail Mikhailovich (HSU)	32
KOMEL'KOV, Mikhail Sergeevich (HSU)	32
KRASNOV, Nikolai Fedorovich (HSU)	32
RYAZANOV, Aleksei Konstantinovich	32
STEPANENKO, Ivan Nikifirovich (2HSU)	32
KIRILYUK, Viktor Vasil'evich (HSU)	32
GOLOVACHEV, Pavel Yakovlevich (2HSU)	31

The Red Falcons

AKHMET-KHAN, Sultan (2HSU)	30
ARKHIPENKO, Fedor Fedorovich (HSU)	30
BOBROV, Vladimir Ivanovich	30
GLINKA, Boris Borisovich (HSU)	30
LIKHOBABIYI, Ivan Dmitrievich (HSU)	30
LIKHOLETOV, Petr Yakovlevich (HSU)	30
MAKHAROV, Valentin Nikolaevich (HSU)	30
POKRYSHEV, Petr Afanas'evich (2HSU)	30
KHLOBYSTOV, Aleksei Stepanovich (HSU)	30
KIRIYA, Pavel Nesterovich	29
KRAVTSOV, Ivan Savil'evich (HSU)	29
MERKULOV, Vladimir Ivanovich (HSU)	29
MERKUSHEV, Vasilii Afanas'evich (HSU)	29
NAIDENOV, Nikolai Alekseevich	29
NOVIKOV, Konstantin Afanas'evich (HSU)	29
POGORELOV, Mikhail Savil'evich (HSU)	29
ROMANENKO, Ivan Georgievich (HSU)	29
VOSTRUKHIN, Petr Mikhailovich (HSU)	28
ZAITSEV, Vasilii Aleksandrovich (2HSU)	28
IGNAT'EV, Mikhail Trofimovich	28
ZOTOV, Nikolai Aleksandrovich (HSU)	28
KABEROV, Igor' Aleksandrovich (HSU)	28
KOVALOV, Konstantin Fedorovich	28
KOVZAN, Boris Ivanovich (HSU)	28
KULAGIN, Andrei Mikhailovich (HSU)	28
MURAV'EV, Pavel Ignat'evich (HSU)	28
OSIPOV, Vasilii Nikolaevich	28
SELYANIN, Yefgenii Nikolaevich (HSU)	28
SEROV, Vladimir Geogrievich (HSU)	28
CHAPCHAKHOV, Lazar' Sergeevich (HSU)	28
BAZANOV, Petr Vasil'evich	27
GARAM, Mikhail Aleksandrovich (HSU)	27
GRINEV, Mikhail	27
KARPOV, Aleksandr Terent'evich (2HSU)	27
KLIMOV, Vasilii Vladimirovich (HSU)	27
KLIMOV, Pavel Dmitrievich	27
KOZHEVNIKOV, Anatoli Leonidovich	27
KUZNETSOV, Sergei Alekseevich	27
MAIOROV, Aleksandr Ivanovich	27
MAKOVSKII, Spartak Iosifovich (HSU)	27
MERENKOV, Viktor Alekseevich (HSU)	27
SMIRNOV, Aleksei Semenovich (2HSU)	27
ARSEN'EV, Nikolai Lavrent'evich (HSU)	26
BARANOV, Mikhail Semenovich (HSU)	26
BASTRAKHOV, Arsenii Mikhailovich (HSU)	26
GOLOSOV, Ivan	26

KITAEV, Nikolai Trofiomovich (HSU) 26
LAVITSKII, Nikolai Yefimovich (HSU) 26
LEONOVICH, Ivan Semenovich (HSU) 26
MIKHAILEV, Vasilii Pavlovich (HSU) 26
SACHKOV, Mikhail Ivanovich (HSU) 26
KHARITONOV, Vasilii Nikolaevich (HSU) 26
CHIRKOV, Andrei Vasilevich (HSU) 26
BENDELIANI, Chichiko Kaisarovich (HSU) 25
BORISOV, Ivan G. 25
BORODACHEV, Viktor Ivanovich (HSU) 25
VASILEVSKII, Yegor Vasil'evich 25
GUBANOV, Aleksei Alekseevich (HSU) 25
MARKOV, Vasilii 25
SAFONOV, Boris Feoktistovich (2HSU) 25
SUBIROV, Viktor Ivanovich (HSU) 25
SHIKUNOV, V. 25
VEDENEEV, Valentin Ivanovich (HSU) 24
GREBENEV, Arkadii Dmitrievich 24
YERMAKOV, Dmitrii Vasil'evich (HSU) 24
ZINOV'EV, Ivan Ivanovich (HSU) 24
LAVEIKIN, Ivan Pavlovich (HSU) 24
LESHCHENKO, Vyacheslav Sergeevich 24
LOBOV, Georgii Ageevich 24
LOMAKIN, Anatolii Georgievich (HSU) 24
MIKRYUKOV, Vitalii Vasil'evich (HSU) 24
MOROZOV, Anatolii Afanas'evich 24
NAGORNYI, Viktor Sergeevich 24
SOBOLEV, Afanasii Petrovich (HSU) 24
TRUD, Andreii Ivanovich (HSU) 24
FEDOROV, Arkadii Vasil'evich 24
FEDOROV, Aleksandr Yakovlevich (HSU) 24
FEDOROV, Ivan Vasil'evich (HSU) 24
TSIGANOV, Yevgenii Terent'evich (HSU) 24
SHEVTSOV, A. 24
ANDRIANOV, Vasilii Ivanovich (2HSU) 23
ANDRIANOV, Il'ya Filippovich (HSU) 23
BOBIOV, Vasilii Petrovich 23
BURNOZYAN, Sergei Avdeevich (HSU) 23
GNEZDILOV, Ivan Fedorovich (HSU) 23
YEREMIN, Boris Nikolaevich (HSU) 23
KARASEN, Anton Andreevich (HSU) 23
KNYAZEV, Vasilii Aleksandrovich 23
KUTSENKO, Mikhail 23
MANKEVICH, Viktor Mikhailovich (HSU) 23
OGANESOV, Vozgen Mikhailovich (HSU) 23
OSKALENKO, Dmitrii Yefimovich (HSU) 23

The Red Falcons

Name	Score
PILYUTOV, Petr Andreevich (HSU)	23
SIVTSOV, Nikolai Stepanovich (HSU)	23
SIDORENKOV, Vasilii Kuz'mich (HSU)	23
TATARENKO, Mikhail Mitrofanovich (HSU)	23
TROFIMOV, Yevgenii Fedorovich (HSU)	23
SHMELEV, Il'ya Vasil'evich (HSU)	23
ALEKSEEV, Konstantin Stepanovich (HSU)	22
BARSUKOV, Vasilii Nikolaevich (HSU)	22
BATURIN, Aleksandr Gerasimovich (HSU)	22
BLOKHIN, I. (HSU)	22
BORISENKO, Ivan Ivanovich (HSU)	22
GAL'CHENKO, Leonid Akimovich (HSU)	22
GUCHEK, Petr Iosifovich (HSU)	22
DZYUBA, Petr Petrovich (HSU)	22
DOBRODETSKII, Anatolii Vasil'evich	22
YEVTEEV, Mikhail Ivanovich	22
YEGOROVICH, V.	22
ZIBOROV, Vasill Mikhailovich (HSU)	22
KLESHCHEV, Ivan Ivanovich (HSU)	22
KUZNETSOV, Mikhail Vasil'evich (2HSU)	22
LAVRENEV, Aleksandr Filippovich	22
LOBANOV, Aleksandr Vasil'evich (HSU)	22
MASLOV, Ivan Vasil'evich (HSU)	22
NOVOSELOV, Kuz'ma Vasil'evich (HSU)	22
NOGA, Mitrofan Petrovich (HSU)	22
SAVIL'EV, Vasilii Antonovich (HSU)	22
TOKAREV, Moisei Stepanovich (HSU)	22
FADEEV, Vadim Ivanovich (HSU)	22
SHEVCHENKO, Vladimir Illarinovich (HSU)	22
BARCHENKOV, Danil Gavrilovich (HSU)	21
VIKTOROV, Georgii Petrovich (HSU)	21
DOLGAREV, Pavel Mikhailovich (HSU)	21
KOZLOV, Nikolai Aleksandrovich (HSU)	21
KUZ'MIN, Georgii Pavlovich (HSU)	21
MIRONOV, Viktor Petrovich (HSU)	21
MOROZOV, Fotii Yakovlevich	21
MRIINSKII, Yevgenii Pakhomovoch (HSU)	(+ 1 balloon)20
NEKRASOV, Vladimir Petrovich (HSU)	21
RIDNYI	21
STARIKOV, Dmitrii Aleksandrovich (HSU)	21
TISHCHENKO, Aleksandr Trofimovich	21
KHOLODOV, Ivan Mikhailovich (HSU)	21
TSYGANOV, Mikhail	21
ANTONOV, Nikolai Dmitrievich	20
ARTAMONOV, N.	20
BARABANOV, Aleksandr Nikolaevich	20

BILYUKIN, Aleksandr Dmitrievich 20
GRAZHDANINOV, Pavel Andreevich 20
DAVIDKOV, Viktor Iosifovich 20
DEKHTYARENKO, Andrei Nikolaevich (HSU) 20
DRANISHCHEV, Yevgenii Petrovich (HSU) 20
DRYGIN, Vasilii M. (HSU) 20
ZHIDOV, Georgii Nikanorovich (HSU) 20
KAMENSHCHIKOV, Vladimir Grigor'evich 20
LAUKIN, Aleksandr Kirillovich (HSU) 20
LEVITAN, Vladimir Samoilovich 20
LEONOV, Nikolai Ivanovich (HSU) 20
LITAVRIN, Sergei Gavrilovich (+ 2 balloons) 19
NEUSTROEV, Ivan 20
ONUFRIEV, Mitrofan Aleksandrovich 20
PASHKEVICH, Aleksei Vasil'evich 20
PIDTYKAN, Ivan Dmitrievich (HSU) 20
RYANTSEV, Aleksei Fedorovich (HSU) 20
STOROZHAKOV, Aleksei Nikolaevich 20
STROIKOV, Nikolai Vasil'evich 20
SUKHOV, Konstantin Vasil'evich 20
FEDOROV, A. A. 20
TSOKOLAEV, Gennadii Dmitrievich (HSU) 20
CHEREVATENKO, Aleksei Tikhonovich 20
SHISHKIN, A. 20

HSU = Hero of Soviet Union.

Index

Index

Index